THERMOPYLAE

During the Battle of **THERMOPYLAE** in 480 bc, a Greek force of approximately 7,000 faced the biggest army ever seen in the Greek peninsula. For three days, the Persians—the greatest military force in the world—were stopped in their tracks by a vastly inferior force, before the bulk of the Greek army was forced to retreat with their rear-guard wiped out in one of history's most famous last stands.

In strict military terms it was a defeat for the Greeks. But like the British retreat from Dunkirk or the massacre at the Alamo, this David and Goliath story swiftly took on the aura of success. In fact, Thermopylae came to acquire a glamour exceeding any of the other battles of the Persian Wars, passing from history into myth, and it has lost none of that appeal in the modern era.

In *Thermopylae*, Chris Carey analyses the origins and course of this pivotal battle, as well as the challenges facing the historians studying it in their attempt to separate fact from fiction and make sense of the event in the absence of hard evidence. Carey also considers Thermopylae's cultural legacy, from its absorption into Greek and Roman oratorical traditions to its influence over modern literature, poetry, public monuments and Hollywood movies—a legacy which has now come to over-shadow the battle's immediate military significance.

Chris Carey was born in Liverpool and educated at Jesus College, Cambridge. He has worked at the University of Cambridge, University of Minnesota, Carleton College, St Andrews, Royal Holloway, and UCL, and taught in the Netherlands, Hungary, Greece, and Serbia. He has worked on Greek lyric poetry, epic, drama, oratory, and law, and is currently working on a commentary on book 7 of Herodotus' *History*. He was elected Fellow of the British Academy in 2012.

Praise for *Thermopylae*

'Carey is one of Britain's foremost students of ancient history. In this meticulous examination of the story he admits that most of the "facts" we have are speculative ... The value of Carey's book lies in its reflections upon a legend that continues to influence our culture and ideals.'

Max Hastings, *The Sunday Times*

'Highly readable and informative ... Carey's account of [the battle of Thermopylae] provides an absorbing exposition of both the facts and the fictions that underlie and surround it.'

Diana Bentley, *Minerva*

'Very readable, well researched and thought-provoking ... an excellent book and thoroughly recommended.'

Chris May, *Battlefield Magazine*

'Thermopylae is a discerning examination of a still resonant battle and the problems it poses for ancient historians. Its author writes intelligently for non-specialist students of military history, without footnoting controversies. He has walked Xerxes's route.'

Donald Lateiner, *Michigan War Studies Review*

GREAT BATTLES

THERMOPYLAE

CHRIS CAREY

OXFORD

UNIVERSITY PRESS

OXFORD
UNIVERSITY PRESS

Great Clarendon Street, Oxford, OX2 6DP,
United Kingdom

Oxford University Press is a department of the University of Oxford.
It furthers the University's objective of excellence in research, scholarship,
and education by publishing worldwide. Oxford is a registered trade mark of
Oxford University Press in the UK and in certain other countries

© Chris Carey 2019

The moral rights of the author have been asserted

First published 2019
First published in paperback 2022

Impression: 1

Published in the United States of America by Oxford University Press
198 Madison Avenue, New York, NY 10016, United States of America

British Library Cataloguing in Publication Data
Data available

Library of Congress Cataloging in Publication Data
Data available

ISBN 978–0–19–875410–7 (Hbk.)
ISBN 978–0–19–875411–4 (Pbk.)

Printed and bound by
CPI Group (UK) Ltd, Croydon, CR0 4YY

To Pauline, Chrys, Nick, and Laura
with love, admiration, and gratitude to have you in my life

FOREWORD

For those who practise war in the twenty-first century the idea of a 'great battle' can seem no more than the echo of a remote past. The names on regimental colours or the events commemorated at mess dinners bear little relationship to patrolling in dusty villages or waging 'wars amongst the people'. Contemporary military doctrine downplays the idea of victory, arguing that wars end by negotiation not by the smashing of an enemy army or navy. Indeed it erodes the very division between war and peace, and with it the aspiration to fight a culminating 'great battle'.

And yet to take battle out of war is to redefine war, possibly to the point where some would argue that it ceases to be war. Carl von Clausewitz, who experienced two 'great battles' at first hand—Jena in 1806 and Borodino in 1812—wrote in *On War* that major battle is 'concentrated war', and 'the centre of gravity of the entire campaign'. Clausewitz's remarks related to the theory of strategy. He recognized that in practice armies might avoid battles, but even then the efficacy of their actions relied on the latent threat of fighting. Winston Churchill saw the importance of battles in different terms, not for their place within war but for their impact on historical and national narratives. His forebear, the Duke of Marlborough, commanded in four major battles and named his palace after the most famous of them, Blenheim, fought in 1704. Battles, Churchill wrote in his biography of Marlborough, are 'the principal milestones in secular history'. For him 'Great battles, won or lost, change the entire course of events, create new standards of values, new moods, new atmospheres, in armies and nations, to which all must conform'.

Clausewitz's experience of war was shaped by Napoleon. Like Marlborough, the French emperor sought to bring his enemies to battle. However, each lived within a century of the other, and they fought their wars in the same continent and even on occasion on adjacent ground. Winston Churchill's own experience of war, which spanned the late nineteenth-century colonial conflicts of the British Empire as well as two world wars, became increasingly distanced from the sorts of battle he and Clausewitz described. In 1898 Churchill rode in a cavalry charge in a battle which crushed the Madhist forces of the Sudan in a single day. Four years later the British commander at Omdurman, Lord Kitchener, brought the South African War to a conclusion after a two-year guerrilla conflict in which no climactic battle occurred. Both Churchill and Kitchener served as British cabinet ministers in the First World War, a conflict in which battles lasted weeks, and even months, and which, despite their scale and duration, did not produce clear-cut outcomes. The 'Battle' of Verdun ran for all but one month of 1916 and that of the Somme for five months. The potentially decisive naval action at Jutland spanned a more traditional twenty-four-hour timetable but was not conclusive and was not replicated during the war. In the Second World War, the major struggle in waters adjacent to Europe, the 'Battle' of the Atlantic, was fought from 1940 to early 1944.

Clausewitz would have called these twentieth-century 'battles' campaigns, or even seen them as wars in their own right. The determination to seek battle and to venerate its effects may therefore be culturally determined, the product of time and place, rather than an inherent attribute of war. The ancient historian Victor Davis Hanson has argued that seeking battle is a 'western way of war' derived from classical Greece. Seemingly supportive of his argument are the writings of Sun Tzu, who flourished in warring states in China between two and five centuries before the birth of Christ, and who pointed out that the most effective way of waging war was to avoid the risks and dangers of actual fighting. Hanson has provoked strong criticism: those who argue that wars can be won without battles are not only to be found in Asia. Eighteenth-century European commanders, deploying armies in close-order formations in order to deliver concentrated fires, realized that the destructive consequences of battle for their own troops could be self-defeating. After the First World War, Basil Liddell Hart developed a theory of strategy which he called 'the indirect approach', and suggested that manoeuvre might substitute for hard fighting, even if its success still relied on the inherent threat of battle.

The winners of battles have been celebrated as heroes, and nations have used their triumphs to establish their founding myths. It is precisely for these reasons that their legacies have outlived their direct political consequences. Commemorated in painting, verse, and music, marked by monumental memorials, and used as the way points for the periodization of history, they have enjoyed cultural afterlives. These are evident in many capitals, in place names and statues, not least in Paris and London. The French tourist who finds himself in a London taxi travelling from Trafalgar Square to Waterloo Station should reflect on his or her own domestic peregrinations from the Rue de Rivoli to the Gare d'Austerlitz. Today's Mongolia venerates the memory of Genghis Khan while Greece and Macedonia scrap over the rights to Alexander the Great.

This series of books on 'great battles' tips its hat to both Clausewitz and Churchill. Each of its volumes situates the battle which it discusses in the context of the war in which it occurred, but each then goes on to discuss its legacy, its historical interpretation and reinterpretation, its place in national memory and commemoration, and its manifestations in art and culture. These are not easy books to write. The victors were more often celebrated than the defeated; the effect of loss on the battlefield could be cultural oblivion. However, that point is not universally true: the British have done more over time to mark their defeats at Gallipoli in 1915 and Dunkirk in 1940 than their conquerors on both occasions. For the history of war to thrive and be productive it needs to embrace the view from 'the other side of the hill', to use the Duke of Wellington's words. The battle the British call Omdurman is for the Sudanese the battle of Kerreri; the Germans called Waterloo 'la Belle Alliance' and Jutland Skagerrak. Indeed the naming of battles could itself be a sign not only of geographical precision or imprecision (Kerreri is more accurate but as a hill rather than a town is harder to find on a small-scale map), but also of cultural choice. In 1914 the German general staff opted to name their defeat of the Russians in East Prussia not Allenstein (as geography suggested) but Tannenberg, in order to claim revenge for the defeat of the Teutonic Knights in 1410.

Military history, more than many other forms of history, is bound up with national stories. All too frequently it fails to be comparative, to recognize that war is a 'clash of wills' (to quote Clausewitz once more), and so omits to address both parties to the fight. Cultural difference and, even more, linguistic ignorance can prevent the historian considering a battle in the round; so too can the availability of sources. Levels of literacy matter here, but so does cultural survival. Often these pressures can be congruent but they can also be divergent. Britain enjoys much higher levels of literacy than Afghanistan, but in 2002 the memory of the two countries' three wars flourished in the latter, thanks to an oral tradition, much more robustly than in the former, for whom literacy had created distance. And the historian who addresses cultural legacy is likely to face a much more challenging task the further in the past the battle occurred. The opportunity for invention and reinvention is simply greater the longer the lapse of time since the key event.

All historians of war must, nonetheless, never forget that, however rich and splendid the cultural legacy of a great battle, it was won and lost by fighting, by killing and being killed. The battle of Waterloo has left as abundant a footprint as any, but the general who harvested most of its glory reflected on it in terms which have general applicability, and carry across time in their capacity to capture a universal truth. Wellington wrote to Lady Shelley in its immediate aftermath: 'I hope to God I have fought my last battle. It is a bad thing to be always fighting. While in the thick of it I am much too occupied to feel anything; but it is wretched just after. It is quite impossible to think of glory. Both mind and feelings are exhausted. I am wretched even at the moment of victory, and I always say that, next to a battle lost, the greatest misery is a battle gained.' Readers of this series should never forget the immediate suffering caused by battle, as well as the courage required to engage in it: the physical courage of the soldier, sailor, or warrior, and the moral courage of the commander, ready to hazard all on its uncertain outcomes.

HEW STRACHAN

PREFACE

I had for some time been contemplating a book on Thermopylae in tandem with a project on book 7 of Herodotus, our earliest surviving source for the battle. So I was delighted when Hew Strachan invited me to contribute to the Oxford University Press *Great Battles* series. I am very grateful to him for his careful reading and annotation of successive drafts; I have in almost every instance accepted his suggestions. Thanks are due to the Press readers for their comments on the initial proposal and especially to the anonymous reader who subjected the first draft to a close critical scrutiny and offered robust, detailed, and thoughtful comments. I have in all cases sought to address the reader's criticisms, even where I have allowed the thrust of the argument to stand. I am happy finally to be able to express my thanks to a number of friends and colleagues who helped me along the way. Robert Garland kindly invited me to lecture on Thermopylae at Colgate University, NY, several years ago when the project was still its infancy, with support from the Center for Freedom and Western Civilization under its Director, Professor Robert P. Kraynak. This allowed me to begin the process of turning vague thoughts into hard questions. I have fond memories of warm hospitality and of lively debate about ancient Greece and modern America (these were the heady days of the rise of the Tea Party) over a long and leisurely dinner with faculty at Colgate. I owe a deep debt of thanks to Giorgos Telios and his wife Alice for their generous hospitality in Athens and Agios Konstantinos. Giorgos and I walked the Anopaea together on a beautiful June morning, guided by Stylianos Gkekas and Kostas Apostolopoulos, veterans of the Anopaea race, and accompanied by my very good friend Professor Athanasios (Thanasis) Efstathiou of the

Ionian University of Corfu and his colleague Sokratis Poulis. Nike Polychroniadis and her husband Apollonios Gogos shared their detailed knowledge of the area around Thermopylae as we scoped possible entry points to the Anopaea and reported to me on Apollonios' later expeditions. I am grateful to Ian Beckett for sharing sources relating to Rorke's Drift and Isandlwana, the subject of his 2019 volume in the *Great Battles* series. Thanks are also due to the staff at Oxford University Press, from whom I have received excellent support from first to last, and especially to Rowena Anketell, who saved me from errors at the copy-editing stage. But my principal debt is to my wife Pauline, who followed Xerxes' route with me across western Turkey, over the Hellespont and through Greece as far as the Gates, and as if that weren't enough discussed and debated issues large and small with infinite patience as the book developed, then finally read and commented on successive drafts with acute and sensitive judgement both on style and on content.

Writing this book has been a pleasure from first to last, about as much fun as you can have with your clothes on. Whether the same can be said of reading it I leave the reader to judge.

CHRIS CAREY
March 2019

In preparing the paperback edition I have benefited from comments from Simon Hornblower and Paul Cartledge, and from thoughtful reviews by Don Lateiner and Kostas Vlassopoulos; it is a pleasure to record my thanks here.

July 2021

ACKNOWLEDGEMENTS

Where not otherwise specified the illustrations are from photographs taken by me during research visits to Greece and Turkey. The following are thanked for their kind permission to reproduce drawings, images, and text:

Map 4, the Persian Empire from *Cambridge Ancient History*, vol iv (2nd edn., 1988)—Cambridge University Press;

Extract from Margaret Atwood, 'The Loneliness of the Military Historian'—Houghton Mifflin Harcourt and Curtis Brown;

Extract from John E. Brookes 'Thermopylae 1941'—Mrs E.M. Brookes, Mr Jeremy Brookes and The Visitor Ltd, formerly Badger Publications;

Extract from Sylvia Plath, 'Letter in November'—Faber and Faber;

Emily Dickinson, ' "Go tell it"—What a message'—*The Poems of Emily Dickinson*, edited by Thomas H. Johnson, Cambridge, MA: The Belknap Press of Harvard University Press, Copyright © 1951, 1955 by the President and Fellows of Harvard College. Copyright © renewed 1979, 1983 by the President and Fellows of Harvard College. Copyright © 1914, 1918, 1919, 1924, 1929, 1930, 1932, 1935, 1937, 1942, by Martha Dickinson Bianchi; Copyright © 1952, 1957, 1958, 1963, 1965, by Mary L. Hampson;

Figure 15, Hoplites fighting in formation; detail from the Chigi vase—World History Archive/Ann Ronan Collection/age fotostock;

Figure 22, *Leonidas at Thermopylae* by David—Ann Ronan Pictures/ Heritage Image/age fotostock;

Figure 28, *Ruins of Monte Cassino*—ARNOLDO MONDADORI EDITORE S.P./Mondadori Portfolio/age fotostock;

Figure 29, Photograph of Dimitri Hadzi, *Thermopylae*—Robin Levine.

The following images are reproduced under Creative Commons licence or as public domain images:

Figure 12, Persian coin ('Daric') showing the king as archer. Digital image courtesy of the Getty's Open Content Program;

Figure 13, Persian archers, possibly members of the elite Immortals, Wikimedia commons/Carole Raddato/CC-BY-SA-2.0;

Figure 17, Persian and Median troops from Persepolis with the smaller Persian shield, Wikimedia commons/Arad/CC-BY-SA-3.0;

Figure 18. Darius III wearing the *tiara*, Wikimedia commons/Carole Raddato/CC-BY-SA-2.0

Figure 23, Statue of Cambronne at Nantes, Wikimedia commons/ Adam Bishop/CC-BY-SA-3.0

Figure 24, Alamo mission, Wikimedia commons/Daniel Schwen/ CC-BY-SA-4.0;

Figure 25, Last stand hill Little Bighorn, Wikimedia commons/ 1025wil/CC-BY-SA-3.0;

Figure 26, Ruins of Stalingrad, RIA Novosti archive, image #2251/ Zelma/CC-BY-SA 3.0;

Figure 27, Kohima Memorial, Wikimedia commons/Isaxar/CC-BY-SA-4.0;

Figure 30, Achaemenid king killing a Greek hoplite, Marco Prins;

Figure 6, Aerial View of the Middle Gate, was edited from an image downloaded from Google Maps.

In addition, a number of maps were digitally redacted by myself and redrawn by staff at OUP from previously published maps. Map 1, Greece and the Aegean, was based on Map 1 in Robin Waterfield's translation of *Demosthenes* for the Oxford World Classics (Oxford, 2014), p. xxxii. Map 2, Thermopylae 480 bc, is based on the online illustration on the Livius website created by Jona Lendering. Map 3, the Middle Gate at Thermopylae, was ultimately based on the map in D. Müller, *Topographisches Bildkommentar zu Herodot, Griechenland* (1987), 379 and heavily revised under the influence of S. Marinatos, F. Stählin, E. Meyer, and W. K. Pritchett. Map 5, Possible routes for the Anopaea, is based on the map of P. W. Wallace, 'The Anopiaia Path at

Thermopylai', *American Journal of Archaeology* 84 (1980). Map 6 of Salamis was reproduced from Hignett, *Xerxes' Invasion of Greece* (OUP, 1963).

Translations are my own, though for style and accuracy I have also consulted published translations. In the case of Old Persian documents I drew on the translations of Maria Brosius and Amelie Kuhrt (listed in the Further Reading, p.219), which I revised using the online resources of the University of Texas at Austin Linguistics Research Center (https://liberalarts.utexas.edu/lrc/).

CONTENTS

LIST OF FIGURES

LIST OF MAPS

ABBREVIATIONS

Diod. Sic.	Diodorus of Sicily
Hdt.	Herodotus
Isoc	Isocrates
Lycurg.	Lycurgus
Lys.	Lysias
Paus.	Pausanias
PMG	D.L. Page, *Poetae Melici Graeci*
Stob.	John of Stobi
Thuc.	Thucydides
Tyrtaeus Fr. West	Tyrtaeus fragments cited from M. L. West, *Iambi et Elegi Graeci*

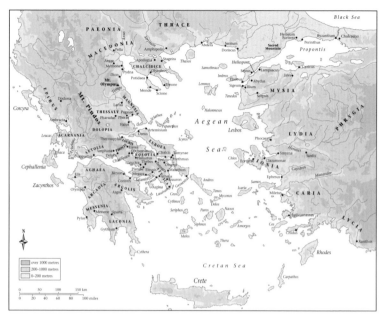

Map 1. Greece and the Aegean

1

Introduction

As you pass Lamia on the road south through Thessaly a vast mountain chain, with Kallidromon straight ahead and Mount Oeta to the right, looms up like an impassable wall (Figure 1). Even the modern traveller can get a sense of the massiveness of the obstacle. But this is a pale shadow of the sight which opened itself to Xerxes in 480 BC. Where now there stretches a wide alluvial plain there was a narrow pass (Figure 2). And the pass was occupied by a Greek force in a well-prepared fortified position. The army opposing him was contemptibly small, six or seven thousand, while Xerxes had brought the biggest army ever seen in the Greek peninsula. But the Greeks had chosen their position well. For two long days Xerxes threw in division after division only to have them thrown back with heavy losses. He was then informed of a narrow route through the mountain which would allow him to outflank the Greeks and take them in a pincer movement. He sent a Persian force with a local guide by this path to descend in the rear of the Greek army. After heated debate the Greek commander Leonidas sent away most of his troops before the net closed. The contingent which stayed, with a small band of Spartans at its core, held its own in fierce fighting against vastly superior odds until it was wiped out by arrow volleys from the Persians.

The story is well known and easily told. The battle was over in three days. The Greeks lost and the Persian army, mauled but victorious, rolled on to overrun much of central Greece. Their victory was short-lived. A month later the Greeks inflicted a massive defeat on the Persian navy in the narrow strait between the island of Salamis and

Figure 1. Thermopylae seen from the plain of Malis

Figure 2. Thermopylae from the hills above

the coastline of Attica. The Persian fleet—and the king—withdrew after the defeat, leaving the army to winter in Greece. A year later in a hard-fought and shifting battle the Greeks faced and defeated the Persian army at the Battle of Plataea in Boeotia. The Greek victory was sealed in a further battle at Mycale on the southern coast of Ionia in what is now Turkey, when the Greeks both defeated a Persian army and destroyed the fleet.

Salamis and Plataea changed the course of history. The immediate trigger for the invasion was the defeat of a Persian expedition against Athens at the Battle of Marathon ten years before. But the scale of the invasion made this more than a reprisal. Persia was the dominant regional power. It had been steadily expanding its empire since the middle of the sixth century BC. By the end of the century it had gained a foothold in the northern part of the Greek peninsula, in Thrace, an area largely inhabited by non-Greek tribes, though with settlements from different Greek cities strung along the coast, and in Macedonia, where the ruling family were Persian vassals. So movement southward into Greece was a natural next step. Our earliest source, the Greek historian Herodotus, claims that this invasion was itself a first step toward the ultimate conquest of Europe (Hdt. 7.5.3; 7.8.γ.2; 7.50.4). Persian expansion had been incremental and it is very unlikely that dominance of Europe was part of any grand strategic plan at this stage. But Xerxes and his advisers must have been aware that once they had gained a solid foothold in eastern Europe expansion westward was a possibility. One could play out the 'what-ifs' endlessly. But Greece was about to embark on a cultural era which would see the dramatic forms of tragedy and comedy gradually move outward from Athens to become a pan-Greek and ultimately a world possession. Oratory had yet to flourish as a literary form and with it rhetoric, the systematic study of persuasion. Historiography had not emerged (that in fact was in part a direct result of the Persian Wars, which inspired the quantum leap of Herodotus' history). The study of the physical world which had emerged in western Anatolia had not yet given rise to the study of moral (and then political) philosophy which would occur in

3

democratic Athens. The Persian empire was a 'thin' empire. The ruling power interfered relatively little in the cultural and religious life of the peoples it conquered, and Persian domination had not stopped the Greek states on the west coast and coastal islands of what is now Turkey (what the Greeks collectively called Ionia) from making great strides in the study of the natural world. Democracies had been tolerated. But even had Xerxes and his successors drawn a line west of the Greek peninsula, Greece (and by extension Europe, given the impact of Greek culture on Rome) would have looked very different. And had they eventually moved west, then . . .

All that stopped in 480–479. Greece remained what it had always been, a small peninsula of squabbling city states. The Persians withdrew to the Asiatic side of the Dardanelles and were then pushed back from the Aegean coast by a successful Greek retaliatory campaign under Athenian leadership. This was what victory at Salamis and Plataea meant. Thermopylae in contrast was a military defeat for the Greeks. Yet it is Thermopylae, far more than Salamis or Plataea, that has embedded itself in the memory of Europe and its diaspora. Like the massacre at the Alamo or the British retreat from Dunkirk in the Second World War it was a defeat which took on the aura of success in retrospect. Thermopylae has the compelling power of a loose tooth; it continues to attract debate and this will certainly not be the last book on the battle. The David and Goliath quality of the encounter, in which the greatest military power in the world was stopped (briefly) in its tracks by a vastly inferior force, gave the incident enormous appeal. The story was further seasoned with betrayal, in the shadowy local man Ephialtes who volunteered to show the Persians a route round the back of the defenders, and the courage of the final decision by a core element to fight and die at the highest cost possible to the enemy. The battle became the yardstick for the heroic stand against impossible odds and for a readiness to accept the ultimate sacrifice. It has been used and abused to celebrate genuine acts of courageous resistance against an invader such as the Battle of Tirad Pass in the American–Philippine War or dogged tenacity under fire like the Polish capture of Monte Cassino, and to glorify or palliate catastrophic imperialist or expansionist failures such as Little Bighorn, Isandlwana, and Stalingrad while casting resistance as aggression.

Thermopylae was one of those events which pass from history into myth and it made the transition immediately. It acquired a glamour exceeding the other battles of the Persian Wars and it has lost none of that appeal in the modern era. Though the Persians won on the ground, in the court of history the Greeks have been the winners—we see Thermopylae through their eyes.

2

Reading Thermopylae— The Problems

For the historian Thermopylae presents a clutch of challenges from start to finish. Any attempt to make sense of the battle struggles with a paucity of hard evidence. There was an almost total absence of (credible) survivors on the Greek side, at least for the last act. The Spartan contingent were almost all dead. This included the main protagonist, the Spartan king Leonidas. Our most important source, Herodotus, is happy to put thoughts into Leonidas' head. Although some of them may reflect his real motives and intentions, it is likely that what we have is inference, Herodotus' own or that of his informants. There were in fact two Spartan survivors from the battle according to Herodotus (Hdt. 7.229–32), but as the Spartans told it, neither survived long. One hanged himself on his return. The other chose to die fighting as a berserker at Plataea the next year. But even if they had lived long enough to repeat their story, both were disgraced by the sin of survival and so neither was likely to get a hearing in Sparta. Some of the Theban contingent probably survived. But since they survived by surrendering they had no good reason to trumpet the events on the last day and no audience outside Thebes for their account.

This of course applies only to the last stand. Leonidas dismissed most of the survivors when the Persian encirclement was confirmed, with the result that there was a large contingent which survived the battle. This was an allied force and Leonidas no more had absolute control over the contingents than commanders of coalition forces in modern times. Strategy had to be debated among the commanders. So there was ample opportunity to hear Leonidas' intentions. Herodotus actually gives us an account of the debate among the Greeks on the arrival of Xerxes, when some wanted to withdraw (Hdt. 7.207), and the debate after the encirclement (7.221.2–222.1) before the departure of the greater part of the force. There was also debate among the Greek allies before the collective decision was made to send the force to Thermopylae (Hdt. 7.175–7). And the Spartans had to deliberate before they decided how many to send, when, and whom. We do not know for sure when Herodotus began his research. We do know that he was still alive and writing at least at the beginning of the Peloponnesian War which split Greece in the last third of the century from an incident early in the war (the capture and execution by Athens of Spartan envoys to Persia in 430) which he mentions at 7.137. But the sheer scale of his narrative and his travels suggests that he must have begun work at least in the 440s. A man of twenty or thirty in 480 would then be in his fifties or sixties. So Herodotus could have spoken to survivors or to their sons. We cannot know (since Herodotus never tells us) whether he spoke directly to any ageing survivors or their descendants. He may also have had access to a poetic source contemporary with events. We know that the poet Simonides mentioned Thermopylae in a lyric poem of which only a small fragment now survives. Whether there was a more extensive treatment in the lost poem is unknowable. But Simonides also composed narrative poems on other great battles of the Persian Wars for post-war celebrations and it has been suggested that he might have written a narrative on Thermopylae. He certainly composed a narrative on the Battle of Artemisium and this too will have included references to Thermopylae. Finally, there were Greeks travelling with the Persians who gave him information directly or indirectly, such as the Athenian Dicaeus (Hdt. 9.65) and Thersander of Orchomenos (9.6). So he had access to events in the Persian camp. It is also likely that Greeks in the vicinity of Thermopylae were able to view the site after the Persian military machine rolled on and for reasons from the macabre to the patriotic many may have done so. Since Persia used the corvée system of pressed labour, probably locals were drafted in to bury the dead. Some of these (or again their children) will have been alive when Herodotus visited the battlefield. So he was in a position to check his story. That he did have access to some reliable information is confirmed by a simple fact. His account of how and where the remaining corps died is confirmed by archaeological evidence.

What we cannot do unfortunately is take the leap from what we can substantiate to the rest of the narrative. Herodotus' reliability has been the subject of endless discussion. Scholarship has moved a long way from Cicero's enthusiastic description of Herodotus as the 'father of history' (*Laws* 1.5). The extreme edge of the arc of academic discussion is in the 'liar' school, which views many elements of the narrative and the authorial claims to autopsy and enquiry as fiction. This perspective was already anticipated in antiquity. Plutarch in the Roman period devoted a whole essay to demolishing him in *On the Malice of Herodotus*. Plutarch had every reason to dislike Herodotus. He came from Boeotia and its leading city Thebes had enthusiastically 'Medized', i.e. collaborated, with the Persian invaders (the Greeks never fully distinguished between the Medes and the Persians), which earns it a bad press in Herodotus. More tongue-in-cheek is the satirist Lucian of Samosata, roughly contemporary with Plutarch, who in his *True History* (itself an elaborate fantasy) makes Herodotus one of the sinners punished in the underworld for telling lies (3.31). The most sustained modern critic of Herodotus' veracity is Detlev Fehling, who in an important monograph argued that Herodotus' claims to autopsy and to support from informed sources are a literary device. Herodotus is not writing what we would call 'history' and his audience knew how to read these gestures. Few now would subscribe to extreme revisionism of this kind. But even readers more sympathetic to Herodotus would struggle to guarantee every detail of his narrative on Thermopylae or anything else. Herodotus stands at a crossroads in the history of European literature, which his introductory paragraph makes clear:

> This is the presentation of the *historie* of Herodotus of Halicarnassus, so that events may not be lost to mankind through time and that great and marvellous deeds, some performed by Greeks and others by barbarians, may not lose their glory, including the reason why they went to war with each other.

The word I leave untranslated, *historie*, is the origin of our word 'history'. But it is not literally history in our sense, 'the study of past events, particularly in human affairs' (*Oxford English Dictionary*). It means 'enquiry' and by extension here 'results of enquiry'. It is less precisely devoted to the past, though the past is its main focus and is the glue which holds the book together, as Herodotus' introduction makes clear. But Herodotus is also interested in ethnography and geography—a whole book (book 2) is devoted to contemporary Egypt, while another (book 4) contains extensive descriptions of the Scythians of the steppes of eastern Europe. The narrative control which draws together such diverse material is itself a remarkable achievement, since the linear narrative (in a world which has yet to invent the footnote or the appendix) pauses to allow enormous digressive loops which incorporate the prehistory of events or the cultural background to peoples and characters. But the net result is that the simple strand of the Graeco-Persian Wars which he advertises in his brief preface as the subject of his narrative is embedded in a phenomenally rich tapestry, which takes its reader to the remotest corners of the world and looks at the shape of the world and the nature of its inhabitants.

There are two other terms worth flagging in Herodotus' opening paragraph. The first is 'marvellous deeds', *thaumasta erga*. 'Marvellous' is unambiguous enough, 'deeds' less so. Though I translate *erga* as 'deeds', it can also mean 'works', and Herodotus is also interested in other magnificent achievements such as engineering works, like the bridges and the canal which allowed Xerxes to invade Greece, and great monuments. And his sense of the wondrous extends to his account of fantastic places and creatures at the end of the world. This taste for the marvellous caused the Roman satirist Juvenal to dismiss both

Herodotus and Greek historians in general as purveyors of the incredible (*Satire* 10.173 ff.), and even Herodotus' admirer Cicero, almost in the same breath as he names him father of history, also notes his love of the fabulous. There is relatively little of this to trouble us at Thermopylae but we have to be alert to the possibility of exaggeration. The area where this matters most is arithmetic, which we will revisit in Chapter 4. Herodotus had no access to Persian muster lists for the expedition. His Greek sources had little opportunity to count Persians and every motive to multiply the actual figures, since the bigger the Persian army the more remarkable both the courage of those who faced them at Thermopylae and the glory of the Greek victory a year later. Herodotus did try to work out the size of the invasion force and he is not just confident but also rather proud both of the method and of the result. But for the land army he was working back toward numbers already in the tradition and his figures are generally regarded with something between extreme doubt and outright disbelief.

The other word to watch is 'glory'. Both the notion of glory and the words he uses here have a strong and specific resonance in their Greek context. His explicit aim is not just to preserve events but to preserve the fame of great achievements. And the terms he uses point to a particular model immediately visible to a Greek audience. His aim is to ensure that great achievements of Greek and barbarian may not become *akleë*, that they may not be deprived of *kleos*, 'glory'. The ultimate model in the Greek world for preserving glory is heroic epic. The heroes of Homer's *Iliad*, the ultimate war epic of the Greek tradition (and the most influential single text in the history of Greece), seek *kleos aphthiton*, 'undying glory'. This is what the poet bestows. And this by implication is what Herodotus gives to his subject. He insists that his theme is the single greatest war in the history of Greece when he introduces Xerxes' expedition near the beginning of book 7 (§20), immediately after the Persians have ratified the decision to invade:

> Of all expeditions we know of this was by far the greatest. The one that
> Darius led against the Scythians is nothing compared to this; nor is the

Scythian expedition, when they invaded Median territory in pursuit of the Cimmerians and conquered and held almost all the upper lands of Asia (for which Darius afterwards attempted to punish them); nor according to what we are told the expedition led by the sons of Atreus against Troy; nor the expedition of the Mysians and Teucrians, who before the Trojan War crossed the Bosporus into Europe, conquered all the Thracians, and came down to the Ionian sea, driving southward as far as the river Peneius. Not all of these nor all the others added to them rank alongside this single expedition.

Though Herodotus gives a list here of the earlier invasions, only one receives a comment on its source. That is the Trojan War, where he qualifies the reference to Troy with a disclaimer about the tradition. The comment is revealing. Troy and epic are the main competitors for his theme and the passage insists that in scale and significance Herodotus' story dwarfs that of Homer. This sense that fifth-century Greece has witnessed something analogous to the great deeds of the heroic age has obvious implications for his narrative. And it is especially significant for his account of Thermopylae, where we find recurrent elements drawn from epic, most notably in the treatment of Leonidas. As we will see, Leonidas' status, psychology, and courage, as well as the details of his death, are modelled visibly on the heroes of epic poetry. We cannot just dismiss this out of hand; it takes a remarkable level of courage to stand and face certain death. But we cannot simply accept all of this as unvarnished fact.

But although Herodotus is not quite, or not simply, offering history as we would define it, he cannot be dismissed as a source. Even modern authors who are highly critical struggle not to use him as their primary reference, for want of any comparable means of access to the events and people. After Aeschylus, who dealt in part with the war in his play *Persians* (whose focus is only on Salamis) in the 470s, he is the earliest source we have; and he did have access to sources close to the events of the war, including Thermopylae. But in using Herodotus we are not just making the best of a bad job. In the process of giving us the results of his enquiry Herodotus invents analytical history. His roots may be in epic but the result is very distinct from epic poetry in key respects. There is a third key term or concept which emerges right at the beginning of his narrative—cause, *aitie*. He did not invent the notion of cause. Greek poetry from Homer onward was aware of cause and effect. But the insistence on causal explanation as the primary job of the narrator is a new emphasis. And we only have to move a few sentences into his account proper to discover that his view of cause differs radically in focus from that of epic. His causality is emphatically human in emphasis, unlike epic poetry, where the narrative focus shifts frequently between the human and the divine level. The other significant feature of his introductory paragraph is an absence. The most common opening for an epic narrative poem is an appeal to the Muse: 'Sing, goddess the wrath' (*Iliad*), 'Tell me of the man, Muse' (*Odyssey*). Herodotus never appeals to the Muse. The significance of this cannot be overstated. The epic poet gets his inspiration and the authority for his account from a divine source. Herodotus gets his information from human informants and monuments. He gives us at one point (Hdt. 2.99) the bases for his story— autopsy (*opsis*), report (*akoe*, things heard), *historie* (enquiry), and judgement (*gnome*). Amid material which would not make it into a history book as it would be written now he offers us what is inescapably history. He tests his information where possible either by comparing or by judging on grounds of plausibility. He looks for reliable sources where he can, while aware that any source can be biased. In turning events into a coherent narrative he subjects those events to analysis in terms of explanatory models of behaviour. He also realizes that any one selection of events is an artificial sample from a much larger narrative. We can quibble, and we often do, about how he goes about his job. But this is a serious attempt to verify, understand, and evaluate.

There are inevitably further problems over and above those noted above, problems which are just part of writing history, and writing history in a particular historical context. Like any modern historian he brings to his story preoccupations which shape his narrative and his evaluation of acts and characters. The historian who does not has yet to be born. Like any Greek of his day he was prone to see the hand of the gods in human affairs, and is explicit about this. For many moderns this has been an obstacle to taking him seriously, though in fact he never invokes the gods as the exclusive explanation of the world. He approaches human history in empirical terms, as something explicable in terms of human psychological, social, and political tendencies. The gods supply an additional level of explanation, not a competing alternative. It is a level of causation which Herodotus himself intermittently espouses but one which his reader is (explicitly) free to take or leave, notably in his discussion of the forces which shaped the pass at Tempe (Hdt. 7.129.4):

> The Thessalians themselves say that Posidon [the god of earthquakes] created the defile through which the Peneius flows, plausibly. For anyone who believes that Poseidon shakes the earth and that fissures are the result of quakes caused by this god would on seeing this say that Poseidon caused it. For the gap between the mountains is the product of earthquake, as it seemed to me.

And he had his passions. He was fascinated by the prevalence of change in human affairs. His narrative also displays both a fascination with and a readiness to explain historical developments in terms of reciprocity and revenge. Notoriously he tends to explain great events in terms of individual experience and motives, but for wholesale escape from this tendency we have to wait until the twentieth century. So we have to sift his narrative in terms of internal consistency and plausibility, as he sifted his sources.

Though our earliest, Herodotus is not our only Greek source for the events. Later historians also provide accounts of Thermopylae and the events leading up to it. We have a narrative of the battle in the enormous Greek history of Diodorus of Sicily in the first century BC. And Thermopylae recurs intermittently in the work of the Greek essayist Plutarch writing into the second century AD in Rome. It is also treated briefly by the Latin writer Justin, again in the second century, who produced a summary of the expansive history of Pompeius Trogus, written in the first century BC. We cannot dismiss these authors on simple grounds of chronology. Ancient historiography, like modern, is fundamentally geological in nature; it builds up in layers and earlier works provide the underpinning, often the direct source, for later. Diodorus, Plutarch, and Justin/Pompeius are drawing on earlier sources, especially the fourth-century historian Ephorus. So late is not inevitably worse. Diodorus for instance gives us different numbers for the Greek combatants at Thermopylae. We do not know the origin of his figures, but we cannot dismiss them out of hand. Ephorus may have had at least one source for the battle which was independent of Herodotus in the poet Simonides. But some of what we meet in the later sources is suspect and is unlikely to come from Ephorus. Both Diodorus and Plutarch give us what they claim to be exchanges between Leonidas and the Spartan authorities at the time he was departing for Thermopylae. They are inspiring anecdotes. But they look like products of the biographical tradition, and Greek biography was prone to mythologize its subjects. So caution is needed.

Usually we might look to the victors for an account of the action. History notoriously is written by the winners. And for Xerxes and possibly for all or almost all of his subjects the invasion was a success. He had set out to conquer Greece. But an important part of his purpose was to punish Athens for its defeat of his father's army at Marathon and its earlier interference in Persian affairs. He had broken the opposition at Thermopylae; with vastly superior numbers, it is true, but war is about winning, not about playing with equal odds on a level playing field. He had killed a king of Sparta, the greatest military power in Greece. He had burned Athens. He had of course lost at Salamis. But that responsibility could easily be passed down the line to those at a more expendable level. Modern politicians and senior executives do it all the time. It was what Xerxes did when he ordered the execution of the engineers overseeing his bridges across the

Hellespont when the first attempt was destroyed in a storm (Hdt. 7.35.3). Those can be wild waters, as anyone will attest who has seen a storm there, and the bridges he finally built were damaged beyond repair within months of his descent into Greece. But for Xerxes the problem was not the technical difficulty of the task he set but the failure of his underlings to deliver.

So Xerxes had every reason to view his expedition as a success. He would not be the last (as he was not the first) ruler to spin glory out of more base matter. But on Thermopylae and indeed on the invasion as a whole the Persian voice is silent.[1] There was no Persian tradition of historiography in the Greek manner, which ultimately has become our way of writing history; that is, one or more independent researchers collecting information and absorbing it into an overarching analytical narrative. The Persians did have narratives. But the narratives were brief and biased royal assertions designed to project their power, wisdom, and achievements. A magnificent example is offered by the monumental inscription of Darius I, Xerxes' father, at Bisitun, describing the main events of his reign, starting with his rise to power. This or a comparable text was ultimately behind the story of his accession which found its way into Herodotus' third book. Self-glorifying narratives of this sort are a long way from the questioning historiography of the Greeks. But they do supply perspective and they do supply fact, even if the factual information is subjected to a ruthless control. Though our sources are far richer for Darius than for his son, Xerxes—like his father—celebrated his achievements in monumental form, as we can see from the famous 'Daiva' ('demon') inscription at Persepolis:

1. A great god is Ahuramazda, who created this earth, who created yonder sky, who created man, who created happiness for man, who made Xerxes king, one king of many, one lord of many.

2. I am Xerxes, the great king, king of kings, king of countries containing many men, king on this great earth far and wide, son of Darius the king, an Achaemenid, a Persian, son of a Persian, an Aryan, of Aryan lineage.

3. Xerxes the king says: By the will of Ahuramazda these are the countries of which I was king apart from Persia. I ruled over them. They brought me tribute. What was said to them by me, that they did. My law, that held them firm: Media, Elam, Arachosia, Armenia, Drangiana, Parthia, Aria, Bactria, Sogdia, Chorasmia, Babylonia, Assyria, Sattagydia, Lydia, Egypt, Yaunâ [i.e. the Greeks][2] those who dwell on this side of the sea and those who dwell across the sea, men of Maka, Arabia, Gandara, India, Cappadocia, the Dahae, the Saka [Scythians] who drink haoma, the Saka wearing pointed caps, Skudra [Thrace], men of Akaufaka, Libyans, Carians, and the Nubians.

4. Xerxes the king says: when I became king, there was among these countries which are inscribed above one that was in rebellion. Afterwards Ahuramazda brought me aid. By the will of Ahuramazda I struck that country and put it down in its place.

And among these countries there was a place where previously demons (*daiva*) were worshipped. Afterwards, by the grace of Ahuramazda I destroyed that altar of demons, and I proclaimed: 'The demons shall not be worshipped.' Where previously the demons were worshipped, there I worshipped Ahuramazda and Truth reverently. And there was other business that had been done ill. That I made right. That which I did, all I did by the will of Ahuramazda. Ahuramazda brought me aid until I completed the work.

You who will live hereafter, if you think 'Happy may I be when living, and when dead may I be blessed', have respect for the laws which Ahuramazda has established. Worship Ahuramazda and Truth reverently. The man who has respect for that law that Ahuramazda has established and worships Ahuramazda and Truth reverently, he both while living becomes happy and when dead becomes blessed.

5. Xerxes the king says: May Ahuramazda protect me from harm, and my house, and this land. This I ask of Ahuramazda. This may Ahuramazda give to me.

Particularly important is the account here of his crushing of rebellion and deviation from proper religious observance. Precisely what we are to make of this in personal terms has been disputed. The identity of the place or places in question again is problematic. What is clear is that Xerxes in Persia was a success story, and that the irreligious Xerxes who defies the gods in Herodotus is the product of Greek thought. One possible explanation for the Persian silence is that the invasion of Greece was a minor matter for them. It was a defining moment for Greece but in the context of an empire which stretched (at least in 479) from the Aegean to the Hindu Kush Greece was a very small area. Still, Xerxes by spending the best part of a year in person on the fringes of the empire had made Greece a big project, and his own. So the silence may be in part due to the accident of survival. One suspects, with or without archaeological evidence or any explicit pointer in our sources, that a monument somewhere trumpeted Xerxes' invasion of Greece as a success story. How much we might have learned from such a text is uncertain; but we would at least have heard Xerxes' voice. The stonemasons who created the text will have worked from a master copy ultimately sanctioned by Xerxes or his advisers and functionaries. In addition, the Persians were careful planners, as we can see from the awed way Herodotus singles out the supply dumps which they deposited in northern Greece prior to Xerxes' expedition (so unlike the haphazard Greek approach to provisioning troops) and the engineering works at Mount Athos and the Dardanelles. They were also meticulous record-keepers and enormous quantities of administrative documents have survived, including copious financial bookkeeping for various kinds of official business. So even if we lack the kind of subjective voice which the Greek sources offer, which might have given insight into Persian motivation, evidence from the administrative records could have supplied us with logistical information about troop mobilization, movement, outfitting, and provisioning. It might also have allowed us to get beyond Herodotus' colourful depiction in his extensive catalogue in book 7 of the diverse and exotic contingents from the Persian empire to see who actually fought in Greece. Sadly none of the royal accounts relates to this campaign.

We do have a source which was a little closer to Persia than Herodotus: the Greek physician Ctesias of Cnidus, who worked at the Persian court toward the end of the fifth century. His history of Persia survives only in secondary references in later authors, including a summary in the *Library* of Photius, Patriarch of Constantinople in the ninth century AD, a wonderful digest of the books read by his circle. Ctesias was long dismissed as hopelessly unreliable. Death is no bar to advancement and ancient careers, like modern, rise and fall. Ctesias' star has been rising of late. It may be, as has been suggested, that on some, perhaps many, issues he represents the view of Persian history prevalent among the Persian elite at the end of the fifth century. His work is, however, unreliable on chronology and often fantastic. He may on occasion get right what Herodotus gets wrong, but whether by accident or access to the facts is uncertain. It would be interesting to have his full narrative of Thermopylae. It features briefly in Photius' summary but what we read looks heavily derivative, and derived from Herodotus. It adds little if anything of substance and introduces some striking implausibilities, such as the vast number led by Hydarnes over the mountain path to take the Spartans from behind (it now becomes 40,000). He takes from Herodotus the repeated Persian attacks and adds only a neat linear escalation (attacks first with 10,000, then 20,000, then 50,000). He overdramatizes the disparity in the losses of both sides ('the vast Persian force was cut to pieces [*sc.* in the first encounter], while only two or three of the Spartans were slain'). He manages to lose all the allies (only the Spartans are mentioned). And he offers in his account of Plataea the next year figures and origins for the Greek combatants which make no sense at Plataea but perfect sense at Thermopylae. Somewhere in all of this there may be genuinely independent and useful information. But taken as a whole it looks more like an attempt to outdo Herodotus by reworking him than a serious attempt to offer a different view of events drawing on Persian sources.

So for Thermopylae, as for the invasion as a whole (indeed for descriptions of Persian culture and values more generally), we read the Persians through Greek eyes. But the Greek accounts themselves are transmitted through partisan filters which reshaped events in retrospect and neither Herodotus nor his informants could escape these. Chief among these is the back projection of a sense of Greekness on to a period where the notion of Greek identity was more cultural than political. Though the states of southern and central Greece (at least in part) managed to create and sustain a fragile alliance despite tensions, the sense of a loyalty to a larger Greece was to some degree a product of the success against the invader. At the end of book 8, between the battles of Salamis and Plataea, when the Persian situation is not what it was during Xerxes' juggernaut progress through Greece, Herodotus has the Macedonian king Alexander 'the Philhellene' (ancestor of Alexander the Great) bring a message from Mardonius the Persian general inviting Athens to defect. The Spartans intervene, anxious that the Athenians may accept the invitation. The Athenians reject Mardonius' offer, and in a reply to the Spartans heavy with reproof insist that they will not betray the cause of freedom nor the shared Greek identity, based on a common blood, religion, and culture (Hdt. 8.144). Conceivably the Athenians did speak like this. The Greeks did have ideals. And the sense of identity is real enough, as witnessed for instance by the Greek athletic games, which from the start in the eighth century BC were open only to Greeks. But this sense of identity did not run deep enough to prevent a whole range of pragmatic accommodations with non-Greeks. The Greeks had tolerated for a century or more the domination of the Greek colonies of western Anatolia, first by the Lydians and then by the Persians, and had offered only token support for the revolt by those Greek cities which began in 499, to be crushed decisively at the Battle of Lade in 494. It was common for Greek rulers when ousted to appeal, or just abscond, to Persia. Greek states in the path of Persia in 480 were willing to change sides out of a very real and realistic desire to escape the inevitable consequences of resisting an enemy which for any single Greek state was overwhelming. And those states not immediately threatened tried collectively to stop the Persians as far north as they could and keep the enemy from their own doorstep, always in the knowledge that they were abandoning fellow Greeks to Persian occupation. Even after Salamis, there was an influential view in the Peloponnese in favour of fortifying the Isthmus of Corinth as a viable defensive line and leaving the rest of Greece to its fate.

Things changed after the war. There was a concerted effort to remove the Persians from the whole of the Greek peninsula, finally realized when the Persian garrison at Eion on the river Strymon in Thrace was starved into surrender by a Greek coalition under Athens in 475. The Athenian alliance, known to us as the Delian League from the location of its treasury on the island of Delos in the Cyclades, then systematically swept the Persians from the Aegean. The League was soon to harden into an Athenian empire. But in the heady days of the post-war campaign of liberation the freedom of Greece and Greeks was an ideal which could command wholesale support. The war of 480 was inevitably read against this backdrop of unanimous commitment to Greek freedom. Memories were long and conduct in the war had enormous and lasting propaganda value. Where this matters for us is the way it impacts on Herodotus' presentation of Thebes, the arch-Medizer. Viewed in retrospect Thebes was a traitor to Greece. This is felt in both the account of Leonidas' motives in bringing a Theban contingent to Thermopylae, which ignores the realities of Theban politics, and the realities of war. It also impacts on his account of the fate of the Thebans in the final phase of the battle.

Another distorting filter was the conflict between the Greek states which began less than a generation later, which sharpened animosities between some of the participating states. Athens, like Sparta, had a good war and Sparta, long the dominant power in Greece, was wary from the start of a potential rival strong in precisely the area where Sparta was weak. The Athenian walls had been destroyed by the Persians and this suited Sparta nicely; Spartan jealousy manifested itself already in the 470s, when they tried unsuccessfully to prevent the refortification of Athens. The hostility only increased in the decades after the war as Athenian expansionism brought increasing friction and intermittent warfare with Sparta from the late 460s onward. The hostility culminated in the Peloponnesian War between the two power blocs, the Athenian empire and the Spartan-controlled Peloponnesian League, which lasted (with a break for a period of phoney war) from 431 to 404, ending with the defeat of Athens and the dismantling of the Athenian empire (and briefly of Athenian democracy). All this enhanced an inevitable tendency to see the Persian Wars in terms of 'Athenian' and 'Spartan' successes. This was not entirely untrue but it did oversimplify. For us what matters is that non-Spartan elements in the Greek force were obscured in subsequent perceptions of the battle as part of this binary presentation of the Persian Wars.

And the story itself changed over time. There was probably never a moment when one could look coolly at the battle. Possibly there never has been and never will be. Thermopylae passed into legend almost at once. And the mythologization grew with time. This too had implications for both the perspective of Herodotus' informants and his own, as well as for the reception of the battle in subsequent ages down to the present.

The accretion of legend which obscures events and motives is matched by the literal accretion of soil on the battlefield. Battlefields are often elusive things. Precise location of the action is not always easy. And change in land use or water patterns can obscure or destroy physical remains, especially in the modern era, when so much open space has been swallowed up by urban development. At Thermopylae change in the level of the sea due to deposits from the Spercheius river and the hot springs has added several kilometres to the coastline, so that the narrow pass is no longer a pass but the edge of an alluvial plain; and soil build-up has raised the ground by about 20 metres, turning the hill of the final stand into a low knoll. This is not just a difficult battlefield to read. The terrain has changed beyond recognition and it requires an enormous effort of imagination (or digital imaging) to see the pass as they saw it.

There is one final problem to stress. We read history backwards but people in time live it forwards. When we look back we lose our sense of history as granular process, and as process in which at any point things might turn out differently. Hindsight is profoundly vulnerable. It confers an illusion of inevitability on events which could have turned out differently. We know that the Persians turned the Greek flank and we suppose therefore that the flank would be turned whatever Leonidas or his forces did. This in turn invites us to superimpose our inevitability on to the perspective of the participants and turn results into intentions. We risk losing the sheer untidiness of situations as they unroll. Hindsight invites us to ignore accident, luck, and error, and overemphasize the degree of knowledge and control exercised by those involved. We need to view history, and especially military history, as process. By that I mean that we have to see a campaign or a battle not as a static clash of structures, systems, resources, values, or ideologies but as an evolving situation in which individual decisions at different stages based on information available expand or contract the options open to the participants and adjust the balance between contenders. This may seem too obvious to mention but the heffalump trap is not too obvious for researchers to avoid.

3

The Pass

Coming south, before you reach Thermopylae you pass through the open terrain of Thessaly and enter the plain of Malis at the head of the Malian Gulf. The Malian plain is enclosed to the west by the steep slopes of Mount Oeta and the precipitous gorge of the Asopos river just north of Oeta, and to the south by the vast bulk of Mount Kallidromon, across the river Spercheius. As seen by the modern visitor, the plain of Malis spreads for several kilometres toward the sea and the slopes of Mount Kallidromon descend to a continuation of this plain. The flat land north of Kallidromon and the eastern end of the Malian plain are the result of seismic action and silting from the Spercheius and deposits from the springs of sulphurous hot water which gush down the slopes of Kallidromon. In the fifth century BC the soil level was about 20 metres lower and Kallidromon, like many Greek mountains, descended steeply down to the sea.

The modern highway runs parallel to the northern edge of Kallidromon through what is still a pass, though much wider than it was in antiquity. The pass as it now is runs on level ground west to east along the southern shore of the Gulf. The name Thermopylae, 'Hot Gates', refers to the warm springs which still gush from the rocks in the pass (Figure 3). Today there is a thermal spa there. Ancient sources sometimes speak simply of 'the Gates' (*Pylai*), which reflects the importance of the pass as a point of entry to central Greece. The shorthand is revealing. This is *the* gateway to the south. It is not the only way into central Greece, as is sometimes thought. There are other routes from

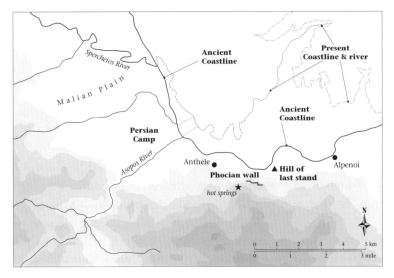

Map 2. Thermopylae 480 BC

north to south. One alternative route, which figures at the end of Herodotus' account of the action in the pass, runs through the Dhema Pass in the south-western corner of the Malian plain. It involves a detour to the west just north of Thermopylae, heading south round Mount Oeta then south-east along the Cephisus valley to enter Boeotia. But the route through the pass was (and is) the more direct route, which is why the main road from Athens to Thessaloniki still runs through it.

Though the landscape has changed dramatically in the intervening millennia, one can still recognize the way the undulating edge of the mountain creates pinch points in the terrain. The multiplicity of pinch points explains the plural, not 'Hot Gate' but 'Hot Gates'. There are, or were, three. Herodotus describes the pass as follows (Hdt. 7.176):

> The entrance through Trachis into Greece is half a plethron [about 15 metres] wide at its narrowest point. It is not at this point, however, that the coastal area is narrowest, but in front of Thermopylae and behind it;

24

at Alpenoi, which lies behind, it is a just a cart-road, and in front at the Phoenix river, near the city of Anthele again just a cart-road. West of Thermopylae is a high mountain, inaccessible and precipitous, stretching up to Oeta. East of the road lie marshes and sea. In this pass are hot springs for bathing, which the locals call the Basins, and an altar of Heracles stands nearby.

Herodotus here seems to envisage the pass as running north to south. This could reflect ignorance but the level of detail in his description suggests the authority of an eyewitness. He had been there. His loose language probably reflects the pivotal role of the pass for anyone entering Greece from the north like Xerxes. The terrain he describes is shaped like a double bow. The pass is narrowest at the east and west entrances, 'in front . . . and behind' in Herodotus' language, where there is a road only just wide enough for cart traffic,

Figure 3. The hot springs at Thermopylae

that is (to judge by other ancient cart-roads) no more than 5 metres and possibly as little as 2. The pass proper as he sees it is in the middle, where he places his Greeks. The hill where the final cohort died can be identified with confidence as (what is now) a low mound across the road and directly opposite the modern memorial to the battle with its statue of Leonidas. The excavations conducted by a Greek archaeological team under Spiridon Marinatos in the 1930s found arrowheads datable to the fifth century and of an oriental type (Figure 4); interestingly they found only one spearhead. This agrees with Herodotus' statement that by this stage almost all the Greeks spears were broken. It also confirms that the Persians did not finish them off at close quarters. All this is consistent with Herodotus' claim that the Greeks retreated to a hill in the pass before being shot to death by archers. So we have a solid piece of topographical evidence to prove that he got the details of the final massacre right in both the manner and the place.

It has been argued that the road along the Dhema Pass between Oeta and Kallidromon, not the route through Thermopylae, was the northern end of the main north–south route from the Isthmus of Corinth to northern Greece (the so-called Isthmus Corridor).

Figure 4. Arrowheads found at Thermopylae

This rests both on archaeological research into settlement patterns along the Cephisus valley and on geological research at Thermopylae itself. There is no reason to doubt that there was a significant arterial route west of Kallidromon. It is the status claimed for the route—and particularly the conclusions about the role of the western route and about the state and status of Thermopylae in the archaic and early classical period—which has met with resistance. On the basis of the geological sampling it was argued that the pass at Thermopylae was not open to large-scale traffic in the fifth century BC because of the sea level. The case has been hotly contested. Apart from the difficulty of dating geological data with the precision needed for historical research we would have to ask why, if Thermopylae was impassable, the Greeks did not know it. This is not merely a problem with writers like Herodotus who described actions in the pass but generals who tried to break through and opponents who sought to prevent them. The Spartans sent several hundred troops to risk their lives in the pass and the numbers were swelled by thousands more from southern and central Greece. And as we shall see later, this blocking action was repeated time after time in subsequent ages. The repeated manoeuvres and battles are not fiction. The pass through Thermopylae was both open and of crucial strategic importance.

This whole debate may, however, be misconceived. If you were to ask anyone who has travelled in modern times between central and northern Greece to picture Thermopylae in the age of Xerxes, they would probably envisage a route, whether a built road or simply a beaten path, running along the shoreline more or less at sea level, running parallel to the slopes of Kallidromon (like the modern road) between the hills and the waves. I certainly did. This is how the modern movies imagine the site. This would in turn mean that our battlefield lies somewhere below the silt on which the modern road rests, though closer to the hills.

This is not inconceivable. But it raises real problems. The first is the so-called Phocian Wall. In his description of the terrain Herodotus says at 7.176: 'In this pass a wall had been built, and in early times it had

Figure 5. The 'Phocian' Wall

a gate. It was the Phocians who built it for fear of the Thessalians.' The Greeks decided to restore this wall and it plays a role in the Greek defence, as we shall see. But for now what matters is its position. It is generally identified with a long line of wall foundations on a hill slightly south (that is inland) and west of the hill of the final stand. The two hills must have been separated by a valley before the deposits lowered the hills and filled the gaps between them. The remains of the wall run zigzag east–west along the hill for about 200 metres and there was a tower at the western end, possibly matched by another at the opposite end, though there is now no trace of this (Figure 5).

Though all maps and almost all studies identify these remains as the Phocian Wall, the identification is anything but certain. But if it is right, and the materials and construction would fit a date in the archaic period, this is far too high above the ancient shoreline to offer a defence or even a useful base to any Greek forces downhill to the north. Reinforcements would have to trek 20 metres down a steep slope to engage the enemy. This is not just a test of physical fitness. The German scholar Stählin pointed out almost a century ago that a Greek position 20 metres downhill would be exposed to a flanking manoeuvre from above at just this point. The Persians would not need a path through the hills behind Kallidromon to get into the rear of the Greek position. If this is the Phocian Wall, the fighting must have taken place in the hills above the shoreline. Even if we dismiss the claim of these remains to be the Phocian Wall, we still have problems. Herodotus' description of the coastline as 'marsh' or 'shallows' (*tenagea*) does not suggest a sandy strand. Accounts of the later actions in the pass agree. Pausanias in recounting the later battle against Brennus and the Celts in 279 BC (Paus. 10.21.3) speaks of 'swamp' (*telma*), while Livy writing on the battle of 191 BC speaks of 'swampy mud' (*palustris limus*) and 'quicksands' (*voragines*), and Dexippus in the third century AD speaks of 'mud' (for these engagements, see Chapter 7). Our sources suggest that the line of hills dropped steeply to the sea and that the shoreline was made up of muddy shallows. Pausanias offers us another clue in his account of the fighting against the Celts. The Athenian triremes bring much-needed aid to the Greek forces by coming close to shore, despite the risk of grounding in the mud, and attack the Celts with missiles. Finally many of the Persian and the Celtic invaders 'fall' into the sea and drown (Hdt. 7.223.3; Paus. 10.21.4); the language suggests not that they are pushed sideways into the shallows at sea level (where rescue would anyway be relatively easy) but that they are pushed by the sheer mass of fighters to tumble down the slopes and are unable to scramble up the steep banks out of the muddy water. And the water was deep enough to drown a man and (just) to take the shallow draught of a trireme. All this suggests that the road had to climb the coastal hills below Kallidromon for part of its way rather than following the shoreline. The key point for us is that, even if the water lapped up to the foot of Kallidromon, it is unlikely that the pass was ever closed in antiquity.

But where did the road go? Probably it went uphill along the contours between the West Gate and the Middle Gate. The slope along the line of the hill to the west of the Middle Gate is relatively gentle. The fact that some of the Persians fell into the sea during the third day's fighting could suggest that the battle took place to the north of the wall and the road passed over this shoulder of land before dropping down to the south to turn back on itself in the direction of the sea through the defile between the fortified hill and Kolonos, the hill of the final stand. It then turned east on lower ground to continue to the East Gate. One advantage for the defenders on this view is that anyone passing the wall from west to east has his vulnerable sword/spear side exposed. The problem is that the wall as we have it faces south. South of the wall the ground drops and there is a gully below the eastern end. This and the orientation of the wall suggest that the road passed south of the wall into this gully before turning toward the coast. The gully would be a natural place for the Greek camp. This seems at odds with the claim that some of the Persians fell into the sea on day three, which would make more sense if the road passed north (on the seaward side) of the wall. But the fighting that day took place west of the area protected by the wall. At the east end of the gully there is a spring, which (on either reconstruction of the road) gave the Greeks access to fresh water as long as they held the Middle Gate. At this point the road turned to pass between the

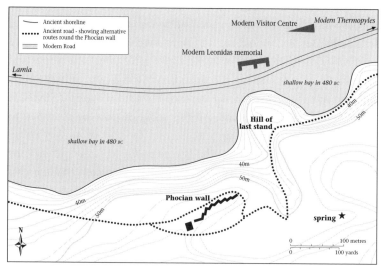

Map 3. The Persian Empire

walled hill and the hill of the last stand, to continue on its way at or near sea level. Whether we take the road north or south of the wall, this route means that the battlefield is not completely lost. It is not, as I had long thought, buried beneath 20 metres of silt. It has lost its contours and its context but is still there waiting for us.

This route for the road explains the orientation of the wall parallel to Kallidromon, not at right angles (Figure 6). The maps in most modern studies tilt the wall by 90 degrees to make it run broadly on a north–south axis. This imaginative redrawing reflects an understandable desire to have the wall at right angles to the shoreline to block the

Figure 6. Aerial View of the Middle Gate

pass. Sadly there is no archaeological evidence to support it. Unless we are prepared to move the stones, these maps are just wrong. The wall as we have it did not block the road but dominated it, though in its original form it could have continued to the 90-degree turn the road took at the Middle Gate. In earlier times it had a gate, though we don't know precisely where; but this 90-degree turn would be a good location. Wherever it was, Leonidas' troops in rebuilding the fallen wall probably did not retain the gate, since in Herodotus' account of the final battle the Greeks retreat from the open area to the west of the Middle Gate, 'passing the wall', to take refuge for their last stand on Kolonos hill (Hdt. 7.225.2). He does not say that they passed through it. They followed the road and turned to pass the end of the wall through the defile between the two hills.

One detail still puzzles. The Persians tore down the wall as the Greek survivors retreated to Kolonos. Why destroy a wall parallel to the road, now that they controlled the road itself? The answer is probably that the wall was still an obstacle. They had to divide around it to pursue the Greeks. Without it, their troops could move en masse both along the road and along the higher ground where the wall had stood.

In one key respect the proponents of the Isthmus Corridor are right about Thermopylae. The absence of a road at sea level, the slope, and the narrowness of the entry and exit points to the pass meant that it was not an ideal route for large troop movements and poor terrain for wheeled traffic. But Herodotus told us long ago that the pass was narrow. It is, however, just a short distance, about 6 kilometres. The going would be rough, but Greek and Persian armies alike must have often manhandled wagons on demanding ground. And Herodotus' language at 7.200 ('there is . . . a cart-road constructed'—*dedmetai*, the same verb he uses for the Phocian Wall at 7.176) makes clear that there was a man-made road of some sort there. What it looked like is uncertain; it will almost certainly not have been paved; but the soil may have been levelled in places, some rocky outcrops flattened and perhaps some cutting back of the base of the cliffs at the narrowest points. It cannot have been as ambitious as the road built a century later by Philip II of Macedon; but it was not just a dirt track.

The location of the battleground means that the Greeks in the last stage of the fighting retreated a very short distance. But they relocated to a narrow-topped and steep-sided hill, quite unlike the low knoll which the alluvial deposits have left us in its place, where badly armed as they were they presented a formidable target. For the Persian bowmen finishing them off it must have been like shooting fish in a barrel. Not sporting but a pragmatic way of dealing with tough and determined men who now had nothing to lose.

It is worth asking why if there was an alternative route, Thermopylae continued to play such an important role. Why not simply bypass Thermopylae, as the Germans did with the Maginot Line in their invasion of France in the Second World War, and just take the longer road into Greece? Part of the answer is that Thermopylae was and is the most direct way to penetrate central Greece. And even for an invader ready to adopt the roundabout route, bypassing Thermopylae was not really an option, since to ignore the pass risked leaving one's rear exposed to attack. Xerxes had to eradicate the resistance in the pass, irrespective of any route he planned to take into Greece.

The other topographical feature of note is the Anopaea path. The route taken by Hydarnes through the hills, like almost every other feature of the battle, has long been the subject of vigorous debate. But we can save that until we start the battle. For now all we need to remember (as if we could forget) is that there was a route over Kallidromon behind the Greek position.

One final note is worth making before we follow the Persians to Thermopylae in Chapter 4. Herodotus has Xerxes seated in a position where he can observe the action (Hdt. 7.212). He jumps up three times as he watches the failure of his troops. We can accept that Xerxes would be as close to the action as possible. The king's presence was important for morale and Herodotus' account of Salamis stresses the importance of the king's gaze to the Persian forces (Hdt. 8.86; 8.90.4) for fear or favour. Scholars have suggested that there may be a position at the western end of the pass on a spur of Kallidromon which would allow Xerxes to obtain a good view of the fighting. But we need to be a little cautious. The detail reflects Herodotus' desire to create a vivid narrative and to tie together different strands in his story in order to make a moral and psychological point. As the invasion force prepares to cross the Dardanelles near Abydos on the south shore, Herodotus' Xerxes has a viewing platform built in a position where he can see the whole of his vast army and fleet (Hdt. 7.44). There is in fact no position which would allow his gaze to take in the whole of the strait and the large area of the adjacent land which would be occupied by his troops. He again watches the army as it crosses (Hdt. 7.56). Herodotus is there setting up Xerxes for his fall. Just as he watches his army in its prime, so he has to see it fail with his own eyes. The detail at Thermopylae is in turn a foretaste of the climactic viewing at Salamis (Hdt. 8.90.4), where Xerxes will watch the destruction of his fleet. There is another relevant act of viewing in the narrative. In book 4 Darius watches his army as it crosses the Bosphorus on the bridge he has had built on its way to his invasion of the land of the Scythians (4.88). That invasion was a costly disaster. The viewing at Salamis was given to Herodotus by tradition from an authority contemporary with the events (Aeschylus, *Persians* 465–7). That both Xerxes and Darius would want to view the crossing is plausible enough. That does not make it ascertainable fact and one suspects that here (as almost certainly at Thermopylae) Herodotus has intervened to add details and sharpen the lessons of his account of Xerxes' pride and fall and his failure to learn from his father's expansionist mistakes.

4

The Persians

The Long Road to the Pass

By the time he reached Thermopylae Xerxes had been on the road for over a year. But the journey began much earlier. His presence in Greece was the end stage of a long chain of events which stretched back into the sixth century. By its close Persia had become the most powerful state in the east Aegean and Anatolia, encroaching eastward and westward to build an empire which stretched from the eastern shores of the Aegean to the Indus. In the west the expansion had come at the expense of the Lydian empire, whose king Croesus had unwisely provoked Persia and lost. The empire had a toehold in Europe, since Thrace had fallen under Persian control in 513 and Macedonia shortly after. Herodotus claims that Darius, who ruled Persia from 521 to 486, contemplated expansion into Greece (Hdt. 3.134). Certainly the idea may have occurred to him. But there were no aggressive moves. The Persian empire on its western edge included the Greek colonies strung along the coast of what is now Turkey and the offshore islands. It was the Greek element in the Persian empire which ultimately brought about the Graeco-Persian Wars. But the mainland Greeks showed no particular inclination to meddle with Persian control in its own sphere of interest. So it was anything but inevitable that Persia and Greece would come to war. Greece was anyway at this stage divided into a large number of city states, each controlling a small part of the peninsula in territory largely determined by geographical features, each with its own interests to pursue and often in conflict with each

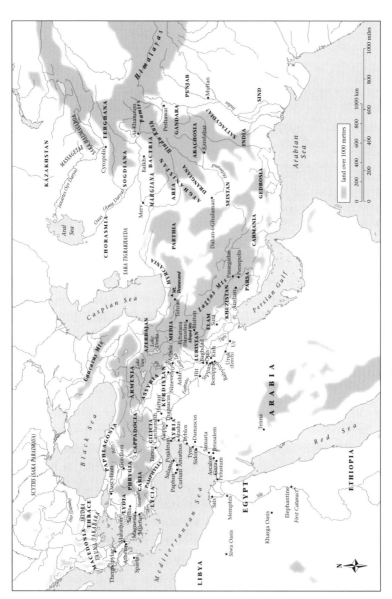

Map 4. Middle Gate (Greek position) at Thermopylae

other. There was a firm sense of Greek identity but this was always in tension with local and tighter loyalties. So Greece was unlikely to meddle collectively with Persia. It was not Greece but part of Greece, the city state of Athens, which provoked Persia in the first instance.

The conflict between Athens and Persia arose from political change in Athens. For the second half of the sixth century Athens had been ruled by a dictatorship (what the Greeks called a *tyrannis*, 'tyranny') under Pisistratus and then his son Hippias. The regime was finally overthrown in 510 with the aid of Sparta. In the political struggle which followed, Sparta again intervened, this time in support of the anti-democratic faction, in a failed attempt to put down the nascent democracy. Like other Greek states Athens was happy to work with non-Greek powers against their Greek neighbours. So the Athenians appealed to the Persian satrap (governor) of Lydia on the east coast of Asia Minor for support (Hdt. 5.73.2). The satrap, Artaphernes, seems to have offered little in the way of explicit guarantee, but he demanded that the envoys give earth and water. This was the standard ritual for acceptance of Persian authority. It was not capitulation to Persian rule as such; but it was an acknowledgement of inferior status as a subordinate ally of Persia. Herodotus claims that the envoys were criticized on their return for exceeding their brief in this respect. The claim that the envoys made the concession on their own initiative could be Athenian rewriting of their history in order to recast themselves as inveterate opponents of Persia from the start. It is possible that the envoys were empowered in advance to make such a gesture, since the Athenians, when they sent them, must have had some inkling of the way Persia dealt with other peoples. Possibly the situation at Athens had changed in the time it took the envoys to cross the Aegean and travel inland to Sardis and then reverse their steps; Persian aid may have seemed less urgent and so the concessions demanded by Persia less acceptable. If the envoys acted on their own initiative in accepting Artaphernes' demands, it may be that the Athenians were willing to accede retrospectively to a gesture of subservience which had no practical implications; this might be true even if the envoys were criticized and even if they were brought to trial, a not uncommon fate for incautious envoys under the democracy. Whatever the facts, we do not hear that the Athenians formally repudiated the gesture. From the Persian perspective both the appeal for assistance and the sealing of some sort of formal relationship were cost- and risk-free, since there is no evidence that Artaphernes made any move to assist the Athenians and the Athenians were able to block Spartan interference in the process of democratization without any external assistance. Athens was a long way away and there was little to be gained for Persia at this stage from military interference in local Greek squabbles. Possibly for Athens Persia was only ever meant to be a sabre to rattle in the face of Spartan pressure. For Artaphernes (and possibly Darius, if he was consulting the king) it provided a potentially friendly state in Greece, a useful card to have even if Darius had no clear idea how it might be used.

The relationship changed a year later. After failing in its attempt to put the oligarchic faction in power Sparta had reversed its hostility to the tyrant and backed Hippias, the exiled son of Pisistratus. The plan to reinstate him came to nothing in the face of opposition from Sparta's allies. With no real hope of effective support from Sparta Hippias turned to Persia. The Athenians sent a counter-embasssy, again to Artaphernes, who instructed them to take back Hippias under threat of war. The Athenians refused and considered themselves at war with Persia (Hdt. 5.96). Little changed on the ground, however. Persia made no move to punish Athens for non-compliance (Persian support was as much use to Hippias as it had been to Athens against Sparta) and Athens for its part made no move to provoke Persia.

The situation changed in 499 when the Greek cities on the eastern shore of the Aegean rebelled against Persian domination. Attempts by the leader of the revolt, Aristagoras, the tyrant of Miletus, to raise support in Greece were mostly unsuccessful. Unsurprisingly his first stop was at Sparta, the most formidable fighting force in Greece at this date. Unlike most Greek states, which fought using a citizen militia called up as needed, Sparta had something resembling a standing army. With a large quasi-serf population (the helots) to undertake the farming (and any other labour) needed to support them, the Spartan elite were free to devote much of their free time to military training. They trained from youth and from their youth were subjected to a ruthless discipline. Sparta was also leader of the Peloponnesian League, a coalition of southern states, and so able to bring a substantial army into the field. But there was evidently no appetite in Sparta for intervention in Ionia. Sparta was at this stage aggressively extending its influence in Greece and they may have felt that they had their hands full without taking on overseas adventures in addition. They may also have felt that the prospects of success for the revolt were poor or simply that the seaboard of Asia Minor was too remote to be of interest or use to them. As Herodotus tells it, Aristagoras was virtually run out of town (Hdt. 5.51.3). He received a better reception in Athens. What motivated the Athenians to intervene is unclear. Possibly they could not resist the opportunity to hit back at Persia for the support given to the exiled tyrants. Whatever the reason Athens provided twenty ships and troops. The only other Greek city to give support was Eretria on the island of Euboea, which provided five ships. The rebels with their allies marched inland from the coast, and captured and burned Sardis, the old Lydian capital and now the seat of Persian government in the region. When the enemy rallied they retreated in haste, pursued by a Persian army which defeated them in battle near Ephesus. The Athenian ships returned home and Athens abandoned the cause, refusing repeated requests for help. The revolt continued and even gained ground until the Ionians were decisively defeated at the Battle of Lade in 494. Persian reprisals against Miletus, the state at the head of the rebels, were savage.

We are told that Darius' reaction to the news of the burning of Sardis was first to ask who the Athenians were and secondly to fire an arrow into the air while making a prayer that he might avenge himself on them. So incensed was he that he ordered a servant to say to him three times a day, as his meals were set before him: 'Master, remember the Athenians' (Hdt. 5.105). As often, there is gold here, if we know how to look. The emphasis on personal anger is normal for Herodotus, as is the eye for the dramatic detail. The anger may be real in a culture where state policy is an extension of the king's will. But there *was* for Persia a policy issue beyond any personal response. For the best part of a century the Greeks of the mainland had acquiesced in the domination of the eastern Greeks by a foreign power. The support from the west set an unwelcome precedent. Darius could not allow intervention from Greece in support of the Greeks of Asia. And the disparity between the belligerents (reflected in the question which Herodotus puts into Darius' mouth—'who are the Athenians?') exacerbated the affront. To us looking back, Athens is the most memorable city in Greek history. At the beginning of the fifth century there was little sign of what was to come. The fleet which would win the Battle of Salamis had yet to be built. The democracy was new. The great cultural achievements lay in the future. The power of Persia had been challenged by a small state on the edge of the world. It was almost inevitable that Persia would punish Athens to make clear that the west coast of Asia Minor was exclusively Persia's sphere of interest. Greek support for the revolt had been lukewarm at best and the mainland Greeks simply needed a reminder of the cost of meddling. The reaction came in 490, when Darius sent an expedition under the joint command of Datis and Artaphernes to attack Athens.

The Persian force stopped briefly to sack Eretria before landing at Marathon in south-eastern Attica. The expedition was accompanied by Hippias, the exiled tyrant; Marathon was in an area where Hippias' family had long been influential and this may in part have influenced the choice of place to land. The other factor was that the terrain favoured the deployment of the Persian cavalry. In the event neither the Persian cavalry nor the archers seem to have played any part in the battle, which was an infantry clash of the sort the Greeks favoured. The Athenians supported only by troops from the small city of Plataea in Boeotia defeated the Persians and drove them into the sea, where the butchery continued as the Persians fled.

The scale of the expedition, the precise targeting, and the fact that it came by sea only with no land support, make clear that this was primarily a punitive raid. It may also have occurred to Darius that a sea raid across the Aegean allowed him to reciprocate neatly in kind for the ships from Greece. But success in the raid might have opened up further possibilities. Darius had sent the general Mardonius to northern Greece in 492 (Hdt. 6.43–5). His mission may simply have been to reinforce Persian control in the north. But even so a firmer hold in the north opened the option of expansion further south, if opportunity offered. Hippias did not accompany Datis and Artaphernes simply to provide local knowledge; he expected to be reinstated with Persian support. A friendly vassal in Athens would have been very useful if Darius decided to expand into Greece. None of this amounts to evidence of a plan. But it does look like an expansion of options and for those who like the 'what-ifs' of history it is tempting to imagine what might eventually have followed a Persian victory at Marathon.

The Athenians must have been aware that the Persians would be back. If Darius was prepared to send an army across the Aegean in response to Athenian aid to the Greeks of Ionia, he had all the more reason to retaliate for the defeat at Marathon, which was a second blow to Persian prestige. This must have been in the minds both of the Athenians collectively and the politician Themistocles, when he persuaded them to invest in their navy in the years after Marathon. The state owned the silver mines under the soil of Attica and, when a new vein of silver was discovered in the 480s, he persuaded the Assembly to spend money on ships instead of distributing the proceeds among the citizen body (Hdt. 7.144). The immediate rationale for Herodotus was that Athens needed to build up the fleet in order to have an advantage over the neighbouring island of Aegina, with which the Athenians were at war. There is no good reason to doubt this. But the recent experience of a Persian invasion by sea must have played a role in the decision. In the event, though the fleet proved decisive at Salamis, Xerxes frustrated expectations by coming by land.

Darius never did get to punish the Athenians. The assault on Greece was postponed by other more pressing business. The intractable Egyptians revolted from Persian rule. Herodotus' focus on the Graeco-Persian conflict leaves no room for Egypt, whose revolt makes only a perfunctory appearance in the *History*. From a Persian perspective, however, Egypt was far more important. Egypt was one of the great grain-producing areas in the Aegean. Control over Egypt mattered for the Persian food supply; Egypt also paid a high level of tribute. But maintaining control was not easy. Egypt had been conquered in 525 but two years later a rebellion had to be put down. And the revolt in 486 was not to be the last. Egypt was also more urgent. On seizing power Darius had faced a chain of revolts and there was always a possibility that other regions would follow Egypt and secede. So rapid and decisive action was needed. While Darius was preparing for the expedition he died. His unfinished business was picked up by his son Xerxes. We are badly informed about the campaign but resistance was probably stiff. Once he had settled Egypt, he was free to turn his attention to Greece.

Though Egypt was more urgent, we should not dismiss the importance which Herodotus gives to the Greek campaign as nothing but Greek self-absorption. Xerxes accompanied the expedition to Greece in person. This involved an enormous journey of about 4,000 kilometres from Persepolis to Athens by land and an absence of more than a year from the seat of government. The expedition against Greece mattered to him. Both Aeschylus and Herodotus offer psychological explanations for Xerxes' decision to invade Greece. The two key themes are personal ambition and the desire to rival his father. They are putting thoughts in his head and words into his mouth but what they say makes sense. Xerxes' policy was to present himself as a mirror image of his father in order to emphasize continuity with the past. Darius had seized power in a well-orchestrated coup and his accession to the throne had been followed by widespread revolt. He then took pains both to create an aura of legitimacy around his accession and by a series of astute marriages to prevent the emergence of claimants to the throne. A policy of insisting on stability and seamless continuity both helped with the process of retrospective legitimization of the regime and encouraged satisfaction with the status quo. This policy dimension is very visible in the expedition. Darius was a very effective campaigner and an expansionist ruler, and the expedition with Xerxes himself at the head made the invasion a continuation of his father's policies, especially as Darius had himself sent an expedition against Athens. It also allowed Xerxes to mirror his father's engineering achievements. He bridged the Dardanelles to enter Europe as Darius had bridged the Bosphorus in his abortive campaign against the Scythians. The bridging in both cases reflects practical needs but the similarity cannot have been lost on observers. The same applies to the canal which Xerxes commissioned through the narrow neck of Mount Athos, the most northerly of the three prongs of the Chalcidice peninsula in north Greece (visible on Map 1). Mardonius had lost a fleet off Athos on his expedition into northern Greece. The canal allowed his ships to avoid the storms which blow round the headland. So Xerxes' canal had a practical role in facilitating the movement of troops and supplies. But again there is an echo of his father. We know from the Chalouf stele which Darius set up in Egypt that the canal which he commissioned there was a source of pride (as well as practical politics):

> King Darius says: I am a Persian. From Persia I seized Egypt. I ordered this canal dug from a river that is called Nile and flows in Egypt, to the sea which begins in Persia. Afterward this canal was dug as I had ordered and ships went from Egypt through this canal to Persia, as I wished.

Again one is struck by the resemblance to his father. But in a monarchy like that of Persia the political is always also personal and we should not dismiss Herodotus' account out of hand. Xerxes was a new ruler keen to establish himself; and his own accession had been contested by his half-siblings before Darius declared him his heir (Hdt. 7.1.2–3). His propaganda stressed this formal acknowledgement by Darius. An addition to the empire would be good for Xerxes' standing. The invasion of Greece allowed Xerxes both to present himself as a dutiful son in personally punishing the Greeks for the affront to Darius and at the same time to outdo his father by pacifying an enemy which had defeated him. Xerxes' physical presence at the head of the army in the field presented him as a worthy successor, while at the same time going beyond what his father had done in sending underlings to capture Athens.

The Persians were meticulous planners. The level of planning is reflected in the engineering works. Two bridges close together were put in place at the narrowest point of the Dardanelles (Figure 7), where the strait is little more than a kilometre wide (Hdt. 7.33–6). This is an area which can suffer from violent and sudden storms and the first attempt at bridging failed. Xerxes had the engineers in charge executed and ordered the work to begin again. A further bridge was put in place over the river Strymon in Thrace (Hdt. 7.24). We are not given a

Figure 7. The Hellespont (Dardanelles) at its narrowest, site of Xerxes' double bridge

timescale but the second bridge pair at the Hellespont was probably begun in late winter of 481/480 in time for Xerxes to cross in the spring. Herodotus gives a very detailed description of the bridges and was both fascinated and deeply impressed by the engineering, as he often is by ambitious construction works. Each bridge was made by lashing warship hulls in line to make pontoons (360 ships for one and 314 ships for the other), with a palisaded causeway laid down on top and gaps to allow merchant shipping to pass through. Herodotus claims that the canal was begun three years before the expedition (Hdt. 7.22). The timescale is probably exaggerated, since the neck of the Athos peninsula is low-lying and narrow and the ground presents no geological problems (Figure 8). For the Persians this was not a novel engineering feat. But the organization was typically thorough. The work was done by local pressed labour working in relays. Some Greeks by the Roman period doubted that the project was ever finished and some modern scholars have supposed that the canal was dug through only part of the isthmus and combined with sections

Figure 8. The southern end of Xerxes' canal through Mount Athos

of causeway (*diolkos*) for dragging ships. But recent research has confirmed that the canal was completed. It appears to have fallen rapidly into disuse and this probably explains the later doubts. The defeated Persians had no subsequent need of it and the depth may have made it unsuitable for laden cargo vessels. So it was probably left to silt up. The extensive engineering work probably served a collateral propaganda purpose, apart from the practical task of facilitating the movement of men and animals. It gave ample warning of the Persian invasion plans and their capacity and determination to deliver. The scale and elaboration of the preparation were unlike anything experienced in warfare in Greece and the implied message was that resistance would be futile. Surprise was never part of the plan. And until they met resistance at Thermopylae the strategy of intimidation worked.

The other aspect of the preparation which impressed Herodotus was the supply depots which were set up along the route in friendly territory (Hdt. 7.25.2). Greek armies did not usually carry substantial supplies. They tended to rely on markets en route and in general they operated with a highly devolved arrangement for buying provisions rather than having a central quartermaster securing the food supply. So forward planning on this scale was remarkable. As long as the Persian army moved through territory which they controlled, they were guaranteed supplies. Beyond that they could rely on the Greek states which came over to the Persian side as they advanced. Beyond that again they would rely on plunder.

By the winter of 481/480 Xerxes had progressed from Persepolis through Anatolia to rendezvous with his troops at Critalla (precise location unknown), before marching to the coast. His progress was unhurried. This was a good opportunity for a royal progression to allow the western regions of the empire to see the new king, and the king to get a clear sense of this part of his empire. Xerxes spent the winter in Sardis not far inland before continuing north and crossing into Gallipoli in the spring and beginning a slow march through Thrace, pausing just beyond the river Hebrus to marshal his troops before they moved toward Greece proper. Herodotus gives a slow and detailed account of the march into Greece which both reflects the leisurely progress of the army and creates the impression of a gradually gathering storm relentlessly advancing south and collecting momentum (in the form of fresh levies) as it moves. It was this relentless movement that brought Xerxes in August 480 to the Malian plain north and west of Thermopylae, where he found the Greeks waiting. It is surprising that Xerxes (or his generals) did not send an advance guard to secure the pass. The Thessalians certainly understood the strategic importance of Thermopylae. Xerxes may not have realized its importance until he had Thessaly under his control and access to better local knowledge, by which time it was too late. The Greeks had taken control of the pass while the Persians were still in Macedonia (Hdt. 7.177).

His progress so far had been unimpeded. Thrace and Macedonia were already broadly under Persian control (insofar as the Thracian tribes could ever be fully controlled). Thessaly was divided. The Aleuadae, the ruling family of Larissa, wanted Persian support against rivals and had urged Xerxes to enter Greece (Hdt. 7.6.2). According to Herodotus, the rest of the population had no desire to be subject to Persia, but after support from the south petered out they had acquiesced in the Medism of the Aleuadae for want of any alternative (Hdt. 7.172–4). All this meant that Xerxes' advance had been more of a royal progress than a military march. The ready capitulation of everyone in his path had the advantage that he had suffered no losses. It also meant that he had acquired territory which was not impoverished by war and therefore capable both of providing supplies for the army and of paying tribute once absorbed into the empire. But he had yet to meet the Greeks in battle and he did need a military victory, if he was to prove worthy of his father. So he was probably not disappointed finally to face action at Thermopylae.

Though Herodotus tells us that the Persians recruited as they marched, the bulk of the forces were those he brought from or through Asia (Hdt. 7.115.2). Just how big and how diverse the Persian forces were is unclear. Herodotus offers a catalogue of the contingents from the empire which occupies a full sixth of book 7 (§§61–99). His list includes troops from as far north as the steppes of eastern Europe, down to Egypt and Ethiopia, and as far east as India. Its job is not just to give us fact but to contribute to the atmosphere and the themes of his history. The list is both vivid and exotic. It serves to slow down the narrative in order to create suspense and to underscore his insistence that this expedition was unprecedented in scale. But when the fighting starts almost all we see are the Iranian forces in action (the Medes, the Persians, and the nomadic tribes of the central European steppes which the Greeks called Scythians and the Persians Saka). So we cannot be sure how many of the other peoples figured on the expedition, if at all, and in what numbers. But the list of divisions (which mirrors his list of the Persian satrapies in book 4) contains a great deal of authentic fact and must reflect a Persian source of some sort. It looks as though Herodotus has combined Aeschylus' claim in Persians (1–60), that Xerxes has drained the empire to assemble his forces for Greece, with a muster list of potential contingents available to the Persian king. It could be that any presence from the peripheral regions of the empire was a token contribution. It may be, as has been suggested to me, that Xerxes found it politic to take leaders from subject territories to ensure that they did not get up to mischief in his absence and that the regions donated troops both to demonstrate loyalty and to share in the glory. But the upshot is that the army may not have been as diverse as Herodotus maintains, possibly either essentially or predominantly Iranian.

This has a bearing on the odds at Thermopylae. Herodotus reaches a figure of 1,700, 000 for the Persian infantry (Hdt. 7.60.1, 7.184.4; to which he adds 80,000 cavalry, Hdt. 7.85, 7.184.4, none of whom fought at Thermopylae). He is frank that he lacks precise numbers for the different contingents (Hdt. 7.60.1) and therefore (though he does not say this) for the whole force. He is clearly working partly on tradition and partly by estimate. Tradition had handed him a huge figure in the epitaph for the Peloponnesians at Thermopylae (see Chapter 8)—no less than three million. His figure is only a little over half of this. But unsurprisingly even this lower figure is generally rejected. It would make this invasion over one-third the size of Operation Barbarossa, the German invasion of Russia, the largest invasion in history, which used all the mobilizing force and logistical resources of a modern industrial state. Greek tradition had every reason to exaggerate the scale of the Persian forces after the event, as (for purposes of intimidation) did the Persians beforehand. Different approaches to the arithmetical problem have been tried, ranging from an assumption of arithmetical error to logistical projections based on the need to secure water supplies in a dry climate. All reconstructions are conjectural. Most end up with an army roughly in the region of 200,000. Even this may be too large. An army even half that size would be enormous by ancient standards. But it would still leave the Greek forces at Thermopylae facing odds of about fifteen to one. Halve that conjectural figure again and the imbalance between the sides would still be dramatic.

So on any calculation the Persians had an overwhelming advantage in terms of numbers. They did, however, have a serious disadvantage in terms of position. The Greeks were occupying a narrow pass where the Persians could not use their vast numerical superiority to envelop them. They could only advance in a column with the rear unable to engage the enemy usefully, while piling pressure on the front ranks, hindering both manoeuvre and retreat, and potentially increasing any casualties.

The Persians had to clear the Greeks out of the pass, if they wanted to continue south. Even if they chose to take the westward route down the Cephisus valley, they could not leave a hostile force in their rear. At the very least Xerxes would have to leave a large force behind to neutralize them, and even a small Greek force left in the pass could be swelled at any time by reinforcements to form a genuine threat. They also had to take it reasonably quickly. They needed to keep a vast invasion force supplied and provisioned. Any figure we reach for the combatants by whatever means has to be swelled by a host of support personnel: guides and scouts, armourers, butchers, bakers, cooks and servants, farriers, wheelwrights, carpenters, sappers, herdsmen, medics for man and beast, priests, and other camp followers such as wives, mistresses, whores, slavers, and other merchants to deal with booty. The royal entourage alone must have been enormous, since the king and other members of the elite would need a small army of servants. This elite included not just the extended royal family and the Persian nobility but also the various Greek exiles accompanying the expedition in the hope of reinstatement, such as the Spartan ex-king Damaratus and the new generation of the Athenian tyrant family (Hdt. 8.52). They also needed fodder for cavalry mounts, baggage animals, and horses or oxen pulling the carriages of the elite non-combatants, such as the Greek woman who accompanied the army as the mistress of a high-class Persian and who abandoned the Persian army after Plataea (Hdt. 9.76.1). And they had now moved beyond their supply dumps in Thrace and northern Greece (Hdt. 7.25). The Greek fleet had taken up a position at Artemisium in northern Euboea, threatening the entrance to the Malian Gulf and preventing the army from being provisioned from the sea. The Persians were now reliant on local supplies by land. They were in friendly territory, and so they could look to the local allies for supplies. But the more time passed, the further they would have to go to source them. The same would apply especially to grazing such a large animal stock, both military and baggage. Water too would become a problem. The plain where they were camped was drained by several rivers. Thus far water supplies had presented no difficulties, but in the hot Greek summer they could anticipate growing problems, not just in securing water but in getting clean water. The constant trampling of men and beasts would gradually foul the rivers, as would urine and faeces from the animals drinking. The Greeks in contrast had a water supply behind their position and their far smaller numbers and few if any animals made their situation far more sustainable. And they had ensured a ready food supply base in the village of Alpenoi not far behind their lines (Hdt. 7.176.5). It has been suggested that it might only take a week to make the Persian position untenable. This may be over-optimistic; but the Greeks could reasonably hope to use the Persians numbers against them logistically as well as in the fighting on the ground.

In another respect time was on the Greek side. It was now late summer (around the end of August) and the Persians needed to maximize their gains before the end of the campaigning season. They also had to reckon with the possibility that the Greeks would send reinforcements to strengthen their defensive position, perhaps even (for all they knew) that reinforcements were already on the way. They needed to take the pass and to take it quickly. This probably explains why Xerxes opted for a frontal assault on terrain which favoured the defenders instead of sitting and waiting out the enemy or pounding the Greeks with day after day of unremitting volleys from the Persian archers to break their will. Xerxes or at least his generals would be well aware that the casualties could be high. What they could not gauge in advance was the determination of the troops facing them. Thus far the Greeks had not offered battle. They could anticipate that the Greeks would be intimidated (as they undoubtedly were) by the sheer scale of the forces facing them, and it was entirely possible that resistance would crumble rapidly. If not, they could expect to wear the Greeks down by force of numbers. The sheer persistence of the Greeks probably was a surprise. On this Herodotus is almost certainly right.

Xerxes did not launch an attack immediately on his arrival at the pass. Instead he waited four days (Hdt. 7.210.1). Herodotus tells us that he expected the Greeks to retreat. Though a victorious fight would be better both for Xerxes' reputation and as a demonstration of the futility of resistance, a Greek retreat would allow him to advance south more rapidly. So we should not dismiss the idea. Later sources go further and have Xerxes send messages to the Greeks inviting surrender and the Greeks refuse. The narratives smack of mythologizing, but, stripped of legend, they are not incredible. Xerxes had plenty of Greek-speakers to act as intermediaries. But the silence of Herodotus is a serious obstacle. A firm rejection of an invitation to surrender would only enhance his tale of immense courage against overwhelming odds. It looks as though no such stories existed in the fifth century.

Whether or not Xerxes considered the possibility of a Greek retreat, probably the main reason for delay was the need to get his forces in place. A large army straggles and Xerxes was not in a position to launch an immediate attack. He must have waited for the whole force, or at least his key units, to arrive and settle in camp before deploying. He must also have conferred with his commanders. He sent scouts to spy out the Greek camp (Hdt. 7.208) and he probably also sent scouts to search for routes around the pass. It required little experience to reason that the best way to unblock the pass was to look for a way round it. If he did try to scout out a flanking option, the attempt was unsuccessful. This option only became real after two days of hard fighting. Xerxes was probably also waiting for news of the arrival of his navy. He needed the ships in place to hold down the Greek fleet and leave him free to concentrate on the Greek land forces. In addition a successful engagement at sea would allow him to land men in the Greek rear and overwhelm the opposition in the pass. The navy had been hit by storms on the way down the coast of Mount Pelion and he may have wanted to reassure himself that it was still capable of dealing with the Greeks at sea. On the fifth day, evidently satisfied that all was ready, he sent the Medes and the Cissians into the pass.

5

The Greeks

In the rear-view mirror of history the stand at Thermopylae looks inevitable. But Thermopylae was not the first choice. The Greeks always knew that they needed to face the Persians as far north as possible, if they were to limit the encroachment into Greece and maximize the forces at their disposal. The only question then was how far north was feasible. Greece was not a single nation (it owed its eventual unification to Rome) but a collection of independent states divided by natural features, mostly mountains, each with its own government and laws and its own variation on the shared religion. Resistance to the invasion required a coalition and the coalition was confined to a number of states on the mainland with a little assistance from some of the Aegean islands. Attempts to recruit ethnic Greeks from further afield, including Sicily and Crete (Hdt. 7.153–62, 169–71), had proved unsuccessful, and some Greek states on or near the mainland preferred to remain neutral, including Argos in the Peloponnese and the island of Corfu off the west coast of Greece (7.148–52, 168), while others either favoured Persia or hedged their bets. They did, however, manage to put together an alliance based at the Isthmus of Corinth to plan the defence, led inevitably by Sparta, the strongest power on the peninsula and the leading state in the Peloponnesian League. Xerxes had sent envoys demanding earth and water from the Greek states and some had complied. This did not necessarily mean they had gone over to the enemy. It was more of an insurance policy. But the Persian army was formidable and the Greek alliance could anticipate that the Greek states in the path of its advance would go down in succession like dominoes. Each state which surrendered added to Persian strength and weakened the Greeks' position, and potentially their collective resolve. The alliance was shaky throughout; though the Greek states declared a suspension of inter-Greek hostilities (of which there were always several at any one time) in the face of a common threat (Hdt. 7.145), the natural tendency of Greek states to think in terms of local interest meant that the southern states always had one eye at least on the option of withdrawing south of the Isthmus of Corinth. So it was important to deny the Persians as much of Greece as they could.

This was the Spartan reasoning according to Herodotus in his account of the decision to send troops to Thermopylae (Hdt. 7.206.1). The native tribes and Greek cities of Thrace in the far north had never really stood a chance. Macedonia was long lost to the Greek cause, since it was a Persian dependency before the invasion. So the focus shifted to central Greece and Thessaly. Thessaly was important, since its cavalry offered a means to counteract the Persian strength in this area. So the first Greek attempt to check the Persian advance in 480 sought to deny them Thessaly. The rulers of Larissa, the Aleuadae clan, were keen to have the Persians in Greece to boost their own power against the rival rulers in other parts of Thessaly. But there was enough opposition, for whatever reason, to make it worthwhile for the Greeks to deny Thessaly to the Persians. According to Herodotus, the anti-Aleuad factions sent envoys to the Greek alliance at the Isthmus and urged them to send military support to prevent Thessaly falling to the Persians (Hdt. 7.172.1).

So the first line of defence was at the valley of Tempe between Macedonia and Thessaly, flanked by the massive bulk of Olympus to the west and Ossa to the east (Figure 9). The logic in the choice of Tempe was simple. The valley is narrow and could be held by a relatively small force; Persian numbers would be of no use. The Greeks sent a force 10,000 strong there. Herodotus places the allied expedition to Thessaly before Xerxes had passed into Europe (Hdt. 7.174), but it must have been undertaken after he arrived in northern Greece, or

Figure 9. The valley of Tempe

the army would have had to camp there for months. This was predominantly a land operation, unlike the more ambitious joint operation which was to follow at Thermopylae. Ships were used to take the land forces up to Halos on the Gulf of Pagasae, to allow them a short march up through Thessaly to Tempe, and then were left at the port. But a combined operation, at least like the one at Artemisium and Thermopylae, was impossible. The river Peneius flows through Tempe to the sea and there is good anchorage just south at (what is now) Agiokambos on the coast of Mount Ossa. Greek warships simply beached for the night and the beach there is extensive. But the shoreline faces the Aegean. So the Greek fleet would meet the Persian fleet in open water, where the Persians would be at an advantage both in numbers and in skill. The fleet did, however, remain in position in the Gulf (Hdt. 7.173.4). If it was meant to play an active role, its task may have been (as has been suggested) to prevent the Persians from landing forces behind the Greek position. An encounter in the confines of the Gulf would be less threatening for the Greeks, though they did risk being blockaded there.

The Greek force remained at Tempe only for a few days. They were visited by messengers sent by the king of Macedonia, Alexander the son of Amyntas, urging them to abandon the position because of the overwhelming numerical superiority of the Persian army. Alexander was later known as the 'Philhellene' but here, as elsewhere, his role is ambiguous. He was a vassal of Persia and it may have suited Xerxes and his Aleuad allies to push the Greeks further south and add the Thessalian cavalry to their forces. More to the point, the Greeks realized that there were alternative routes which circumvented Tempe. So they risked being cut off. They withdrew in haste. In the event the same was true of Thermopylae, since there was a track (Anopaea) over Kallidromon which could circumvent the Greek position, but the allies did not realize this until they reached the pass. The withdrawal from Tempe made excellent sense but it cost them Thessaly. Herodotus seems a little sniffy about the Greeks' decision (Hdt. 7.173–4) but they had no choice.

It was a subsequent meeting of the League that decided on Thermopylae. Thermopylae had all the topographical advantages of Tempe. It was again a confined space which allowed a small group of defenders to face a much larger army, and, as Herodotus pointedly remarks (Hdt. 7.177), the Persians would be unable to deploy their cavalry. Just how much use the Persians made of their cavalry in battle has been debated. But the opportunity to use cavalry was instrumental next year in Mardonius' decision to fight in the open terrain of Boeotia at Plataea (Hdt. 9.13.3) and the cavalry proved very effective in the subsequent battle. Cavalry were of limited use in direct attack on tight formations, but they could be very effective in disrupting communications and interrupting supply lines, and devastating in cutting down infantry in flight. If (as was argued in Chapter 3) the battle took place on the slopes above the shoreline and not on the flat, then not just the confined space but also the uneven nature of the terrain ruled out any cavalry action.

One important advantage for Thermopylae was that, unlike Tempe, the new position allowed an amphibious campaign to meet the twin land and sea threats from Persia. We tend to think of Thermopylae in isolation but there were two actions going on simultaneously and they were interdependent. The Greeks stationed a fleet of 271 triremes plus a number of lighter ships at Artemisium on the northern tip of Euboea. Their job was to protect the land army by preventing the Persians from disembarking a force in the Greek rear and also to cut the link between the Persian fleet and their land forces. The topographical advantages applied both to the land position and the fleet, since the location at Artemisium placed the Greek fleet in the strait between northern Euboea and the south coast of Pelion, allowing them to avoid an engagement in the open sea while also watching for any attempt by the Persian navy to sail east around Euboea to attack them and the land army from the south. The distance between the position at Thermopylae and the naval station was only 60 kilometres, allowing for communication between army and fleet by messengers in light craft (Hdt. 8.21).

We are given different numbers for the Greek force in our sources. Herodotus lists the contingents at 7.202–3 as follows:

> (from the Peloponnese) 300 Spartans; 500 each from the Arcadian cities of Tegea and Mantinea, 120 from Orchomenus and 1,000 from the rest of Arcadia; 400 from Corinth; 200 from Phlius; and 80 from Mycenae

> (from central Greece) 700 from Thespiae and 400 from Thebes (both in Boeotia); 1,000 from Phocis; and 'the total fighting force' from Opuntian Locris.

The contingents listed come to 5,200 (3,100 from the south, 2,100 from central Greece). Without a figure for the Locrians we cannot gauge the total force as Herodotus sees it. When examined alone Herodotus' list looks like a very meagre turnout. But it excludes the naval forces at Artemisium, which he does not enumerate until he begins his account of the battle at Artemisium. The fleet was provided by Athens (which fielded by far the largest contingent and whose crews included their long-standing allies, the Plataeans of Boeotia), Corinth, Megara, Chalcis, Eretria and Styra in Euboea, Aegina, Sikyon, Sparta, Epidaurus, Troezen, Locris, and the small island of Keos in the Aegean.

This is still a patchy turnout and some of the contingents were small but the naval list explains some obvious absences from the forces in the pass.

Diodorus (Diod. Sic. 11.4) offers different figures for the forces at Thermopylae. He gives no breakdown of the Peloponnesian levies, simply a global figure of 3,000, not far from Herodotus' 2,800 for the Peloponnese other than Sparta. From central Greece he omits the Thespians and adds 1,000 Malians, that is, from the territory west and north of Thermopylae, while keeping the 400 Thebans and 1,000 Phocians. He also gives a figure for the Opuntian Locrians of 1,000. But the most striking difference is in the Spartan contingent. There is some ambiguity about his figure, since he starts with a firm statement that Leonidas took 1,000 'Lacedaemonians' but then speaks of '1,000 Lacedaemonians, with them 300 Spartiates'. This would most naturally mean 1,300 in all, of whom 300 were Spartiates, that is, members of the hard core of full Spartan citizens, and 1,000 'Lacedaemonians', Spartans outside this elite group. But it can mean 1,000 including 300 Spartiates and this seems more likely in view of his opening statement. He is unlikely to have contradicted himself on a key detail within just a few lines. And except for the Thebans he is working consistently in multiples of 1,000. Diodorus' numbers give us a total of 7,400.

It is impossible to tease out authoritative figures from these two accounts. Confidence in Diodorus' arithmetic overall is reduced by his loss of the Thespians. This is not a negligible omission. The Thespians were wiped out with the Spartans. They are the other heroes of Thermopylae. So unless something has fallen out of the manuscripts at some stage, we have a glaring omission, especially since he includes the Thespians in his account of the last stand (Diod. Sic. 11.9), with the strange detail that Leonidas 'detained' them, which looks like a confused recollection of Herodotus' explanation of the presence of the Thebans at the last stand (Hdt. 7.222). Faith in Diodorus' figures is further dented by his inclusion of 1,000 Malians. The Persians were already occupying Malis, which must have simply capitulated like most states in Xerxes' path. It is conceivable that this was an anti-Persian faction or that a force sent by Malis before the Persians reached the plain was now cut off with the central and southern Greeks. If so, it is odd that we never hear of it elsewhere. His figure for the Locrians is valuable if true. Herodotus claims that they sent their entire army and 1,000 seems implausibly low for the total complement of adult males of fighting age. Centuries later Pausanias (Paus. 10.20.1–2), who otherwise simply reproduces Herodotus' figures, worked out that they might have sent about 6,000. As the next state in the path of the invader (and the state where the battle took place) they had good reason to turn out in force. But they also had to defend their own territory in the event of defeat in the pass. So we might well work with a guesstimate of 2,000, which would still make them the largest Greek force in the field.

In view of his inaccuracies we might be tempted simply to dismiss Diodorus. But his figure for the Peloponnesians has one big advantage—it brings their numbers into line with the only contemporary (literally) solid evidence, the grave inscription for the Peloponnesian fighters at Thermopylae cited by Herodotus at 7.228:

Against three million here once fought
from the Peloponnese four thousand.

Unfortunately Diodorus' agreement with the inscription cuts two ways. It may give us access to an authoritative source independent of Herodotus, whether oral tradition or the poetry of Simonides. But he or his source, presumably Ephorus, may simply be trying to arrive at a figure (1,000 Spartans and 3,000 other Peloponnesians) which fits the verses. The issue is complicated by the fact that Isocrates in the fourth century BC twice gives a figure of 1,000 for the Spartans at Thermopylae (*Archidamus* 99; *Panegyricus* 90). It is difficult to know where Isocrates got his number. In both contexts there are inaccuracies and this could be his own invention; Athenian orators are free in their treatment of historical fact. But the count could be from the same source used by Ephorus. What we can say for sure is that the number 1,000 had entered the tradition at least by the middle of the fourth century and this strand of the tradition is probably the basis for Diodorus' arithmetic.

If Diodorus' figure for the Spartans is correct, then his total of 1,000 could include either the enslaved helots serving the Spartan hoplites or they could be drawn from the *Perioikoi*, literally 'those who live around', free Spartans who lacked the full rights of the Spartiate elite. There were certainly helots at Thermopylae, as Herodotus repeatedly tells us (Hdt. 7.229.1; 8.25.1); a Spartan would always take one or more to serve him when in the field. At Thermopylae it looks as though Herodotus believed that there was one helot to every Spartan hoplite—when a blinded man insists on returning to the fight, he is led by 'the helot'/'his helot' (not 'a helot') (Hdt. 7.229.1). But it would be very surprising if the helots were included among the Greek totals for the fighters, either in the inscription or anywhere else, in view of the ingrained status distinctions throughout Greece between slave and free and the Spartan contempt for the helot population. It would be equally odd if Diodorus simply bundled the free with the unfree without comment. The Spartans certainly started to use helots as troops later in the century, and their presence among the dead after the battle (Hdt. 8.25.1) indicates that some, perhaps many or all, fought in the last stand on the hill. But Herodotus' only firm reference to their role at 7.229 suggests that even if they assisted in the fighting they were there to serve the warriors. Perioikoi were more likely than helots to be included, either in the inscription or in Diodorus, and this may be the easiest way to square the numbers. But we are then left with a worrying hole in our information and our sources. Herodotus insists (Hdt. 7.224.1) that he managed to obtain the names of all 300; and the traveller Pausanias 600 years later saw a monument bearing the names (Paus. 3.14.1). This inscription could have been Herodotus' source or (as has been suggested) it may be a later compilation. Herodotus does not mention any inscription. Whether his claim is a statement of fact or just an authorial boast designed to emphasize the thoroughness of his research, it suggests that Herodotus could find no evidence for more than 300 from Sparta. What happened to the other

700? If they stayed and died, why did their sacrifice disappear from the record? If they did not stay and die, the withdrawal of a substantial Spartan contingent, even non-Spartiate, makes it more difficult to account for the awe that surrounded the last stand among the Greeks, especially when the Thespians in contrast stayed on and died to a man, and twice as many as the Spartiates. And even if the other Spartan contingent withdrew, common sense suggests that some of these 700 must have died in the first two days of fighting, since they must have taken their turn in the line either alone or with the Spartiates; yet no names were remembered in Sparta.

But simply dismissing Diodorus and his source does not solve our problems; we would still be left with the mismatch between Herodotus' 3,100 Peloponnesians (including the Spartans) and the 4,000 of the inscription. Herodotus knew the inscription; he is our earliest source for it. His precise figures for the contingents involved may just mean that he had done his arithmetic and concluded that the number in the inscription was wrong. In including it in his text he is simply, as so often, offering competing versions and leaving the reader to decide. In just the same way at 7.60.1 and 7.184.4, he gives a figure for the Persian infantry (1,700,000) which is radically different from the three million of the inscription. But we still have to explain the discrepancy in the Greek numbers, even if he doesn't. We cannot exclude the possibility that the author of the inscription has simply rounded up the number to produce a terse and elegant tribute. The number for the Greek forces is in the original 'four chiliads' (*chilias* being the Greek collective noun for 1,000). The Greek words which I translate as 'three million' actually say '300 myriads', *myrias* being the Greek collective noun for 10,000. The collective nouns create a neat contrast between the Persians and the Greeks: four chiliads face 300 myriads. Three chiliads would be neater still but it was easier to round up to four than down to three chiliads. Greek verse worked not with stress patterns but with sequences of long and short syllables (that is, depending on how long it takes to pronounce) and the second line of the Greek elegiac couplet (the norm for epigrams by this date) was _uu_uu_ _uu_uu_ (where _ is long and u is short). Within this schema the word for 'four' (*tetores*) will fit, the word for 'three' (*treis*) will not. It has also been suggested that the inscription mistakenly includes a contingent from central Greece. But the southerners had no reason to dilute their numbers with Greeks from further north. Another possibility is that one or more of the Peloponnesian states overestimated their numbers in order to burnish their patriotic credentials in the aftermath of the war. It could be, however, that Herodotus' total is wrong and that either he has missed out one or more Peloponnesian contingents (for instance from Elis, Sikyon, or Epidaurus) or the reference fell out of his text during the many centuries of transmission by manuscript copy. Whether or not Herodotus or his manuscripts erred, his precise counting in contrast to Diodorus' broad-brush arithmetic suggests that he did try to check his facts and that on the specific issue of the Spartan numbers his 300 is more likely to be correct, even if we struggle to square his tally with the inscription.

The reader who has waded through this morass of conflicting arithmetic and competing options is left with a very uncertain figure. But we probably have a Greek force of around 7,000 troops on any count. Whatever figure we reach, the Greek army in the pass was dwarfed by the Persian forces.

The Greeks, however, arrived ahead of the Persians (Hdt. 7.207). How far ahead we are not told. But they had plenty of time to establish and strengthen their position. Though they were outnumbered on both land and sea, their early arrival gave them an advantage. At Thermopylae they were able to seize and fortify the pass. They found a ruined fortification wall there and they had enough time to rebuild or reshape it to their own purpose (Hdt. 7.176), giving them a secure base which could control the road. Their early arrival also allowed them to compensate for their poor advance intelligence. They had not realized the danger of encirclement until they arrived. But they were able to scout the terrain and question locals, who informed them of the existence of the path through the hills (Hdt. 7.175.2). This allowed them to take precautions against a flanking manoeuvre by putting a guard of 1,000 Phocians in place behind Kallidromon (Hdt. 7.212.2). The size of the Phocian contingent means that it was a serious attempt to block an enemy force advancing through the hills; but the Greeks had planned for the possibility that it might be forced back. The location of the Phocians at the eastern end of Anopaea prevented them from being cut off from the main force. It allowed the garrison there to retreat and warn the troops in the pass of imminent encirclement (though here too events did not turn out as planned). The Greeks also set lookouts in the hills (Hdt. 7.219.1), presumably either light-armed Locrian troops or even local shepherds familiar with the hill paths. These could warn the army below if the Phocian garrison was overwhelmed. The Greek commanders ensured that their army in the pass could be adequately supplied at a short distance from behind from the village of Alpenoi (Hdt. 7.176.5).

Herodotus says nothing at all about the route through the Dhema Pass between Oeta and Kallidromon to the Cephisus valley, though he knew of it, since he mentions it after the battle in his account of the subsequent movement of the Persian army (Hdt. 8.31). Presumably the Greek forces either knew of it already or learned of it on arrival. The Phocians certainly knew it, since it offered access to Phocian territory. Leonidas did not have enough men to garrison this route and he may have relied on the Phocians to bar it; part or all of the Phocian army (excluding those serving with Leonidas, stationed on Anopaea) may have been stationed somewhere on this route. Whether or not there was a Phocian force there, in the event the Phocians decided after the Greek defeat that lone resistance was not feasible and melted into the hills to avoid the Persian advance (Hdt. 8.32). Here at least flight was just good sense.

At sea the early arrival of the Greeks meant that they were able to occupy the better anchorage in the wide bay of Artemisium, modern Pefki, which has ample space to beach a large fleet of warships (Figure 10). This left the Persians with inferior anchorage opposite them at Aphetae, what is now Platania, on the south coast of Mount Pelion. The position at Aphetae is narrower, more exposed, and less

Figure 10. Artemisium/Pefki, the site of the Greek anchorage in 480 BC

convenient for rapid boarding (Figure 11). But the Persians had little choice. They needed to be able to hold down the Greek fleet and the position directly opposite was the best available.

It is much easier to understand the Persians than the Greeks at Thermopylae. The Persians knew they had to take the pass if they were to advance south. And until they learned of the path through the hills they had to take it by frontal assault, regardless of cost. They did what they had to do. The Greek side is less clear. We know what the Greeks did. But what did they think they were doing?

Herodotus does not discuss the Greek thinking in detail; but he does make it abundantly clear that the aim was to bar the invaders from advancing into central Greece (Hdt. 7.175): 'This then was the passage they decided to guard to prevent the barbarian from entering Greece.' And he repeats at 7.176.5 that this was the spot where they decided 'to keep the barbarian out of Greece'. When Leonidas arrives at

Figure 11. Aphetae/Platania, the site of the Persian anchorage in 480 BC

Thermopylae he calls for reinforcements on the ground that his force is too small to 'check' the enemy (Hdt. 7.207). So Herodotus' Leonidas unambiguously intends to stop the Persian advance in its tracks. Herodotus makes the same point about Artemisium (8.15.2). This is also the view of other commentators from the classical period (Lysias 2.30; Isoc. *Panegyricus* 90), though they may be influenced by Herodotus.

We might simply accept this as fact. But this was not the only ancient view. Some later sources saw a suicide mission, a tradition which still persists. It is an idea with an appeal, especially for those of us who have had two and a half millennia to absorb the story of the last stand. This is certainly the view of Plutarch, writing in the Roman period, who records several exchanges between Leonidas and others at Sparta on his departure for Thermopylae (*Sayings of the Spartans, Moralia* 225A):

> When his wife Gorgo asked him, as he was leaving for Thermopylae to fight the Persian, if he had any instructions for her, he said, 'Marry good men and bear good children.'
>
> When the Ephors said that he was taking few men to Thermopylae, he said: 'No, in fact too many for the task on which we march.'
>
> And when again they said, 'Do you perhaps have some plan other than to bar the barbarians from the pass?' 'Ostensibly that,' he said, 'but in reality to die for Greece.'

These anecdotes take it for granted that Leonidas not only expects but intends to die from the outset. The same applies to the most detailed account of Thermopylae, from the historian Diodorus of Sicily, writing earlier in the Roman period, whose Leonidas, when asked about the numbers he is taking with him (in a variation on the same anecdote which we find in Plutarch, who is almost certainly drawing on Diodorus), replies that the ostensible purpose is to guard the pass but the real mission is to die for Greece (Diod. Sic. 4.11.2–4):

> When Leonidas received the command, he ordered just one thousand men to follow him on campaign. And when the Ephors said that he was leading extremely few soldiers against a great force and urged him to take along more, he replied to them in secret that for preventing the barbarians from getting through the passes they were few, but still for the task for which they were now marching they were many. Since this reply was riddling and obscure, he was asked again whether he believed he was leading the soldiers to some easy task. He replied that ostensibly he was leading them to guard the passes, but in reality to die for the common freedom; so, if the thousand set out, Sparta would be the more renowned

for their death, but if the Spartans took the field in full force, Sparta would be utterly destroyed. For not a single one of them would dare to take to flight to save his life.

This reading still persists. In part it belongs to the heroicization of Leonidas which was already firmly in place by the time Herodotus wrote. We can see this for instance in the lion statue set up near the hill of the last stand at Thermopylae at some point between the battle and Herodotus' visit to the site (Hdt. 7.225.2), perhaps as early as the 470s. The sacrifice at Thermopylae becomes more heroic if the warriors go knowingly to their deaths in the service of Greece. But the suicide story also reflects the fact that Greeks looking back on the Persian Wars experienced history in retrospect just like us. And retrospect creates the illusion of inevitability. We usually know who won and who lost. The participants do not. The tendency to read the outcome as both inevitable and predictable increased as subsequent accounts focused more and more on the Spartan contingent, since the disparity between the opposing armies became still more dramatic. Certainly when the Greeks knew that they were surrounded, Leonidas was determined— or at least ready—to die. But we cannot simply retroject that decision on to the whole expedition from the start. This does not allow us to reject the suicide reading out of hand. It does mean, however, that in looking at the battle we need to guard against unconscious fatalism.

But the sense of Thermopylae as a kamikaze mission did not come from nowhere. It has its roots in Herodotus. He records (Hdt. 7.205.2) that Leonidas took with him only fully grown men who had sons. The reason for this has been debated in modern times. It has been suggested that there is a ritual reason. We are told by Herodotus that the Spartans were celebrating the feast of the Carnea and it is possible that family representation was needed. But Herodotus himself gives no ritual reason, though he mentions the festival, and he does not specify the age of the children. So we should probably conclude, as most readers have, that this is to ensure a successor and prevent the extinction of the families. Actually Herodotus does perhaps offer an implicit answer to the question, when he goes on to discuss the decision of the prophet Megistias to stay with the Spartans rather than escape, before they are surrounded; Megistias insists on staying but sends home his only son (Hdt. 7.221). In a world where the survival of the family is paramount the father is expendable as long as there is a son. But the detail about the choice of mature men with sons could be in part the origin of the view that Leonidas is taking his men to their deaths. Why take only expendable men, if they are expected to come back? But we may not need a suicide mission to explain this. This was on any interpretation a high-risk expedition in which casualties would be high. The Spartans were vastly outnumbered by a hostile serf population. They had subjugated not only the non-Dorian population of Laconia but also the people of neighbouring Messenia. By the end of the century Sparta was suffering from severe manpower shortages. Though the problems became critical some decades after our period, citizen numbers were always a cause of concern and it would make sense to limit the potential damage from losses in the campaign.

One of the more memorable moments in Herodotus' account of the preliminaries to the battle is when the spy sent by Xerxes is surprised to see the Spartans combing their hair and exercising while waiting for the Persian attack (Hdt. 7.208.2–209.3). The anecdote has all the hallmarks of the mythologizing tradition surrounding the battle. But this detail too may have fed the legend of the suicide mission. It was not unknown for warriors who died gloriously in battle to receive the cult status of heroes after death (for more on this, see Chapter 8) and one feature of this kind of cult was athletic games of the sort we find in the funeral of Patroclus in Homer's *Iliad*. Plutarch claims (*On the Malice of Herodotus* 866b) that Leonidas' troops staged their own funeral games before they set out, watched by their parents. This looks like an elaboration of Herodotus' tale of the games at Thermopylae, which could be seen as their own funeral athletic festival, with the beautification as a variation on the dressing of the corpse. This is not, however, the way the exiled king of Sparta, Damaratus, who was travelling with the Persian army, explains it to Xerxes. He tells him that it is the Spartan custom to beautify themselves, 'when they are about to risk their lives'. And the games are an indication of the Spartan calm in the face of danger. The funereal link remains; homoeroticism and admiration for male beauty were ingrained in Sparta to a degree beyond most Greek states and these men wish to die beautiful. The (literally) beautiful death was instilled in the Spartans by the poet Tyrtaeus as early as the seventh century BC (Fr. 10 West, ll. 19–30):

> And the older men, whose knees are no longer nimble,
> do not abandon them in flight, the old men.
> Shameful is this, that an older man should lie fallen
> in the front ranks in front of the young,
> his hair already white and his beard grey
> breathing out his brave life in the dust,
> holding his bloody privates in his own hands—
> shameful is this and repellent to see—
> and his skin stripped. But for the young all is seemly,
> while he has the flower of lovely youth,
> looked on with admiration by men and desired by women
> while alive, and handsome among the dead.

Damaratus, however, sees them as fighting for their lives, not going out to die. Death is a stark prospect, even a probable outcome, but not a conscious goal.

The other point in Herodotus which probably fed the idea of the suicide mission was his account of the response which the Spartans received from the oracular shrine at Delphi foretelling the death of a king as the price for success (Hdt. 7.220):

> For you, dwellers in spacious Sparta,
> either your great glorious city is by Persian men
> laid waste, or if not that, from Heracles' line
> the bounds of Lacedaemon will mourn a dead king.
> The might of bulls or lions will not check him
> with matching strength; for he has the might of Zeus. And I say
> he will not stop until he rends one of these utterly.

But oracles such as this which predict the future with uncanny precision form part of the process by which the Greeks impose order on the events of history. They are more likely to be manufactured in retrospect and to form part of the accretion of myth which surrounds the war in general. In this case the story may be drawn, as has been suggested, from a pattern we find in Greek myth, the story of the king or surrogate (prince, princess) who must sacrifice him or herself for the salvation of the people. It may even, as has been suggested, be part of the Spartan myth-making after the war. Scholars have written much about the Spartan mirage, the public image which Sparta cultivated and which has captivated generations of readers over two and a half millennia. Thermopylae was very good PR for Sparta, as we shall see in Chapter 8; and the king who dies so that Greece can be saved increases the moral and political capital from the battle. But even if we were to accept the historicity of the oracle, the sequence in Herodotus' narrative matters. For Herodotus this is part of the explanation for Leonidas' final decision, when they are surrounded and the position is lost; it is not part of the decision to take to the field.

Except for the oracle, where few will be willing to accept the uncanny prescience of the priestess at Delphi (any more than we accept that the god Apollo gave her this preternatural access to the future), none of this amounts to a knockout blow against the suicide reading. But there are more practical obstacles to this view which emerge when we take it off the page and treat it as serious strategic decision-making by a people fighting a real war. The Spartans were by any standards men of great courage, remarkable fitness and tenacity, and highly developed fighting skills. They were ready to face death and the authorities back home were ready to send men to face death in battle, as were all states in a world where fighting was done by a citizen army. But the three hundred, irrespective of any other troops who might or might not have come from Sparta, were full Spartan citizens. Sacrificing 300 members of the elite is not something they would contemplate unless they saw a practical advantage. If Diodorus is right to add another 700 (or 1,000) fighters, and if they were Perioikoi, the loss becomes more dramatic. Suicide tactics can be very effective, if the strategic advantages outweigh the loss, as for instance with modern suicide bombers or Japanese kamikaze pilots in the Second World War, where a small outlay in men and materials can cause grossly disproportionate damage to the enemy. But in this case their deaths did not stop or slow the Persian advance. Nor did it put any core element of the invading army out of action and the Greeks had no good reason to suppose that it would. There was of course a potential gain for morale from an heroic stand, but this cut two ways. Although it was conceivable that the Greeks collectively would see a glorious martyrdom as an inspiring call to arms, the Spartans could not be sure that it would not just make them despair. It did in fact reinforce the fears of the Peloponnesian contingent (Hdt. 8.40) and in the end it was only a trick by the Athenian Themistocles which induced the Greeks to take a stand at Salamis. This looks like too much of a crap shoot to justify a loss on this scale.

There is another problem. The ancient suicide narratives focus entirely on the Spartans. But this was an allied force, and we are probably looking at an army of at least 7,000 men. This is a very large number to send to their deaths on a mission with no strategic outcome. In fact most of the allies retreated when the position became indefensible; so for them this was never a suicide mission. Diodorus is explicit (in the passage quoted above) that Leonidas told the Ephors of his suicide plan in secret. So we could argue that he simply kept the allies in ignorance. This does not help, however. The leaders of the allied contingents were presumably in most cases seasoned campaigners. To go with him they had to believe that the expedition could achieve something beyond their deaths and the loss of their men. The purpose of the expedition must also have been debated at the meeting of the Greek League which decided on Thermopylae. The representatives of the Greek states too must have thought that the expedition could deliver an outcome other than the death of its members.

This argument becomes more telling if we throw in Artemisium. The allies had to be persuaded to mobilize the fleet, a massive, complex, time-consuming, and very expensive operation, which left the areas to the south vulnerable to a Persian attack by sea. For this too they needed a strategic objective. If the land forces or even just the Spartans were sent to die, the mobilization of such a large fleet looks pointless. So too do the naval engagements at Artemisium, which cost Greek lives and ships—simply to allow the Spartans a glorious death?

We have to conclude that the Greeks in 480 thought Thermopylae could be held. They were not alone. For two and a half millennia after the battle Thermopylae remained the preferred site to stop enemy forces advancing into Greece even for people who knew the story of 480. Generals do not choose battlefields out of sentiment. The Greeks of 480 and all subsequent defenders tried to prevent a flanking movement, usually without success. But this was and is a position with strengths. Thermopylae was chosen by the Greeks as the place to hold back the Gauls who invaded in 279 BC and again in 191 BC by the Seleucid king Antiochus the Third to stop the Romans. Thermopylae was considered worth garrisoning and fortifying at great cost in the early Byzantine era. It was initially chosen as the place to check the German advance in April 1941. The position usually failed in its job but for human reasons rather than because it is inherently indefensible. But it did not always fail. An Athenian force used the pass to stop Philip of Macedon in his tracks in 352 BC. I return to these engagements in Chapter 7. For now the point that matters is that serious commanders long after Leonidas thought that this was a good spot to mount a defence.

Thermopylae also fits into a larger Greek strategy. It repeats a manoeuvre which the Greeks has attempted earlier that year, when they tried to stop the Persians further north at the valley of Tempe. Tempe clearly was not a suicide mission, since the troops withdrew before the enemy could arrive. The logic is the same in both cases, to bring the Persians to battle on terrain where their numbers were neutralized. The location at Thermopylae makes sense especially when we consider it alongside the parallel naval operation at Artemisium. Both positions placed Persian numbers at a disadvantage or at least nullified the disparity. So Greek thinking was both sound and consistent. It just failed, at least at Thermopylae.

We are not yet done with problems. Seven thousand men or thereabouts may have been too many to send to their deaths without a tangible benefit. But the number still looks too small for the defence of Thermopylae against a very large Persian force. It has therefore been suggested that the real aim was to hold back the land army while the Greek ships defeated the Persian navy. This again is history read through the rear-view mirror. We know that Athens engineered the naval victory at Salamis and became the leading naval force in Greece. But again the Greeks did not yet know that. Sparta, the leader of the alliance, was a land power and there is no reason to suppose that the Spartans would see the navy as the critically important wing. This is reflected in the command hierarchy: the land force was commanded by a Spartan king and the navy by a Spartan general, Eurybiadas. Moreover, since a naval victory would still leave a large army in Greece, reliance on the navy could only produce a limited success.

This still does not explain the numbers. The Greeks sent 10,000 to Tempe earlier in the year. They seem to have believed that with the right terrain this was all they needed. By these standards the numbers at Thermopylae were not negligible, but it still remains difficult to understand why the force at Thermopylae was smaller. It has been suggested that the expedition was a gesture intended to retain the loyalty of Athens and the other free cities of central Greece, while allowing the southern Greeks to fortify the Isthmus. Retreat to the Isthmus must always have been at least part of the thinking, since there could be no guarantee of success at Thermopylae. But there was no other good position north of the Isthmus and losing the whole of northern and central Greece would deprive the allies of their navy, which was heavily reliant on states north of the Isthmus, especially Athens. So this can only have been a fallback position.

According to Herodotus Leonidas announced to the Greeks that a larger force would follow. Herodotus twice calls the force at Thermopylae an advance guard (Hdt. 7.203.1, 206.1–2). The reason he gives for the failure of the Spartans to send a larger force is that they were celebrating the Carnea in honour of the god Apollo (Hdt. 7.206.1).

This was a major festival among the Dorians, the branch of the Greeks to which the Spartans belonged. So it had enormous implications both for the worship of the gods and for the sense of tradition, self-definition, and origin. That a military campaign should wait on a religious festival may seem bizarre to a secular age like ours. But in Greek belief the gods could deal ruthlessly with those who failed to honour them and it was especially unwise to provoke them while engaged in a fight for survival. We are also told (Hdt. 7.206.2; 8.26) that the invasion did not stop the Greeks collectively from celebrating the Olympic games in honour of Zeus. Though the Olympics never stopped a Greek state from going to war (the 'Olympic truce' did not impose a pan-Greek peace but simply protected the site of the games and athletes en route to or from the festival), the principle is the same: the gods must be given their due. In 419 the Spartans again postponed military action to avoid interrupting the Carnea (Thuc. 5.54). And ten years before Xerxes' invasion they had delayed sending help to the Athenians at Marathon for the same reason (Hdt. 6.106.3). So there is nothing remotely implausible about Herodotus' explan-ation. The Spartans did of course send troops despite the festival. This looks like a pragmatic compromise and presumably the authorities at Sparta found a way of squaring the decision with the claims of religion. Leonidas may for instance have asked for volunteers to remove any blame from the state as a whole.

The Carnea must have been over by the time the fighting started. The Greeks were in the pass long enough to reconnoitre the terrain, deploy the guard on the Anopaea path, and rebuild the Phocian wall. How long this took we cannot say: possibly a week or more on top of the six days' march from Sparta to the pass. The Carnea lasted nine days and we don't know where in those two weeks or more the festival fell (Herodotus simply says that it was 'in the way'). A larger force would take longer to mobilize and march than the small task force with Leonidas, so that, even if the festival began only a couple of days after Leonidas set off, a relief force could not have arrived in time to join battle. But that does not let the Spartans off the hook. Herodotus never indicates that a second force ever set out or even mobililized. This is quite unlike Marathon ten years earlier, when again religious observance delayed the Spartans but an army still marched, only to arrive too late (Hdt. 6.120). The Spartan authorities seem to have been much less prompt in 480. We are told that they did not expect the fighting at Thermopylae to end so soon (Hdt. 7.206.2). They may have assumed that a disciplined and determined force could hold the pass effectively for quite some time. And so it could, as the fighting on the first two days proved. They were of course ignorant of the flanking route through the hills. And they could not know the precise time of the Persian arrival at the pass, nor how soon after that they would attack. However, the lack of urgency in Sparta suggests reluctance to commit all their forces outright. It is difficult to avoid the suspicion that they were waiting to see if Middle Greece held firm before sending reinforcements. They could still extract their own forces, if the states in the immediate path of the invader failed to support the expedition.

No religious explanation is offered for the numbers from the rest of the Peloponnese. These too (except for Arcadia, whose cities turned out in force) were Dorian states with the Carnea to celebrate and it may be that his focus on the Spartans has led Herodotus to ignore their motive. But with or without any religious reason the Peloponnesian cities were ambivalent about the whole enterprise. Before and after Thermopylae a strong body of opinion in the Peloponnese favoured falling back on the Isthmus of Corinth as the front line, including some at least of the forces with Leonidas. The other southern states were probably waiting on Sparta before they committed more troops.

In the event the action was over before any additional force could be sent. This was not the last time when the situation at Thermopylae changed too rapidly for the defenders to hold on. In the Second World War, General Iven Mackay, commander of the Australian 6th Infantry Division, said of the Allied position at the pass as the Germans swept through Greece: 'I thought that we'd hang on for about a fortnight and be beaten by weight of numbers.' We should not be surprised if the allies of 480 BC too were overtaken by events. Leonidas sent messengers asking for support, presumably to the cities of central Greece (Hdt. 7.207). The turnout from central Greece was not strong. In part this may reflect a desire to hold the bulk of their forces for defence of their own immediate territory but it may also reflect ambivalence about the relative merits of resistance or capitulation. Thebes in particular had sent only a small force. The city was seriously divided and those Thebans who arrived may have represented a pro-Greek faction, as Diodorus believed (Diod. Sic. 11.4.6). Herodotus claims that Leonidas was suspicious of Thebes (Hdt. 7.205.3). But he may also have felt that a show of solidarity from Sparta might swing it behind the coalition (cf. Hdt. 7.206.1). With an improved turnout from central Greece he would be better able to hold the pass pending reinforcements from the south.

But we are still left with a key question: what could they hope to achieve? Here more than anywhere the lens of hindsight risks distorting history. Once the Persians were defeated the Greeks set about clearing them out of Europe and liberating the Greek cities of the western seaboard of Asia Minor. The freedom of the Greeks became a driving ambition and a watchword which was to impact both on Graeco-Persian relations and on Greek interstate politics for the next century and a half. Victory in 480 probably meant something much more modest. The Greeks could not seriously hope to roll back the Persian gains. The aim was probably simply to stop the relentless advance. This would have left the Persians in possession of northern Greece. But the Greeks in Asia had been under Persian control since the middle of the preceding century without troubling the conscience of free Greeks. At this stage there was no ideological reason to drive the Persians from Greece. That came later, after the victories at Salamis and Plataea, when resistance metamorphosed into a war of liberation. For now they just needed to deny the Persians the route into Greece, and that meant stopping them from taking the pass. They may not have thought much beyond that need. The Persians could in theory still have turned west and advanced down the Cephisus valley, but they would have left their rear vulnerable to a Greek attack. So the Greeks could be reasonably confident that success at Thermopylae would prevent the Persians from continuing south. For this they did not need outright victory—indeed outright victory against these odds was never a feasible outcome. They just needed to fight the Persians to a standstill.

This would not have solved all their problems. With a large army the Persians might very quickly have had difficulties with supplies of food and water, and this in turn might have induced them to halt the advance at least for this campaigning season. They would not have quit Greece entirely, even if the bulk of the forces withdrew. The north of Greece would have been garrisoned and placed under a Persian governor or simply left under client rulers, as was already the case in Macedonia. The Persians would have stayed on the doorstep and would have been ready to press further as circumstances allowed. And there were enough Greeks ready to call on Persia to help them deal with their local enemies to ensure that circumstances eventually would allow the Persians to resume their advance. But the League in Corinth would have been happy enough to stop the onward movement and leave larger questions for another day. Not all strategy is long-term.

For the Greeks in the pass the issue was simple if brutal. They just had to beat back Persian attacks until some help came from the south, or from central Greece, or a combination of the two. As they looked at the plain of Malis filled with Persian tents, the enemy numbers probably did not look like a strategic weakness. Collectively they were unnerved by what they saw. In the debate that followed the Peloponnesians were minded to fall back to the Isthmus and hunker down there. The Locrians and Phocians with the enemy at their door wanted to summon help and face the enemy at Thermopylae. Leonidas threw his weight behind the locals, as he had to. It would be humiliating for Sparta if they retreated yet again. They would also be handing additional forces to the invader, as the Greeks in the vicinity changed sides. Though his army was made up of independent allied contingents, his authority swung the outcome. All this must have happened as Greek scouts watched the Persian divisions file into the plain one after another and set up a camp that filled the space as far as the eye could see. The temptation to turn and run must have grown in the four days (Hdt. 7.210.1) while Xerxes assembled and deployed his army. It must have come almost as a relief when finally he sent the Medes and the Cissians into the pass.

6

The Battle

The first battle lasted the whole day. This and subsequent attacks probably began with repeated arrow volleys. Herodotus' brief and impressionistic account of the fighting ignores the Persian archers until they cut down the Greek survivors in the last stand. His silence attracts little comment but it sits oddly with his arresting anecdote of the exchange between the Spartan Dieneces and one of the locals (Hdt. 7.226). Warned that the Persian archers were so numerous that their arrows would blot out the sun, Dieneces famously joked that at least they would be fighting in the shade. Yet the archers do nothing, at least in his narrative. The anecdote is one of the many legends around the battle and we will come back to it in Chapter 8. Just now it is the inconsistency that matters. The bow played a central role in Persian fighting, important enough for the king himself to be portrayed as an archer on the coinage (see Figures 12 and 13), and their strategy was to use it to harass and weaken the enemy before moving in.

This is what happened when the encircling force encountered the Phocians on the path through the hills (Hdt. 7.218.2–3): the Persians drew up in battle formation and showered the Greeks with arrows. In this case they simply moved on because they had more important business but normally they would follow with an attack. At Plataea too the archers hammered the Greeks opposite until the Greeks closed in (Hdt. 9.61.3). So it is unlikely that the archers at Thermopylae remained idle before the final battle. Probably they began day one by trying to weaken the Greeks with massive volley fire before they advanced. Any arrows fired, however, had little impact. The volleys

Figure 12. Persian coin ('Daric') showing the king as archer

must have inflicted some casualties but overall Greek losses on the first day were few (Hdt. 7.211.3). The Greeks were protected by the wall and by their heavy shields and body armour. All they had to do was keep their heads down. Here too the advantage of the Greek position showed itself. The bow could only be used at the outset in an attempt to soften up the enemy, since in such a confined space the archers would have no room to draw and fire, and once the two sides clashed, the risk of casualties through friendly fire was too great. So the greatest Persian asset was out of action for much of the fighting and they were forced to adopt the hard slog of fighting at close quarters for which the Greek hoplites were prepared and they were not. All war is brutal but the clash of hoplite lines, like that of the medieval shield wall, was especially so. In the Greek summer and in a drawn-out battle the physical and mental demands were enormous. The relentless effort of

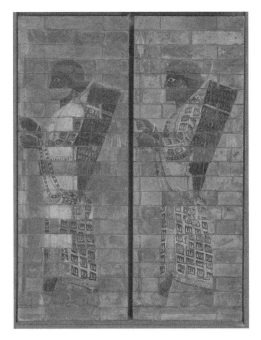

Figure 13. Persian archers, possibly members of the elite Immortals

resisting blows on the shield and dodging thrusts from spear and sword while thrusting at the enemy opposite, the confusion of battle cries, commands and screams, prayers and whimpers from wounded and dying, the smells of sweat, blood, urine and faeces combined to challenge both body and spirit. It must have been horrendous for the Persian troops, thrown into this without the familiarity which their Greek enemies had from early adulthood.

Herodotus gives us virtually no detail of the first impact. The Greeks were good at fighting at close quarters in formation. Hoplite tactics were evolving rapidly at this time and it may be that the hoplite line at the time of the Persian Wars was not the tight line of the classical period (and the modern imagination); and it may have had lightly armed troops mingled with and protected by the hoplites. But the basis was still the line. Maintaining any semblance of order must have been difficult, if the fighting took place on the uneven high ground, although Greek hoplites must have been used to maintaining order on rough terrain. And keep it they must have, since they stopped the Medes and the Cissians in their tracks and inflicted heavy casualties. The first wave was beaten back and the attack was resumed by fresh troops, again to no effect, before the attackers were forced to withdraw. This is the one point in the account of the wars where Herodotus surrenders to the Greek antithesis between themselves and the soft, even effeminate, non-Greeks of the east. In his account of the spoils of Plataea in the following year he stresses (Hdt. 9.82) that the Persians, or at least the high command, enjoyed levels of luxury unimaginable to the Greeks until they saw it. Even so he insists that the Persian defeat at Plataea was not due to any weakness or cowardice on their part (Hdt. 9.62.2). Here, however, he rounds off his account of the first assault with the words (Hdt. 7.210.2–3): 'they made it clear to everyone, especially to the king himself, that though there were so many people (*anthropoi*) there were few men (*aneres*)'. The comment is undeserved, since his own narrative makes clear that in this first assault the invaders renewed their attacks despite severe losses. There was no lack of courage or tenacity.

Xerxes evidently decided that he had underestimated his enemies. His next move was to send in the corps known as the Immortals. This corps was named (so we are told—Hdt 7.83.1) because their number was always maintained at 10,000, with a reserve ready to replace every man lost; presumably other regimental numbers were not necessarily rigidly maintained. They were an elite group. So Xerxes must have been confident that this time the Greeks would be dislodged or destroyed. They too achieved little but took heavy casualties. The day ended with the Immortals too retiring after severe losses. The second day was a replay of the first.

The main reason the Greeks did so well was the terrain. They were fighting in a confined space which prevented the Persians from deploying over a wide front and overlapping the Greek line. So the Persian numerical advantage was neutralized. Worse still, the Persian front ranks were endangered by those at the rear pushing in behind them in the confined space, and the more eager the troops and the more insistent the commanders the greater the danger. Herodotus only mentions the damage inflicted on the front ranks by their comrades pushing from the rear in his account of the third day's fighting (Hdt. 7.223.3). But this is part of his dramatic narrative strategy of dropping in details at intervals and it must have applied throughout. The problem for the attackers was exacerbated by the shape of the pass. Though the battleground was narrow, the western entrance to the pass was much narrower still, which will have created a bottleneck when the attacking forces pulled back or turned to flee. The rear ranks could not respond by pulling back to give them space, especially as they would be stumbling downhill, and so added to the crush of bodies and the resultant casualties.

The Greeks also made very efficient use of their forces by fighting in relays (Hdt. 7.212.2). In such a narrow space deploying the whole force would have produced a long column with the rear lines unoccupied but exposed to relentless attack from archers behind the Persian front rank. The use of relays allowed fresh troops to be deployed and saved the fighting men from being worn down by hour after hour of close combat in severe heat. It also deprived the Persian archers of a target behind the front ranks. How the succession was handled is never made clear. But during the lulls in the fighting, as each Persian division was thrown back, the relief ranks could open to let the retiring troops pass through. If what Herodotus tells us about the relays is true, the obsession with the Spartans in ancient and modern times is all the more regrettable, since the contingents from the various city states all bore the brunt of the fighting over those two days. They earned their place in the memorials later set up in the pass (see Chapter 8), even if history has largely ignored them.

Equipment too played a major part, though it is difficult to get a firm grip on the evidence. The essence of hoplite warfare was the heavy round shield, the cuirass, and the thrusting spear (see Figures 14 and 15). It was common during the archaic period for hoplites to carry

Figure 14. Hoplite shield

Figure 15. Hoplites fighting in formation; detail from the Chigi vase

two throwing spears, a practice which probably persisted into the fifth century. But Herodotus' statement at 7.224.1 that the Greek spears eventually broke indicates that either all or the majority carried the heavy thrusting spear. They also carried a sword as a back-up weapon. The shield, the heaviest and most important piece of equipment, was made of wood covered with a thin layer of metal. Typically it was about 1 metre in diameter and modern estimates put the weight at about 6 kilos, not very heavy to heft and carry but inexorably tiring when held in position to defend or push over extended fighting. The hoplite provided his own equipment and so we should not imagine anything like a uniform size or weight. A man's kit must have varied according to his means; many must have used their father's or grand-father's equipment. This applies even more to the corselet. In the archaic period it was usually made of bronze, at least for those who could afford it. By the fifth century the corselet was becoming lighter and probably leather or linen was preferred. The hoplite also wore greaves, which covered the lower leg below the area protected by the shield, and a helmet. Again equipment would vary but the most common was the 'Corinthian' type with cheekpieces (Figure 16).

Figure 16. 'Corinthian' helmet from the Museum at Olympia

The shape of the helmet restricted visibility and hearing but it pro-tected the head and face from thrusts above the shield rim. Provided that the line held and the soldiers kept their heads down, they were relatively well covered for defence, and the weight of the shield and corselet would give added momentum in a forward push (modern estimates put the whole hoplite kit at about 20 kilos), in the kind of clash which the Greeks called *othismos*, 'the shove', in which battle lines tried to push each other backward.

The Persians had tall rectangular shields with a leather base covered with wicker. These were lighter than the metal-coated wood of the Greek shields but larger. Their size gave them better body cover but made them unwieldy in close combat. This, however, was not their purpose. They were mainly used for engagement at bowshot range. They could be deployed in a tight line to form a movable palisade, as they were at Plataea and Mycale in the following year (Hdt. 9.61–2, 99.3, 102.2–3). The standard tactic seems to have been for the front rank to ground their shields edge to edge to protect ranks of archers behind. The term for warriors fighting in this formation was *sparabara* (from *spara*, the Persian term for the shield). This was probably the formation used at Thermopylae, since before the encounter in the pass the Persians had neither time nor motive to change tactics or equipment. In the right place the *sparabara* formation was devastatingly effective. It had enabled the Persians to dominate the world from the Aegean coast to the Indus and it inflicted heavy casualties on the Greek forces at Plataea before the Greeks advanced (Hdt. 9.61.3). The norm seems to have been for only the front rank to carry the large wicker shields. We do have evidence for smaller Persian shields (Figure 17) and some at least of the ranks behind probably carried these, since they were able to put up a fierce resistance at Plataea even after the wicker palisade was breached (Hdt. 9.62.3). But the tall wicker shields were the main defence and those behind were vulnerable if the wall broke. The wicker shields were not designed to cope with relentless blows, unlike the hoplite shield, since the Greeks were able to hack their way through them at both

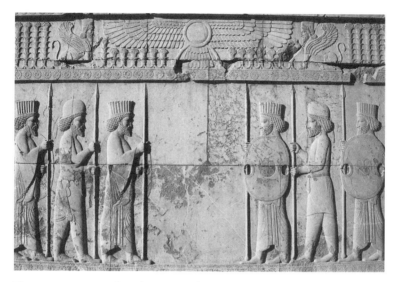

Figure 17. Persian and Median troops from Persepolis with the smaller Persian shield

Plataea and Mycale, where the fall of the shield barricade was pivotal in the Persian defeats.

Some at least of the Persians wore body armour, possibly all. The text of Herodotus' catalogue of the non-Greek participants is corrupt at the key point (Hdt. 7.61.1) but he seems to describe the Persians as having some kind of scale armour, perhaps under their robes, and archaeological finds from the region point to armour made of cloth with small overlapping plates sewn on. The commander Masistius has a corselet under his robe at Plataea (Hdt. 9.22.2); and in fact all the Persians at Plataea seem to have worn body armour (Hdt. 8.113.2). We cannot say that all those who faced the Greeks in the pass were armoured. But absence of Persian body armour cannot explain the Greek superiority. Herodotus in his account of Plataea claims that the Persians were *anoploi*, unprotected, literally 'unarmed' (Hdt. 9.62.3) and he adds (9.63.2) that they were fighting at Plataea 'as lightly armed troops (*gymnetes*) against hoplites'. He is probably referring not to body

Figure 18. Darius III wearing the *tiara*

armour but to the limited protection of the wicker shields in close combat, the vulnerability of the inner ranks of the column, with or without the smaller shields, and the absence of helmets. Herodotus at 7.61.1 describes the Persians as wearing 'unstiffened felt headgear called *tiaras*' (see Figure 18). For an army which relied on archers to soften the enemy before moving in rapidly to attack no more was usually needed. But in hoplite fighting the lack of protective headgear would leave the fighters vulnerable to spear thrusts above the shield, even if the grounded shields protected the legs.

The most difficult piece of equipment to assess is the spear. Herodotus tells us (Hdt. 7.211.2) that the Persian spears were shorter than those of the Greeks. In his general account of the invading forces in book 7 he explicitly describes the Persians as having short spears (Hdt. 7.61.1). Modern research is divided on the subject. Wooden spear shafts rot away, leaving little direct archaeological evidence. So we have to rely on iconography. This is not negligible, since an artistic representation has to bear a resemblance to its subject if it is to appeal to its audience. But unless we know that images are drawn or painted to scale, we cannot rule out artistic considerations, most obviously the demands of the space available. There seems to have been some variation in the length on both sides and the most recent scholarship doubts whether there was any overall difference. If there was, it was probably undramatic. But even a small difference of (say) 30 centimetres, as has been suggested, would be significant when multiplied by tens or hundreds in a serried line, even if individually the mismatch was not great. Greek sources also may be taking account of the use of the spear. It has been suggested that the mode of fighting preferred by the Greeks involved an upward underarm thrust of the spear from the cover of the shield, where the Persian spears were designed to be used as a javelin or for a downward thrust over the shield with the spear held in the middle of the shaft, thus reducing the reach. This has been contested. But the Greek spear may also have been heavier, which would make it less likely to break in combat. It took two and a half days of heavy fighting for the Greek spears finally to break. Like the Greeks the Persians had a fallback weapon in the *akinakes*, a short blade somewhere between sword and dagger common across Anatolia.

Herodotus also offers an intriguing comment about the Greek, or rather the Spartan, tactics for the first day. He has them use a technique unique in heavy infantry fighting. They turn and flee, then turn and fight (Hdt. 7.211.3):

> The Spartans fought memorably. They showed themselves skilled fighters among unskilled in many respects, especially when they would turn their backs and pretend to flee all together. The barbarians seeing them flee would pursue them with shouts and noise. But when the barbarians caught up, the Spartans would turn to face them and slay Persians without number.

He makes a similar point about skill in his account of Plataea (Hdt. 9.62.3, quoted below). But the Persians knew how to fight and Herodotus cannot have supposed otherwise. His point is about hoplite tactics and discipline in face-to-face fighting rather than courage or simple weapon skills. But the specific tactical point here gives an added twist. Diodorus provides a much more conventional account at 11.7.2:

> For since the fighting was in line formation and the blows were struck at close quarters, and the lines were tightly packed, for a considerable time the battle was equally balanced.

This is a standard hoplite slogging match in which the enemy is ground down by weight and determination. Diodorus is probably drawing on the fourth-century historian Ephorus. His story lacks any detail and may be just a generic account of fighting in a narrow space. For most of the battle it must have been true. But Herodotus' account too is problematic. If accurate, it would indicate a remarkable level of discipline, since the soldiers, while pretending to flee, would have had to keep pace so that they could wheel around together. The problem is that the Persians were armed with bows. Heavily armed infantry needed their shields in front of them. To turn their backs was to give the archers a soft target, especially arms and legs; and with the greater distance between the lines the Persian archers would have had an unimpeded sight-line. So the Spartans would not turn and run. We cannot dismiss the possibility that this is just another fragment of legend, designed to display the unique Spartan discipline and to help explain how so few could withstand so many. If there is any truth in Herodotus' claim, it may be that the Greeks gave ground facing the enemy, as though they were forced back, in order to make the enemy break formation in the belief that they had the Greeks on the run. The Spartans knew how to withdraw from battle in good order and this would simply be an elaboration on that move; as mature men all the Spartans were seasoned campaigners. If the Persians were using their tactic of grounding shields to form a barricade, any gap in the wall caused by hasty pursuit would have exposed the more vulnerable ranks behind. Such a tactic might work once, even twice. It would rapidly lose its power to surprise. But the psychological impact of the carnage would have further benefited the Greeks.

One further feature of the fighting which deserves attention is Herodotus' statement that the Persians fought under the lash (Hdt. 7.223):

> Then as they joined battle outside the narrows a vast number of the barbarians fell, for to the rear the commanders of the companies lashed every man with whips, urging them ever forward.

The detail is saved for his climactic narrative of the third day's fighting but it may apply to all three days: with the encirclement complete, there was no more need for the whip now than in the previous two days' fighting. The whip is a recurrent feature of this book. The canal is built by people labouring under the whip (Hdt. 7.22.1); the Persians cross the bridge under the whip (7.56.1). They fight under the whip. This book more than any other contrasts Greek freedom with eastern despotism and the whip motif is part of that contrast. Interestingly, when the Persians fight for their lives next year at Plataea, there is no mention of a whip, only respect for their courage and tenacity (Hdt. 9.62.3):

> Now the Persians were not inferior in spirit or strength, but they had no armour and were inexperienced and no match for their adversaries in skill.

For the Persians Thermopylae was a meat-grinder; the carnage in the pass, and the analogy of modern warfare, including the First World War, when stragglers and deserters in battle could be shot, has suggested to some that the claim may not be outrageous. But the concentration of references to the lash in this book suggests that the whip at Thermopylae may owe more to Herodotus' desire to create a stark contrast between east and west than to historical fact.

By the end of day two, Xerxes was utterly perplexed according to Herodotus. It was then that he was approached by the local Ephialtes who knew a route through the hills. The identity of the traitor was disputed by the middle of the fifth century (to have one's city associated with the arch-betrayal of ancient warfare was an unattractive prospect and the blame must have been shuttled around), but Herodotus gives good evidence to support his identification. Whether it really was Ephialtes' initiative is not now knowable. It would be surprising if Xerxes and his generals did not have scouts looking for locals with good topographical knowledge. And we cannot hope to know whether Ephialtes betrayed the Greek cause for reward or volunteered only after robust interrogation. There was no convention governing the treatment of prisoners or the population of occupied territory. Anyway, Xerxes sent a force through the hills with Ephialtes as guide. The concerted attack by the two forces was set for mid-morning, allowing sufficient time for the encircling force to descend into the pass behind the Greeks (Hdt. 7.223.1). Without any means of communication to allow them to synchronize movements this was the only feasible way to coordinate the attacks.

Herodotus does not give us a number for the troops on the march. But he does say that they are the command of Hydarnes (Hdt. 7.215), and he tells us elsewhere that Hydarnes commanded the Immortals, who numbered 10,000 (7.83.1). He does not actually say that all 10,000 took part and several scholars have doubted that all were involved. Certainly for some sections of the route the track is narrow, and for a pincer movement on a force of 7,000 Greeks 10,000 may have looked like overkill. So it could be that no more than 2,000–3,000 took part. But Xerxes could have decided to attack in overwhelming force in order to end the battle quickly, and the terrain, together with the wall, may have made it difficult for the Persians to assess the numbers in the pass accurately. So we cannot dismiss the possibility that all 10,000 marched.

One of the big puzzles of Thermopylae is the path used by Xerxes' troops to circumvent the Greeks. Though it has probably spilled more ink than any other aspect of the story, this is not a critical issue for us, since—regardless of the route they used—the Persians certainly got behind the Greeks. Herodotus describes a path which goes by way of Mount Kallidromon and descends behind the position of the Greeks at the Middle Gate (Hdt. 7.216.1):

> This path is as follows: it begins at the river Asopus which flows through
> the ravine, and this mountain and the path have the same name, Ano-
> paea. This Anopaea stretches along the ridge of the mountain and ends at
> Alpenos, the Locrian city nearest to Malis, near the rock called Black-
> buttock and the seats of the Cercopes, where it is narrowest.

There are several routes over the mountain and scholars have firm
but different ideas on the route. Herodotus has his Persians set off
'around lamplighting time' (Hdt. 7.215.1), perhaps (since this is summer) about 8 p.m. our time (possibly sooner, since the lamps might
have been lit early). They dislodge the Phocians who are guarding
the path at about dawn (Hdt. 7.217.1–218.3), perhaps 6 a.m. This
detail looks solid, since the Phocians survived to tell their tale. And
they attack 'about the time the market is full' (Hdt. 7.223.1), perhaps
10–11 a.m. This gives them about twelve hours from the start to
their descent to ground level (they then need to march eastward
along the pass).

There are several possible ascent points (see Map 5). The Damasta
route (route 3 on Map 5) is is too short for the time Herodotos gives. It
took me less than five hours, though that was in daylight. It also brings
the army too close to the Greek position, which would allow both the

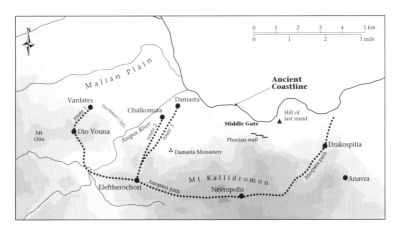

Map 5. Possible routes for the Anopaea

noise and the torches to alert the Greeks to the manoeuvre. And it does not cross the Asopos. Nor does the Chalkomata route (route 2 on Map 5), which otherwise looks plausible. If we take seriously Herodotus' statement that the Persians crossed the Asopos (Hdt. 7.217.1), the obvious route would be the one favoured by a number of scholars, the Vardates route (route 1 on Map 5), starting inland of the Asopos gorge. Ascent through the Asopos gorge itself can be ruled out—it's far too precipitous (see Figure 19). This is not straightforward, however. My friend Apollonios, who walked the Vardates route, told me that it is demanding even in daylight, and the Persians marched by night. He also felt that the terrain is too difficult for a force of 10,000 men; so if this was the route, it may be that not all the Immortals marched. And he doubted that it could be done in the timescale offered by Herodotus. Even with local guides a night march takes time. So we cannot be sure of Herodotus' timing. We need to remember, however, that time is a way of structuring narrative; dusk and dawn are very popular for

Figure 19. Asopos Gorge

this purpose. And dusk is a logical time to set off to avoid discovery and maximize the time available. This could be convenient conjecture by Herodotus. So the Persians could have set off earlier or later and marched for longer—or less—than Herodotus indicates. Regardless of the numbers involved this would be a demanding march by night and there must have been injuries on the march; but the broken legs and sprained ankles have left no mark on the record, as usually in accounts of night manoeuvres in ancient texts.

The night march was not guaranteed success. Leonidas had stationed 1,000 Phocians at the eastern end of the Anopaea specifically to check a move of this sort. He presumably chose the Phocians both because they would know the terrain as locals and because they had good reason to stop the Persians, since their wives, children, parents, and property were at risk from the Persian advance. His faith in the Phocians was misplaced. They seem to have been caught off guard by the Persian advance. The area was wooded, the weather was calm, and they were alerted only by the noise the Persians made in the leaves (Hdt. 7.218.1). Evidently the Phocian commander (unlike Leonidas) had posted no lookouts. So they were caught on the hop. They rushed to arms but were met by a shower of arrows from the Persians. In a mirror image of the later massacre in the pass, they retreated uphill, thinking that they were the target rather than just a temporary obstacle, and expecting to die (Hdt. 7.218.3). With their way cleared without a fight the Persians simply continued their march unimpeded. They had no need to kill the Phocians. Herodotus may be repeating a Phocian rationalization of the failure to protect the rear. But in comparison with his treatment of the Thebans he is remarkably lenient on the Phocians. Whether or not we accept his account of their reaction to the Persian attack, the Phocians failed the Greeks. Their sole job was to watch for and repel an attack through the hills. Leonidas had stationed them at a point which allowed them to defend the path while maintaining a link with the troops below. In retreating uphill they allowed the Persians to cut them off and made it difficult for them to send a warning to Leonidas. The retreat uphill also prevented them from joining the troops below. The Phocians may have decided that they would be more use protecting Phocis itself than joining the troops in the pass. Whatever the reason, they melted away and left Leonidas and his army to their fate. The Phocians should not have been surprised by the arrival of a force they were specifically posted to watch out for. They had the advantage of surprise, since the Persians did not expect to find armed men on their route (Hdt. 7.218.2). A resolute attack might have repulsed Hydarnes' force. As far as we can tell they made no attempt to follow the Persian column, though they were still in a position to harass the rear and at least slow down the enemy advance to buy time for the Greek troops below.

The failure to hold the Anopaea was decisive for the outcome of the battle. It is here that the Greek numbers proved critical. Small as the main force in the pass was, it was enough to hold off the Persians, given the advantages of its position, as the first two days of fighting proved. But the 1,000 Phocians were all that Leonidas could afford to deploy to the path, if he was to have enough troops to man the relays he needed to cope with the hard slog of continuous fighting against repeated Persian attacks. A few thousand more troops from southern or central Greece would have offered a more credible threat to Hydarnes and could have stiffened Phocian resolve at the critical momemt. Whether Leonidas would have used them in this way is of course unknowable.

Even without word from the Phocians Leonidas had ample warning of the Persian advance. In Herodotus Leonidas learned first of their coming death from Megistias, the diviner travelling with the force—all armies needed a diviner to check the omens before engagement or any other major action (Hdt. 7.219.1):

> The seer Megistias, examining the sacrifices, first told the Greeks at Thermopylae that death was coming to them at dawn.

His prophecy was then supported by deserters from the Persian camp. They must have been Greeks who had slipped away from the Persian camp under cover of darkness; the Persian forces included Greeks from the islands and coastal towns of the west coast of what is now Turkey and additional troops pressed into service as they marched through mainland Greece. Certainly Persian troops and troops from elsewhere in the empire had no reason to join a Greek force whose position now looked hopeless. The deserters could not have given any precise information about the position of the encircling troops, but they could presumably have indicated their strength. And they could have informed Leonidas of the time the Immortals set out and the route chosen, which would allow the locals with him to make a rough calculation of their progress and the likely time of their descent. Finally his own lookouts confirmed the imminent arrival of the Persians.

At this point Leonidas did nothing. Herodotus is explicit that the information from Megistias and the deserters was given during the night. Leonidas' inaction at this point makes sense. Prophecies are often vague, in ancient as in modern times, and all Megistias seems to have foreseen is death coming with the daylight. Deserters are always suspect, since one cannot be sure whose side they are really on. The lookouts, on the other hand, came after dawn and they were Leonidas' own men. So now he knew that soon they would be surrounded, unless they withdrew.

This period of inaction lasted for several hours. The Persians to the west did not attack until mid-morning. So there was ample time to escape. The scouts must have been stationed on the descent from the Anopaea path, on lower ground somewhere below the Phocian position. Unlike the Persians, who were marching in column, these were lightly armed runners, able to move fast, and probably familiar with the terrain. They were presumably alerted to the advance by the noise long before they saw the Persians. So the news of the encirclement reached Leonidas hours before the Persians could descend into the pass to close it from the east. The Greek forces were not yet cut off and those who elected to leave were able to escape unhindered before the arrival of the Immortals. Leonidas first debated with his men (Hdt. 7.219.2), which he had to, since this was an allied force. He could not compel. Unsurprisingly opinion was divided; some wanted to stay and fight, others to leave. We can get a sense of the reasoning of the different groups from the breakdown which Herodotus gives us (at least indirectly). The Peloponnesian troops went, except for the Spartans. Some or all of these were the forces who wanted to fall back to the isthmus the moment the Persians appeared to the west of the pass. They had probably concluded that central Greece, perhaps even all of Greece north of the isthmus, could not be saved. But even so they knew that they would be more use alive. The Locrians leave, presumably to protect their homeland.

Leonidas himself elected to stay. He was joined by the contingents of Thespiae and Thebes. Leonidas' decision to stay is another abiding subject of debate. Why sacrifice himself and the lives of his men?

Herodotus gives us two reasons (Hdt. 7.220.1):

> It is said that Leonidas himself sent them away because he was concerned that they would be killed, but felt it was unfitting for himself and the Spartans with him to abandon the position they had come to defend at the outset.

So, a combination of personal honour and concern for the lives of his comrades. The second needs scarcely any comment. The first is glossed further by Herodotus' account of the debate between King Xerxes and the exiled Spartan king Damaratus, who is with the Persian army. When Xerxes expressed disbelief that a force so heavily outnumbered will stay and fight, Damaratus explains that the Spartans, though free men, have a master whom they fear more than the Persians fear their king. It is the law (or custom—the Greek word used, *nomos*, can mean both) which demands that they should never retreat but must stand their ground and win or die. The problem, as commentators have pointed out for a long time, is that there was no such Spartan rule. The Spartans had lost battles in the past without taking 100-per-cent casualties. Which has to mean that they knew the value of retreat. They had withdrawn from the first line of defence at Tempe earlier in the year. They were not obliged to die every time they took up a position. As Evans observed fifty years ago, it is Thermopylae itself which created the legend that Spartans fight until death, and with it this fictitious rule.

Herodotus also gives a further reason, Leonidas' desire for renown (Hdt. 7.220.2–4):

> This is the view I find most convincing, that Leonidas, when he saw that his allies were unenthusiastic and had no desire to share the danger through to the end, ordered them to withdraw but thought it dishonourable for him personally to leave. By remaining he laid up great renown (*kleos*) and Sparta's good fortune was not eradicated. For it had been prophesied by the Pythia when the Spartans consulted the oracle [at Delphi] about this war right at the start when it was looming, that either Sparta would be laid waste by the barbarians or their king would die. She gave this prophecy in hexameter verses which ran as follows:
>
> > For you, dwellers in spacious Sparta,
> > either your great glorious city is by Persian men
> > laid waste, or if not that, from Heracles' line
> > the bounds of Lacedaemon will mourn a dead king.
> > The might of bulls or lions will not check him
> > with matching strength; for he has the might of Zeus. And I say
> > he will not stop until he rends one of these utterly.
>
> Leonidas, with this in mind, and wanting to lay up renown (*kleos*) for the Spartans alone, sent his allies away rather than have them argue different views and the contingents who withdrew do so in an unseemly manner.

Though it has its roots in the mythologization of Thermopylae and Leonidas, this account has to be taken seriously. It has echoes of Greek heroic epic; but Greeks remained highly sensitive to questions of reputation and honour long after the creation of the epic texts. Leonidas was not alone, however. The rest of the Spartans died with him. Even the most loyal followers might hesitate to die just for the personal glory of the king, or even their own. They presumably needed to feel that their death was of some use.

Other explanations have been offered. It has been suggested to me that Leonidas was concerned to restore the credibility of the Spartan kingship, which had suffered in the very recent past. The aggressive expansionism of Cleomenes, king in the previous generation, had alienated Sparta's allies. He had also conspired to taint Damaratus, the other of the two Spartan kings, with bastardy and secure his exile (Hdt. 6.61–70). Whether or not Damaratus was really illegitimate, the image of the Spartan kingship had suffered. A heroic death would be a good counterweight. Another suggestion is that the spectre of the Athenian victory at Marathon hovers in the background. A Spartan retreat against overwhelming odds would be humiliating after Athens had triumphed ten years earlier with the odds stacked against them. Both of these suggestions could have helped sway Leonidas. Yet another reason might have been a desire to set an example in order to stiffen Greek resolve for the contest which would follow. But these suggestions do not explain the decision of the others—Spartans, Thebans, and Thespians—to stay with him. Given that Leonidas held a meeting of the forces (or just the commanders), the decision to stay must have been collective. He must have argued the case and he must have convinced some of his army.

The main reason is likely to have been strategic. Herodotus' account makes clear that the Greek commanders considered but dismissed the option of withdrawing the whole force. The dangers of withdrawal were obvious. The Greek army was perfectly composed for the close-quarters fighting in the narrow pass. Provided they could fight on terms of their choosing, they were unbreakable. But the force was not well geared for an orderly withdrawal over more open terrain in the face of a vastly larger, lighter-armed force equipped with archers and cavalry, including mounted archers (Hdt. 9.49.2). At this point the tables were turned in favour of the Persians. If the pass was left open, the Persians could overtake the retreating army and surround them once they reached more open country east of the pass. If any of the army was to survive, the pass still needed to be blocked. The last stand was a rearguard action designed to hold up the Persians, while the rest of the force got away, like the brief stand by the Allies against the German advance into Greece in 1941.The retreating troops would still have been at risk if the Persian cavalry went in hot pursuit; but a half- or a full day of delay to the Persians would be of some use. And in the end Xerxes proved a very obliging enemy, in that he made no attempt to follow up the advantage and annihilate the escaping hoplites. He may not have realized until too late that he had massacred only a rearguard.

If this was a rearguard action, then the only question was who should stay. In Herodotus Leonidas orders his allies to leave (Hdt. 7.220) but the Thespians insist on staying (7.222), as did the diviner Megistias, who was encouraged to leave by Leonidas but chose to stay, though he sent off his son. But this was an allied, and not a Spartan, force, and Leonidas could not give orders to the non-Spartan troops. Probably he asked for volunteers. The rearguard had to include the Spartans, because they had called the expedition. It would be both humiliating for Sparta and fatal to the Greek cause if the leading state left the dangerous work to others. Herodotus is vague on the motives of the Thespians. He simply tells us that they refused to abandon Leonidas. He is more interested in the motives of Leonidas himself. With the Thebans Herodotus himself complicates the story (Hdt. 7.222), when he claims that they stayed behind under duress, because Leonidas compelled them; he was using them as hostages. Just how Leonidas with such a small force could compel the Thebans to remain as hostages is unclear. Nor do we learn what the hostages were for. If they were to force Thebes to remain loyal to the Greek cause, the gesture was pointless, since the slaughter of their force in the pass was unlikely to stiffen Theban resolve. Herodotus includes the Thebans among the states which gave earth and water to Xerxes at 7.132.1. That could be true, since it was common sense to insure against an ultimately triumphant Persian advance. But he is vague on the chronology and it may be the case that the Thebans only accepted Persian overtures after Thermopylae. But even if Thebes was either wavering or leaning toward Persia, the presence of the Thebans would not prevent an all-out attack from Xerxes, who had no reason to put their lives above his own strategic needs. Herodotus also claims that Leonidas took the Thebans with him at the outset because he suspected them of medizing and wanted to test their loyalty (Hdt. 7.205.3). Centuries later Plutarch (in his essay *On the Malice of Herodotus* 865C) excoriated him for his claims about the Thebans at Thermopylae. Plutarch as a Boeotian had a vested interest. But he is right in this case. Neither detail works. The motive in the first place gives Leonidas an implausibly academic air. In his attempt to reconstruct the perspective of his characters Herodotus tends on occasion to project his own thought processes on to them; this looks like one such occasion. As to keeping the Thebans behind at the end, Plutarch is right to draw attention to the implausibility that Leonidas would keep with him a potentially hostile armed force amounting to about a third of his strength. Any attempt to monitor them would detract from the alertness and efficiency of the loyalist troops, and betrayal on their part would make them a danger to the rest of the force. Herodotus' account reflects the post-war hostility to Thebes as the city which gave strongest support to the Persians. In fact opinion in Thebes as elsewhere was divided and the likeliest explanation of the presence of a Theban contingent is either that Thebes had not fully swung behind Persia or that these were loyalist forces. The same arguments apply to their decision to stay. Both they and the Thespians knew that their cities were next in line and this was an opportunity to slow down the Persians and inflict some more damage. Probably they marched (and stayed) because these were committed to the anti-Persian cause, irrespective of the dominant view in Thebes. Both the Thespians and the Thebans (if Thebes had not yet committed to Persia) might also reflect that they would not be welcome at home if they abandoned their position and allowed the Persians in. The Thebans at Thermopylae changed sides in the end, according to Herodotus; but that was later and we cannot read backwards from that act.

The rearguard elected to stay. But did they expect to die? Was this a suicide mission or a forlorn hope? This final question is impossible to answer. Leonidas knew that the Immortals would soon be advancing from the east in his rear. He was well aware that the trap would shut. But he could only guess about the timescale. He may have thought that he could fight his way out. He could anticipate some delay as the forces in his rear formed up after the straggling march, especially as the Persians expected to catch the Greeks by surprise and had no need to rush. He could have reasoned that a furious assault on the main army might force them to fall back and regroup, as had happened on the first two days, allowing the Greeks to slip away obscured by the hill and the wall. A rapid advance east might then allow them to surprise the encircling forces as they regrouped and force a way through. This would be a long shot at best, since he could not be sure of the position or pace of the forces in his rear. And even if he succeeded, his losses would be enormous. But he now had little to lose. If he did hope to extricate himself, he miscalculated badly. The Immortals may simply have arrived sooner than he expected. But if he was wrongfooted by events, the reason is more likely to have been Xerxes' delay in attacking. The Persian army held back waiting for the time agreed with Ephialtes. If Leonidas hoped to fight his way out after bludgeoning the Persian army, the wait for the main attack probably robbed him of the time needed to retreat. His death would not be any the less courageous for miscalculation.

All this is just speculation. What we do know is that the Greeks now went on to the offensive. Instead of waiting for the Persians to come to them in the Middle Gate, they abandoned their secure position and marched west into the wider part of the pass to meet the attackers head-on. Herodotus' explanation is quite simply that they expected to die. But whether or not they expected or even elected to die, there was good reason to change tactics and position. They were not berserkers. If they stayed where they were, they would be trapped in the Middle Gate and forced to fight on two fronts. The advance west allowed them to fight on one front only, at least at the start. It also allowed them to inflict as much damage as possible on the Persian army. The original position was too narrow for them to deploy all their forces in a line. This had been very useful while they fought in relays and time

was on their side. That was no longer the case. Deployment outside
the central narrows allowed them to bring all their forces into play,
while still allowing them to use the Persians' own numbers against
them, since even in the wider part of the pass the Persians could only
use a small portion of their army, while the disastrous crowding
which had already inflicted substantial casualties on the Persians
continued (Hdt. 7.223.3):

> Then as they joined battle outside the narrows a vast number of the
> barbarians fell, for to the rear the commanders of the companies lashed
> every man with whips, urging them ever forward. Many of them fell into
> the sea and drowned; far more were trampled alive by each other, and the
> losses could not be counted.

The Greeks still had the upper hand in the fighting. It was only the
arrival of the Immortals that tipped the balance, since the Greeks now
had to fight on two fronts. Leonidas must have had lookouts watching
for the Immortals, since he was able to retreat back through the
Middle Gate before they closed in behind him. Whatever the case
before, now it was simply a matter of selling their lives dearly.
Herodotus' account of the deaths of the Greeks is a beautifully tailored
narrative. They retreat to a hill (Kolonos, actually just a Greek word for
hill), now a low knoll but 20 metres higher above sea level in the fifth
century (see Figure 20). They fight on, with their equipment increasingly depleted. First their spears, the key offensive weapon of the
hoplite, break with the relentless fighting. They then resort to swords,
the fallback weapon, and then daggers until these too break. But it is
worth presenting Herodotus' own words, far more moving than my
dry account (Hdt. 7.223–5):

> Since the Greeks knew that they would die at the hands of those who
> were coming around the mountain, they displayed the greatest strength
> they had against the barbarians, fighting recklessly and desperately. By
> now most of them had had their spears broken and were killing the
> Persians with swords. And Leonidas fell in that struggle, showing

supreme courage, and with him other famous Spartans . . . There was a great struggle between the Persians and Spartans over Leonidas' body, until the Greek by their prowess rescued it and routed their enemies four times. This went on until the men with Ephialtes arrived. When the Greeks saw that they had come, the struggle changed; they retired to the narrow part of the road, passing the wall, and took their position all together on the hill, all except the Thebans. This hill is at the opening of the pass, where the stone lion in honour of Leonidas now stands. In that place they defended themselves with knives, those who still had them, and with hands and teeth. The barbarians buried them with missiles, some attacking from the front and throwing down the defensive wall, others surrounding them on all sides.

Herodotus' language ('buried') insists to the end on the impossible odds faced by the Greeks. From the Persian perspective the recourse to the bow is simple pragmatism. They realize that their enemies,

Figure 20. The hill of the final stand (Kolonos)

outnumbered and almost disarmed but still dangerous, are not going to surrender, and that their own forces will continue to suffer avoidable casualties unless the battle is brought to a swift conclusion.

We are not yet done with the forces in the pass. Not all the Greeks died, at least according to Herodotus. After Leonidas' death, when it became clear that the battle was lost and the surviving Spartans and Thespians retreated to the hill, the Thebans surrendered (Hdt. 7.233). Plutarch in his essay *On the Malice of Herodotus* (866D–867A) fulminates at this. Certainly Herodotus is reflecting post-war anti-Theban bias, as elsewhere. He claims that after the surrender Xerxes had the Thebans tattooed with the king's mark. Tattooing for the Greeks was a punishment for runaway slaves. So this is a calculated and lasting humiliation reflecting contempt for behaviour unworthy of free men. But desertion, if there was one, had saved Xerxes trouble. And he had no reason to humiliate potential allies. Herodotus also notes that some were killed before the Persians accepted their claim to be friendly to the Persian cause. This is entirely likely, since surrender in the heat of battle is always risky. And the ancient world lacked any hard rules about the treatment of prisoners of war. But narrative details serve a purpose and here they add to the humiliation of the Theban force, since surrender did not even save all their lives.

Herodotus also adds that the tattooed Thebans included their general, 'Leontiades, whose son Eurymachus the Plataeans later slaughtered when as commander of 400 Thebans he seized the city of Plataea' (Hdt. 7.233.2). There is a sting in the postscript. The incident referred to took place in 431 BC. It was the first act of hostility in the Atheno-Spartan conflict (the Peloponnesian War) which split the Greek world down the middle for the last third of the fifth century. Anticipating war, and wishing to pre-empt support for Athens from its anti-Theban neighbour Plataea, Theban forces made a treacherous attack on the city while still technically at peace, a sort of small-scale Pearl Harbor. The glance forward to the son gives us a family (and a city) deeply mired in treachery. But biased or not Herodotus may be correct about the surrender. There was some disagreement about the identity of the Theban commander at Thermopylae and Plutarch in his attempt to pick apart Herodotus' narrative calls him Anaxandros (*On the Malice of Herodotus* 867A). However, despite raging against him, Plutarch never quite denies the surrender. He offers no solid evidence to the contrary, such as monuments to the Theban dead at Thermopylae, though we know for instance from the later geographer Strabo that the Locrians, who left on day three, had their own monument to earlier casualties there (Strabo 9.4.2). If they did surrender, these were presumably by now the battered remnants, with their numbers reduced by half a day's fighting on top of any previous losses, not the full-scale defection which Herodotus' narrative suggests. They may have concluded that they had done their best for the retreating troops and that their deaths now served no good purpose. Compared with the troops who left the pass on the third day, or with the Phocians who let Hydarnes pass, they had performed well. Compared with the astounding courage of the Spartans and Thespians this was an inglorious moment. But that is a very high benchmark.

Herodotus' account of the endgame was not the only one, however. There was an alternative version in circulation at least by the fourth century BC. Diodorus (Diod. Sic. 11.10.4) tells a story, probably derived from Ephorus, in which the Greeks learn of the flanking march on the evening of day two and decide to raid the Persian camp by night. They inflict great casualties and almost succeed in finding and killing the king. But the Persians realize how few they are and rally and kill them. The same story occurs in Plutarch (*On the Malice of Herodotus* 866A–B), where it forms part of the charge of his indictment of Herodotus, this time for ignoring Leonidas' most courageous act, and in Justin (Just. 2.11). This account was long dismissed by historians but has been accepted recently as at least possible by serious scholars, though it smacks more of modern commando raids than classical Greek warfare. The account has gaping holes. Most significantly it is topographically wrong. Only Plutarch makes clear (what Diodorus and Justin imply) that the Greeks die in the Persian camp, outside the pass to the west. But the archaeology puts their death on the hill in Middle Gate. To get back to the Middle Gate from a night attack on the enemy camp would involve a fighting retreat of at least 6 kilometres while surrounded by vastly superior numbers. This version also has strategic weaknesses. It has the Greeks abandon the pass, where they can hold out, for the Malian plain, where they can be surrounded, and it allows the Persians unrestricted access to the pass and beyond into southern Greece. We can make a desperate attempt to rescue the anecdote by supposing that Leonidas sent a detachment to raid the Persian camp rather than committing his whole force. But this would involve dividing his forces when he had very few men at his disposal. This is not to suggest that Ephorus invented this incident. But he is probably reflecting a tradition which has been embroidered during and after the fifth century rather than a genuine competitor to Herodotus' version.

In Herodotus' account Xerxes took steps after the battle to conceal his losses and polish his success by burying most of his own dead and putting the Spartan dead on display for his naval forces to view (Hdt. 8.24). He left 1,000 on display, when in fact his casualties were about 20,000. The figure seems high, though there is no reason to doubt that the Persians received a mauling, even if we cannot be sure of precise numbers. Herodotus also tells us that Xerxes sought out the body of Leonidas and had it beheaded and crucified (Hdt. 7.238). The story may be true, since he repeats it in book 9 (§§78–9), where the Spartan victor at Plataea in the following year rejects the suggestion that he should retaliate by maltreating the body of the Persian general Mardonius in the same way. This is not anti-Persian bias from Herodotus. He pointedly remarks that it was not normal behaviour for a Persian, since of all peoples they were the most inclined to honour valour in war. But Persian kings could be brutal in punishing enemies both living and dead. The posthumous crucifixion alleged here for Leonidas was inflicted by Artaxerxes in the fourth century on his brother Cyrus, after he crushed Cyrus' attempt to gain the Persian throne at the Battle of Cunaxa (Xenophon, *Anabasis* 1.10.1; 3.1.17). Herodotus attributes Xerxes' act to his anger with Leonidas. But Persian extreme punishments were meant to be exemplary. The insult to the body was designed both to display the Persians' contempt for Leonidas' attempt to stop them and to deter further resistance.

According to Herodotus (Hdt. 8.31), after taking the pass Xerxes turned not east, through Thermopylae then through Locris into Boeotia, but west toward Phocis. The reason he gives is that he was influenced by the Thessalians, who had a long-standing quarrel with Phocis. Xerxes is unlikely to have hung his strategy on a local Greek grudge, even if he found the Thessaians useful. He had his own motives. Phocis was resolutely anti-Persian and the move is best explained as designed to mop up resistance and avoid leaving an unconquered and intransigent enemy in his rear. It is odd that Xerxes, having expended so much energy on the pass, should then ignore it. But even if he always meant to turn west, he still had to eradicate the force in the pass in order to secure his rear. Still, Locris and Boeotia too needed to be secured, even if they had by now gone over to the Persians, and the quickest route into Boeotia was through the pass. Xerxes' army had marched in three columns into Greece. And his strategy on the march had been based on the close proximity of his land and sea forces. A march inland would sever the link just as the Persians moved nearer to hostile territory. So it is likely, if unprovable, that Xerxes divided his land forces at this point, and moved both east and west round Kallidromon. The westward wing further divided, with Xerxes pressing on down into Boeotia from the west, while another section of the army engaged in what proved a fruitless attack on Delphi.

This was, however, a simultaneous land and sea encounter and we've ignored the fleet. While the Persians were attacking the army in the pass, the two navies engaged. Unlike the land forces the fleet held its own against the invader. Herodotus tells us (Hdt. 8.7) that the Persians attempted the same flanking move at sea, sending a squadron round the east side of Euboea to advance up the Euripus channel between Euboaea and the mainland from the south and catch the Greek fleet in a pincer movement. Unlike Thermopylae, the manouevre came to nothing in the end because the encircling ships were wrecked in a storm off Euboea (Hdt. 7.13). The Battle of Artemisium was actually three engagements on three successive days. In the first two encounters the Greeks took the initiative with some success, though without inflicting a knockout blow. On the third the Persians attacked, in what looks like an action concerted with the climactic attack in the pass (Hdt. 7.15–16). Both fleets were mauled in the battle and neither side could claim an outright victory, though the Persian losses were greater. At this point the Greeks received news of the defeat at Thermopylae (Hdt. 8.21). They had stationed a light vessel with Leonidas and had another at Artemisium to allow communication between the army and the fleet. The loss of the pass made their own position both useless and exposed, with only the island of Euboea to the east (mostly) loyalist, while the mainland to the west and south would gradually fall to the invader. So they fell back on the next position, at Salamis. The attempt to hold central Greece was over.

7

Thermopylae Refought

For the Western world the writing of history starts with Herodotus. So for Europe and its diaspora Thermopylae was the very first last stand in world history. The histories of peoples around the world are rich in stories of courageous stands against overwhelming odds. But all, at least in the West, look over their shoulder at the archetype, Thermopylae.

This was not the first action in the pass, however, and it was certainly not the last. Herodotus' account of the 'Phocian wall' which the Greek forces reused in 480 indicates that centuries before the arrival of Xerxes Thermopylae had been used as a barrier between local Greek belligerents (Hdt. 7.176.3–4):

> A wall had been built in this pass, and in early times it had gates. It was the Phocians who built it from fear, when the Thessalians came from Thesprotia [i.e. from Epirus, north-west Greece, through the Pindos range] to occupy the Aeolian land, which they now possess. Since the Thessalians were trying to subjugate them, the Phocians took this precaution, and they diverted the hot water into the pass to make it a watercourse, in an attempt by any means to keep the Thessalians from invading their country.

Whether Herodotus is right to credit the wall to the Phocians is unknowable. His explanation of the origin of the wall has been doubted. But even if Herodotus is wrong about date, builders, and purpose, there was a defensive wall. So generations before Xerxes the pass was an ideal place for Greeks to stop other Greeks heading south.

111

Even when the wall was built, the need to control the pass was nothing new. Greek states were perpetually at war with their neighbours. They probably arrived in the peninsula around 2000 BC and displaced, absorbed, or subjugated the peoples they found already there. And inward migration of Greek-speaking peoples continued for a millennium. Its location and topography meant that Thermopylae must have been fought over before, during, and after the Greek migration and long before the Thessalians took over what became Thessaly; we just lack the written and archaeological evidence.

Not only was this not the first action in the pass, it was anything but the last. In the two and a half millennia since Leonidas' death Thermopylae has seen a succession of hard-fought engagements and rapid retreats. Usually the combatants have looked over their shoulders at the battle of 480 BC. Even here our knowledge is sadly limited. A battle in the pass during the third-century Gothic invasion only came to light in 2007, when a manuscript containing a collection of Christian texts was re-examined using digital technology to reveal an earlier, imperfectly erased, text underneath. Parchment was labour-intensive to produce and so expensive. In the Middle Ages it was often recycled by scraping away the old text to offer a fresh writing surface; but the original text often leaves traces. The undertext in this case turned out to be a piece from a historical narrative (probably by the historian Dexippus) of a battle to stop an invading force at Thermoplyae. I discuss this text further below. But its discovery tells us just how little we really know about the blood spilt in the pass over the last two and a half millennia.

We associate Thermopylae with failure, however glorious, and most of the time it did fail to do its job. But not always. In 359 BC Philip of Macedon came to the throne in a northern backwater whose status as Greek some Greeks at least found (or chose to find) questionable. For the Greek powers to the south the northern lands had been an area to manipulate for their own conflicts. The throne was always precarious and there was no reason to doubt that Philip was just another Macedonian ruler who would spend most of his time

maintaining a precarious hold on his kingdom. But Philip was different. He began a strategy of expansion which within the next twenty
years would make Macedon the dominant power in Greece. Having
secured his position in Macedon he expanded into Thessaly by
exploiting divisions between cities and factions there. This brought
him to Thermopylae, the gateway to the south. The eastward route via
the Cephisus valley was closed to him, since Phocis was hostile. In 352
Philip decisively defeated a Phocian army at the Battle of the Crocus
Field. This secured his hold over Thessaly, although it still left Phocis
closed to him. He followed up the success by advancing on Thermopylae, but the Athenians sent a force to meet him and Philip decided
not to push his luck. This was not really a military engagement but a
test of resolve. A battle would have been costly and part of the cost
would have been in image, given the precedent of 480. An astute
strategist, Philip preferred where possible to get his way by oblique
means and he needed the collective goodwill of the Greeks, if he did
not want to fight his way to power state by state. The dash on
Thermopylae tipped his hand for any Macedon-watchers among the
Greeks; but a battle to force the pass with or without Anopaea would
have been too much like overt imperialism. Above all he might have
alarmed Thebes, whose backyard Boeotia was almost immediately
beyond Thermopylae, and pushed it into the arms of Athens in an
anti-Macedonian alliance. And he would still have a hostile Phocis in
his rear. Just six years later he was able to win over Thebes and break
the power of Phocis, leaving him in a position to advance south. But
he was not yet in a position to force his will on a coalition of Greek
states. Thermopylae was again occupied in 323 by the Athenian
general Leosthenes, leader of the anti-Macedonian forces in the Lamian
War which followed Alexander's death that year, to stop a Macedonian
army under Antipater from entering central Greece.

Much closer to the events of 480 was the Celtic invasion of 279,
when Thermopylae was again chosen as the best location to block a
massive foreign invasion from the north. Sources for the invasion
are limited but our fullest account comes from the travel-writer

Pausanias, writing in the second century AD, several hundred years later. Pausanias' *Description of Greece* is the earliest surviving European travel guide. But it is far more. Pausanias was writing at a time when Greek literature was experiencing a renaissance, the so-called Second Sophistic. Greece was at this stage a political backwater subservient to Rome. The Second Sophistic saw a resurgence of Greek pride in its cultural legacy and an attempt to imitate and compete with the literary achievements of the past. Pausanias' book is a verbal tour of Greece organized by region, describing the rich architectural and artistic heritage of each and locating both within a mythic and historical context.

Pausanias actually tells the story twice, first in his description of the monuments of Athens (Paus. 1.4) in relation to the commander of the Athenian contingent in the campaign, Callippus, then at much greater length in his account of the offerings at the oracular shrine of Apollo at Delphi (10.19–23). The link to Delphi is highly significant. Greek traditions of the Celtic invasion, like those of the Persian Wars, were rich in legend and nowhere more so than at Delphi, which was both the high-water mark and the turning point of the seemingly relentless onward advance of the invaders. The digression on the battle gave Pausanias an opportunity to emulate Herodotus. Pausanias did not invent the comparison with 480. It was a Greek custom to dedicate a portion of the spoils from a battle to the gods, both as a gesture of gratitude and as a monument to success, and the shields taken from the Celts were set up close to those taken from the Persians at Marathon by the Athenians (Paus. 10.19.4). But Pausanias is always looking over his shoulder at the earlier traveller and nowhere more so than in his account of Brennus and his Celts. The shadow of the earlier invasion hangs heavy over his narrative. In some details his account of the invasion is so close to Herodotus' account of the Persian invasion of 480–479 that it has been suggested that he is borrowing from Herodotus. This includes some features of the account of the fighting in the pass. He also goes out of his way to draw comparisons between the two invasions, and even suggests that the Celtic assault was the greater threat. With the memory of the invaders' atrocities fresh in their minds, the Greeks

> saw that the struggle they faced would not be for freedom, as it was with the Persians in the past, and that giving water and earth would not bring them safety.... Every Greek to a man and all the cities collectively were convinced that the choice was victory or death. (Paus. 10.19.12)

Despite the superficial similarities with 480, the Celtic assault on Greece in 279 was a very different kind of incursion. The Persian invasion of 480 was a highly organized amphibious campaign, carefully planned and prepared, and well provisioned. And the aim was to conquer Greece and absorb it into the highly organized Persian empire. Conquest for the Persians did not necessarily involve hostilities. It was in the interest of the empire to avoid both unnecessary losses in the field and unnecessary destruction to the newly acquired territory. As Pausanias rightly notes, it was enough for the invaders of 480 if Greek states were prepared to submit by giving earth and water.

The Celtic invasion in contrast was a combination of population movement and raid for plunder. The Celts had established themselves across a broad area by the fifth century BC, stretching from (what later became) East Anglia in Britain to central Europe as far as modern Hungary and Poland. Though archaeology indicates a shared material culture, we do not know how far this was reflected in shared language or in shared origin, whether ethnic or geographical. We do not even know what they called themselves. Apart from the archaeology we meet them through the words of the Greeks and Romans, who called them *Keltoi/Celti* or *Galatai/Galli* (Gauls). Whether they would have accepted being bracketed together in this way is unknowable. Their culture too (except for settlement patterns and artefacts) emerges only from those who fought them. The Celts were regarded by the Greeks and Romans as savage and warlike. They became the barbarian Other by which the southern cultures defined themselves, like the Scythians of the central European steppes and (later) the Huns. Like the Vikings they raided adjacent lands to the south and occasionally settled. In the fourth century BC they pressed south into the Italian peninsula. Celts/ Gauls under Brennus advanced as far as Rome in 390 BC, when they almost took the Capitol Hill; according to Roman legend they were prevented only when a night attack was thwarted by the sacred geese, who alerted the Romans to their approach. A remnant of this force stayed on the Italian side of the Alps, which the Romans accordingly named Cisalpine Gaul, 'Gaul this side of the Alps'. In the third century they were on the move further east, pressing south through the Balkans.

The serious thrust into Greece came in 279. According to Pausanias the Celts had made two earlier incursions. The first had been a small-scale affair which advanced no further than Thrace in the north and made little impact. It may have been little more than a feeler. The second in 280 was more substantial. The invaders penetrated as far as Macedonia, where they were opposed by the Macedonian king Ptolemy 'Keraunos' ('Thunderbolt'). The Macedonians suffered heavy losses, including the death of their king, but again the Celts withdrew. Then in 279 (a different) Brennus, who had been part of the previous expedition, persuaded the Celts to attack Greece in greater numbers. Our sources give a figure of 150,000 to 152,000 foot and 10,000 to 20,400 horsemen (Paus. 10.19.9 adds another 40,800 reserve riders). The broad agreement on the scale suggests a shared source in a Hellenistic historian. But since the Celts left no literary record, the source for the numbers must be Greek estimates. The figures look wildly exaggerated. But we can be sure both that the numbers were alarmingly vast and that the third expedition was much greater than its predecessors. Unlike the previous raids this looks like an attempt by the Celts to establish themselves in the peninsula, though the devastation caused indicates that this was also a plunder raid on a grand scale. Alexander's death had been followed by wars between his successors and the conflicts had continued into the third century, with different regimes and states in Greece (and Greeks in Asia Minor) locked in seemingly endless struggles for dominance. To the outsider

Greece must have looked ripe for conquest. The Celts were divided into three groups (Paus. 10.19.6), one division moving across Thrace in the north, another to attack Macedon and then move into Illyria in north-west Greece, and the third under Brennus moving due south through southern Macedonia and Thessaly.

Our Greek sources stress the ferocity of the Celts, especially in this invasion. And there is no reason to doubt the tales of atrocities and destruction, even if some of the details are embroidered. But they also had experienced commanders who (if not always) used their resources intelligently. Unlike the Persians before them, however, they had no fleet and this was to prove decisive for the Greek forces in avoiding the annihilation of 480, even if it did not stave off defeat.

The Greeks again fixed on Thermopylae as the point to stop the invader. They had learned from 480. Pausanias stresses the scale of the Greek response in contrast with the force sent against the Persians. This time the combined Greek infantry force (mostly heavy armed) numbered up to 24,000. With it were at least 1,000 cavalry, a significant advance on 480, when the Greeks had no cavalry. Though the cavalry on both sides was useless in the narrow pass, its presence meant that the Greeks had the means to cover their retreat, if necessary. The composition too had changed. The largest contingents came from those with a strong immediate interest in the defence of the pass. The Boeotians, who lay in the path of the Celts once Thermopylae was breached, sent 10,000 hoplites and 500 cavalry. Another very large contingent (probably over 8,000) came from the Aetolians west of the Pindos range. By the third century the Aetolian League had emerged from relative obscurity as the most important power in central Greece and their influence extended into Thessaly, which gave them a strong motive to counter the threat from the Celts. Sparta was absent. Sparta had pursued an active military policy under its expansionist king Areus I and had been at war with the Aetolians just two years before. So Sparta had no good reason to help them now and may not have been unhappy to see them suffer, especially as a weakened central Greece might offer opportunities for Sparta to expand its influence. But the Peloponnese in general remained aloof with the exception of Megara. The immediate danger was to northern and central Greece, and since the Celts had no ships, the Isthmus of Corinth could not be bypassed. So the 'fortress Peloponnese' policy of staying within and fortifying the Peloponnese, which was regularly contemplated but ultimately abandoned in 480–479, now presented no problems. Pausanias puts the Athenians in overall command (and he believed that they proved the best fighters in the battle). This could reflect pro-Athenian bias from Pausanias and it has been suggested that the Aetolians actually took the lead. But the allies may have felt that Sparta, for reasons of pride or rivalry, was more likely to participate under Athens. The states of central Greece may also have been less suspicious of Athens than of the Aetolians.

The logic in the Greek choice of Thermopylae was the same as in 480. They were vastly outnumbered by Brennus' forces and the narrow pass neutralized the numerical advantage of the Celts. It is difficult to tease out detail from Pausanias' account of the battle itself, partly because of its brevity and partly because it is hard to tell how much of the narrative is borrowed from Herodotus' account of 480. His emphasis on Greek order and experience in the face of a disorderly enemy attack (Paus. 10.21.1, 10.21.3), his statement that the Celts were trampled by their own side (10.21.4), and his comparison between the limited protection provided by the Celtic shields and the heavy armed Greek hoplites (10.21.2) are all reminiscent of Herodotus' Persians of 480, as is the drowning of some of the invaders in the marshy shallows, when they slip off the road (10.21.4). On the other hand, the Greeks were drilled in set-piece fighting in a line and they were more heavily armed. The hill fell precipitously to the sea; so the prospect of falling in was real. And in mass fighting at close quarters in a narrow pass men will be trampled. So it becomes difficult to determine where Pausanias or his source (or sources) is drawing on eyewitness accounts and how far he is using a blend of common sense and literary reminiscence to build his account and compete with his model. But he does not simply mimic Herodotus' narrative, and two key aspects of the fighting reflect the very different situation and participants.

The first of these is the intervention of the Athenian fleet, which pulled into the shallows and attacked the invaders from the flank with missiles, a move made possible by the absence of any fleet on the other side, which gave the Athenians unrestricted control of the sea. Quite where in the pass this took place is unclear. It cannot have been at the narrowest part of the Middle Gate, where the road was much too high above sea level to be within easy javelin or even bow range, as well as being too narrow even for the Greek numbers. Probably we should locate the fighting in the slightly wider ground to the west, where the Greeks fought on the last day in 480. But the Celtic forces must have been stretched along the pass, and an attack on the troops pressing forward from behind where the road climbed the steep side of the bay would have caught those of the invaders who had entered the pass in a pincer movement.

The other is the brutal diversionary move by the Celts designed to draw the Aetolians away from the pass and reduce the number of defenders (Paus. 10.22.2–7). The idea is ascribed by Pausanias to Brennus himself; he must have been well informed by locals about the composition of the forces opposing him. A large force (40,000 foot and 800 horse according to Pausanias) turned west through Thessaly and invaded Aetolia, where the Celts systematically ravaged the city of Kallion/Kallipolis. The Aetolians responded by withdrawing from Thermopylae to protect their territory. Together with the population left behind (including not just those of military age but old men and women incensed at the atrocities committed by the Celts), they were eventually able to trap the invaders and inflict enormous casualties. But the Celts had succeeded in weakening the force opposing them in the pass.

It is at this point that history repeats itself. The Celts had tried unsuccessfully to find a way through the hills to encircle the Greek defenders. Finally Greeks from the region alerted Brennus to the Anopaea route. Pausanias generously (and plausibly) claims that they simply wanted to be rid of the Celts (Paus. 10.22.9). Pausanias has Brennus lead a detachment of 40,000 through the hills. The figure looks wildly inflated for the size of the path and grossly disproportionate to the numbers required to outflank a vastly outnumbered Greek force. But the Celts certainly used the path, whatever their numbers. The Phocians had again been left to guard the path. Despite the earlier history this made sense, since they knew the terrain. They were, however, again dislodged, this time after putting up a stiff resistance, though Pausanias' claim that the Celts were upon them before they knew it because of a thick mist on the mountain (Paus. 10.22.11) looks suspiciously like a rerun of the night march of Herodotus' Persians. Even in a mist one would expect the approach of a large force to be audible some way off. That would, however, have made little difference, since there were no reinforcements to summon.

The Phocians did, however, manage this time to get word to the Greeks before they were encircled, and the Athenian fleet was able to evacuate the Greek forces from the pass. History did not entirely repeat itself.

It would be churlish to leave the Celts in control of northern Greece. So a word is needed about the endgame. Instead of advancing through the now open pass Brennus turned his forces east toward the riches of the temple precinct at Delphi, where they were met by massed Greek forces. The Greek tradition was that the god intervened to protect his temple, with thunder and lightning, earthquakes, frost and snow, and rockfalls. And in a repeat of the tradition of the heroes who fought alongside the Greeks at Marathon, the Celts saw apparitions of the heroes Hyperochus, Laodocus, and Achilles' son Pyrrhus, and (some said) a local hero of Delphi Phylacus ('guardian'). Some of the meteorology is probably true. But it is also true that the Greeks knew the terrain and that Brennus had failed to wait for the arrival of the contingent sent into Aetolia, which was held up on the march by Greek guerrilla attacks. The defeated army was relentlessly harried on its withdrawal. The Celts were then further attacked on the return to their camp at the river Spercheius, north of Thermopylae, by the

Thessalians and the Malians from the gulf area. Pausanias tells us that not a man returned from Greece (Paus. 10.23.13). A fine dramatic end, if unlikely. But we can be reasonably sure that a defeated and demoralized force in retreat suffered heavily from attacks by the populations they had overrun, all of whom must have had their own deep grudge to settle.

Since the Greek forces had again been outflanked and had to be evacuated by sea, it is easy to dismiss the military significance of the stand at Thermopylae. But the Celts got no further into Greece. Unlike the Persians, who were determined to take the pass at any cost, the Celts seem to have attempted only one sustained frontal assault on the Greek position, at enormous cost to themselves, after which they left a gap of seven days before they began their attempts to find a way round the pass (Paus. 10.22.1). Pausanias' account suggests that there was a further interval before they learned of the route behind Kallidromon. According to Diodorus Siculus (Diod. Sic. 22.9.1), they had suffered serious losses in the fighting in Macedonia. So their forces may have been reduced by the time they reached Thermopylae, even if they still outnumbered the defenders dramatically. The losses in the first engagement at Thermopylae may have discouraged them from another expensive frontal attack. Though they eventually took the pass, they may have lacked the manpower to push south with confidence. They were presumably relying on systematic plunder for provisions; but foraging raids become more attenuated and more demanding as time progresses and ready sources of food for men and animals are exhausted. So Brennus' attack on Delphi may have been exactly what our ancient sources claim, an attempt simply to plunder the sanctuary, possibly as a last throw of the dice before withdrawal. If so, it was a costly throw. The Greek stand at the pass may not itself have been the pivotal factor in breaking the Celtic advance. But it was instrumental.

The pass next saw action in 191 BC, when it was chosen by the Seleucid king Antiochus III to stop the Romans. The battle is dealt with by Livy in his monumental history of Rome (Livy 36.16–19) and by Appian (*Syrian Wars* 4.16–20), with a colourful and imaginative version also offered by Plutarch in his biography of Cato (*Cato the Elder* 13–14), drawing on a vainglorious account by Cato himself. The carve-up of the short-lived empire of Alexander the Great by his successors had left his general Seleucus in control of eastern Asia Minor. His descendant Antiochus III, who came to power in 222 BC, had been steadily expanding Seleucid control in Asia Minor after initial setbacks and had gradually extended his power west and north through Anatolia until he encroached on Thrace immediately to the north of Greece proper. This inevitably brought him into conflict both with Philip V of Macedon and with Rome. Rome had itself been expanding its influence eastward. It had intervened in Greece in alliance with the Aetolian League as the champion of Greek autonomy to check the power of Macedon. The philhellene Roman general Flamininus had triggered the withdrawal of Roman forces from the peninsula by proclaiming the freedom of Greece at the Isthmian Games of 196 BC. But Rome could not ignore an attempt to annex Greece in whole or in part. Another potent factor was the presence at Antiochus' court of the Carthaginian general Hannibal. After the failure of his invasion of Italy and his defeat at the Battle of Zama in 202, Hannibal had confined his political activity to Carthage until his enemies appealed to Rome. He then fled to the court of Antiochus. The presence of an inveterate troublemaker like Hannibal at Antiochus' court gave Rome an additional reason to block Seleucid expansion in Greece.

Antiochus needed a plausible motive to be in Greece and like Rome he found this in the notion of Greek freedom. The opportunity was offered by the Aetolians, who, fretting at Roman involvement in Greek affairs, elected him general in 192 BC. He crossed into Greece but few Greeks were convinced by his claim to be liberating Greece from Roman influence and he failed to attract much support. The Romans reacted by sending a force under Manius Acilius Glabrio in the following year. Having crossed from Brundisium (Brindisi) to Apollonia in north-western Greece the Romans advanced through

Thessaly to meet Antiochus, who had taken up a position at Thermopylae. As always the choice allowed him to exploit the levelling effect of the narrow pass. The failure of the Greeks to rally to his cause meant that he was outnumbered by a factor of two to one by the Roman army. In addition, though everyone who fought at Thermopylae after 480 had one eye on its history, Antiochus had a good propaganda reason to opt for the pass, since it cast him in the role of the defender of Greece, a commander with impeccable Macedonian ancestry against an unambiguously alien outsider. Commanders do not take up positions for purely symbolic reasons. The main factor was logistical; but the symbolism cannot have escaped the Greeks, even if in the end most of them decided to sit and watch. One key exception was Philip V of Macedon, who after prevaricating decided to ally himself with Rome.

Antiochus established his base at the eastern end of the pass, just inside it. With a head start on the Romans, Antiochus fortified the pass and placed artillery (probably mainly catapults) on the fortifications. He may not have started from scratch. The Aetolians had fortified the pass against Philip in 208 BC (Polybius 10.41) and he may have strengthened and extended their work. He then sat down to wait. With the events of 480 and 279 in mind Antiochus sought to avoid a flanking manoeuvre. So he stationed troops to guard the route through the hills. This time the task fell to the Aetolians. The Aetolians had a garrison of 4,000 at Heraclea in Trachis, about 7 kilometres from the west end of the pass, but their reaction to his request to guard his flank was mixed. Half the force at Heraclea were not confident that Antiochus would defeat the Romans and according to Livy this faction remained where they were in order either to rush to Aetolia to protect their homeland, if the Romans won, or to pursue the retreating Romans if Antiochus broke their attack. As a result only 2,000 Aetolians went to prevent Antiochus' position from being encircled. Thermopylae abounds in 'what-ifs' and (as with the failure to hold the path in 480) it is interesting to speculate what the outcome of the battle might have been, if the Aetolians had turned out in force.

The Aetolians took up three positions according to Livy, two according to Appian. One was on Kallidromon. Appian is quite certain that this was on the route 'where Xerxes attacked Leonidas and his Spartans' in 480. The other two locations, Tichius (Greek *Teichious*) and Rhoduntia (which Appian omits), are placed on Mount Oita. The latter may be in the direction of Gorgopotamos, while the former has been located on the steep ground immediately to the west of the pass, either at or west of Damasta. Glabrio entrusted the assault on these positions to two of his officers, Marcus Porcius Cato (later to become the severest Roman of them all, Cato the Censor) and Lucius Valerius Flaccus.

As before this manoeuvre was to prove decisive. The attack on the western positions involved an ascent on very steep terrain and the Romans were unsuccessful. Cato's attack on the eastern position, however, succeeded. He dislodged the Aetolians, whom he (literally) caught napping (Livy 36.18.8), and they fled before him. Despite the numerical superiority of the Romans, the narrowness of the pass and the entrenched position of the defenders meant that the Romans struggled to dislodge them. Antiochus also made good use of the equipment (particularly the 5-metre-long Macedonian spear, the *sarissa*) and Macedonian fighting techniques developed by Philip II in the fourth century. Our sources differ significantly in their accounts of the fighting in the pass, but they agree that the battle was at best evenly matched from the Roman perspective until the Aetolians poured down from Kallidromon with Cato's forces in pursuit, whereupon the Seleucid resistance crumbled. There is some exaggeration in both directions in terms of the losses on both sides, but the battle was clearly a decisive victory for the Romans. Antiochus withdrew to Asia, where the Romans followed him the next year and defeated him again. The peace terms imposed on him committed him to staying out of Europe for the future.

Thermopylae set the seal on Roman influence in Greece, though they made no attempt to annex the region. The situation changed when Philip V was succeeded by his illegitimate son Perseus in 179. Philip had been forced by the Romans to give up his claims in southern Greece in 197 and had been careful to avoid provoking them. Perseus' increase in his armed forces and his expansion into neighbouring Thrace at the expense of Rome's ally, the Thracian king Abrupolis, led to tension with Rome which erupted into war in 171. In 168 Perseus was defeated and Macedonia was partitioned to prevent it from becoming a major power again. Rome's grip on Greece had tightened. Macedonia rose against Rome in 150 under the pretender Andriscus; it was defeated once more in 148 and in 146 became a Roman province. This provoked an uprising of the Achaean League based in the Peloponnese. The League was quickly defeated and Greece passed under direct Roman control.

We now know that a pitched battle was fought in the pass in the third century AD. The evidence comes from a new fragment of Dexippus' *Scythica* found on a palimpsest and recently published. The enemy were again non-Greek invaders from the north, though tantalizingly the text does not identify them, beyond referring to them as 'Scythians'; that is, the nomadic people of the east European steppes. Probably we are dealing with the Gothic invasions. The Goths had been raiding into the Roman empire since the second century AD. In 267 a Gothic tribe called the Herulians reached far enough into Greece to sack Athens. Like Herodotus' successor, the Athenian historian Thucydides, Dexippus was active in public life as well as in the world of letters. The text mentions a man named Dexippus as one of the Greek commanders. Whether this is the historian himself is contentious. The historian has long been credited with a major role in the defence against the invaders but this too is uncertain. More important for us is the date and the outcome. After unsuccessfully besieging Thessaloniki, the invaders moved south. They were met in the pass by a hastily assembled army. Some were presumably properly armed but 'some carried small spears, others axes, others wooden pikes tipped with bronze and with iron, or whatever each man could arm himself with'. As with Antiochus the defenders did not just rely on the natural advantages of the position but also fortified it. We do not know the outcome, since the account breaks off in the middle of a speech to the troops by the commander. But again the shadow of the earlier action falls across the narrative. In a vague and rather garbled speech the general reminds them of the Persian Wars and the Lamian War in which Athens led a Greek coalition against Macedon immediately after the death of Alexander the Great, and finally the battle of 191, which is represented as a Greek victory (in alliance with Rome) against Antiochus. Whether the invaders ever found the track through the hills, and whether the defenders held out, depends on the vexed problem of the date of the battle. The Gothic tribes invaded several times. The invasion of 267 is a possibility, in which case the defenders lost. But Thermopylae had been fortified successfully at least once in the 250s or early 260s. Our source for that invasion notes that the Goths had unsuccessfully besieged Thessaloniki. It does not mention a battle in the pass but it does have them return home laden with booty but without sacking the cities to the south. So this time the Greeks may have stopped the invaders at the pass. The fragmentary text leaves the motley crew of defenders, and us, endlessly waiting for the barbarians.

We do know, however, from the sixth-century historian Procopius of Caesarea (*History of the Wars* 2.4.10) that the route through the hills was used again in 539, when the Kutrigur Huns swept south into Greece. The pass was by this time walled and the invaders were beaten back by a resolute defence. But they were able to circumvent the Greek defenders before moving south to overrun and pillage central Greece. Procopius maintains that the invaders found the way round by exploring the routes through the hills. He probably has Ephialtes in mind, since his language ('by thoroughly exploring the ways around they unexpectedly found *the path* which leads to the mountain which rises there') takes for granted that that his readers know the history of the pass. This time there was no betrayal. His 'unexpectedly' suggests that the defenders underestimated their enemy and posted no guard in the hills. Procopius links contemporary experience of Thermopylae more explicitly with the events of 480 in his fulsome praise of the defensive measures put in place there by the emperor Justinian (*On the Buildings of Justinian* 4.2.11–22), probably in reaction to the disaster of 539.

Justinian systematically improved the defences in the pass and in the routes through the hills and replaced the local levies responsible for the defence with a regular garrison. Procopius expresses amazement that it took Xerxes so long to find his way around the defensive position at Thermopylae in 480 when there are so many routes. The exaggerated claim serves to highlight by contrast his lavish praise for Justinian's foresight, wisdom, and thoroughness.

Thermopylae was chosen for a brief stand by Leo Sgouros against yet another set of invaders, the Franks, in 1204. Leo Sgouros, the hereditary governor of Nauplion, had taken advantage of the chaos created by the Crusades to make himself effectively the independent overlord of the Argolid in the north-eastern Peloponnese. He had expanded his power into central Greece and the emperor Alexios III had acknowledged his de facto authority by marrying his daughter to Sgouros. Boniface of Verona had established the Frankish kingdom of Thessalonica after the fall of Byzantium to the Crusaders and was pushing south through Greece. Sgouros chose Thermopylae as the place to stop his advance but quickly abandoned his position. Boniface was able to press south and take much of central Greece. Two years later he was dead and twenty years later his kingdom fell to the lord of Epirus.

The route of the main north–south road in modern times means that the Turks inevitably used it in moving troops during the Greek uprising from 1821 and earlier. It was just outside the pass that two of the most significant engagements took place in April 1821. A Turkish force of 8,000 was advancing south to put down the revolt in central Greece and a body of 1,500 Greek insurgents attempted to stop them. The Greek fighters took up three positions, with two groups holding the bridges at Gorgopotamos and Alamana and a third controlling the heights of Chalkomata immediately to the west of the entrance to the pass. The Turks fought their way through and in the process captured one of the Greek commanders, Diakos, who insisted on holding his ground though urged to withdraw. He was brutally executed by the Turks. Here, if anywhere, was the modern Leonidas.

The last engagement at Thermopylae was in April 1941, as the German army swept into Greece, making rapid progress despite difficult terrain and stiff opposition from the Greeks and their allies. The Greek invasion was originally an Italian adventure and the Italians had no desire for German assistance. The Greeks, however, saw off the Italian attack and Germany moved in to fill the void. The logic of the Allied attempt to keep Germany out of the southern Balkans was itself reasonable enough, since it would deny Germany a base for use against British forces in North Africa. But with British and Dominion forces already committed in North Africa, involvement in Greece was contentious from the outset and successful resistance to the German advance was probably never a realistic possibility. The expeditionary force was under-strength and under-resourced, and the campaign degenerated into a prolonged retreat, despite fierce resistance from Greek and Australian and New Zealand forces in Macedonia. There was never any prospect of halting the German advance in Macedonia but it was necessary to hold them back so that the Allied troops could take up a position at Thermopylae. Even so the Germans were at Thermopylae on 21 April, only thirteen days after taking Thessaloniki. The Allied defence focused not just on the pass itself but also on the road up through Brallos leading to the Cephisus valley, where artillery had a commanding view of the plain below. Initially the orders from the commander in the Middle East, Archibald Wavell, to the Commonwealth commander in Greece, General Henry Maitland Wilson, were to engage the enemy and hold the pass for 'some time'. The expectation was that they could check the German advance for several days while the evacuation of the Allied troops was effected by sea from the Peloponnese. Iven Mackay, who commanded the forces dug in at Brallos, later claimed that he expected to hold the line for a fortnight. But Thermopylae too had to be abandoned on 23 April, with a rearguard of two brigades left to cover the withdrawal. The enemy attacked on 24 April. The defenders put up a determined resistance but were forced to retreat after a day of fighting. The immediate trigger for the decision to abandon the position at Thermopylae was the news that the German army had advanced into Epirus. In the event there was no actual attack from the west. But for anyone even remotely familiar with the history of the pass the prospect of a flanking manoeuvre was always a possibility, and in this case the result might have been a repeat of 480. The losses in casualties and prisoners to the forces still in northern Greece would have been severe and the evacuation plan (Operation Demon) would have been threatened. The difference in the nature of the flanking manoeuvre, however, underscores the vast difference in scale and pace which separates ancient from modern warfare. The threatened encirclement came not from a scramble along a path through the hills or an adjacent valley but from a push 250 kilometres to the west.

The memory of 480 was exploited by the German press with the combination of staggering self-delusion and cynical misinformation which characterized Nazi Germany. The success in dislodging the anglophone forces and the rapid capture of Athens was celebrated by the *Völkischer Beobachter* with the claim that the 'circle of world history' had been closed.

> Some 2,500 years ago, the Greek people under Leonidas held out against a numerically superior foe. They were later forced to surrender to the English. Today, with our powerful blows, we have chased the English out of Greece and out of Europe.

Here, with that surreal capacity for grotesque distortion at which the Third Reich excelled, the German invaders masquerade as the native defenders, displacing the Greeks as the true descendants of Leonidas and heirs to his heroism. The alliance between Greece and the British has become an English conquest, and the British and their allies the non-European intruders and heirs to the territorial ambitions of the Persians. This was not the only time the model of Leonidas was to serve the needs of Nazi propaganda. But that is for a later chapter.

8

Thermopylae in the Ancient World

The Battle of Thermopylae passed from history into myth within a few years, perhaps within months. The element of high drama gave the events of 480 a huge claim on the imagination of posterity. Like the pass with its alluvial deposits the events of 480 were lost beneath layer upon layer of fantasy and fabrication as the dead were called on to serve the aspirations and machinations of generation after generation.

Militarily Thermopylae was a defeat, though the Spartans never viewed it as such. Centuries later the traveller Pausanias reports that the Spartan position was that Leonidas won; he just didn't have enough men (Paus. 1.13.5). But a defeat it was and at the time a costly one for Sparta. Herodotus (Hdt. 8.27) speaks of the outcome at Thermopylae as a 'wound'. This is a regular Herodotean image for military losses, not something special to Thermopylae. But to Sparta with its small population, the loss of 300 of its elite must have felt like a physical as well as an emotional wound. It must also have raised anxiety levels in a society dogged by constant fear of a helot revolt. However, in the longer term Thermopylae was an enormous coup for Sparta. The Spartans were a small minority of the fighters in the Greek contingent. They were even in the minority in the last stand. But this was Sparta's great battle. The David and Goliath contest at Thermopylae, and the sheer drama of the decision at the end to stand and die, captured the Greek imagination far more than the conventional battle at Plataea a year later, even though Plataea was, with Salamis, the decisive action. The betrayal by Ephialtes added extra spice; the war or the battle that could have been won (in fact or fancy) but for betrayal has abiding appeal, as we know from Germany after the First World War and American reactions to failure in Vietnam.

Thermopylae passed into legend almost immediately. Herodotus (Hdt. 7.228) records an inscription which was put in place within ten years at most of the battle, possibly not long after the final victory at Plataea:

> Against three million here once fought
> from the Peloponnese four thousand.

The mythologizing process is already visible in the fantastic figure of three million (for the arithmetical problem, see Chapter 5). There was no Persian count available and this was the only contemporary Greek record of the Persian numbers. It set the battle numbers (literally) in stone, and even an author like Herodotus who was prepared to halve the figure ended up working in millions for the total fighting force. The total (indirectly) received the backing of no less an authority than Aeschylus. The Athenian tragedian devoted a play, *Persians*, to the next encounter with the invader, the Athenian victory at Salamis, staged less than a decade after the events. Athenian tragedy was profoundly influential and not just in Athens. Aeschylus was known to have fought in the war. So for later generations he was an unimpeachable first-hand source. His play insists that the whole of Asia has been emptied of fighting men to supply troops for the expedition (*Persians* 56–8, 126–37, 718, 730).

Herodotus says that this inscription was set up by the Amphictyonic League, the interstate body responsible for the shrine at Delphi, which met at Thermopylae. This probably means no more than that they gave permission for the monument. Just how many inscriptions there were is contentious. Herodotus mentions three, the one for the Peloponnesians cited above, an inscription for the Spartan dead, and thirdly a personal memorial from the poet Simonides to the seer Megistias. The geographer Strabo, writing at the end of the first century BC, says that there were five inscriptions at Thermopylae (Strabo 9.4.2). He says that the Locrians had one; his count almost certainly includes one for the Thespians (identified by scholars with a couplet for the Thespians 'killed by the Persians' preserved in the geographical dictionary of Stephanus of Byzantium in the fifth century AD). Unless Herodotus is wrong or just selective, the other inscriptions were put in place later. Herodotus actually says that the monument for the Peloponnesians was 'for all of them', that is all the defenders. But it ignores the Greeks north of the Isthmus. It seems at first sight inconceivable that the Amphictyons would allow the southern states to claim all the credit in this way. But the Phocians had slipped away without fighting, the Locrians had Medized after Thermopylae; the Thebans fighting alongside Leonidas had eventually defected, while the city itself became a staunch ally of the invader. The only serious contenders from central Greece in the immediate aftermath of the battle were the Thespians; they had stood firm but their hoplites had been killed and the city was then burned by the Persians. They may have lacked the means or the will at this stage to press their case with the Amphictyons. The Peloponnesians may have been the only ones pushing for recognition. This was really no different from the various celebratory poems and songs commissioned by individual states to immortalize their distinctive contribution to the common project. So possibly the monuments on the site in Herodotus' day were from the south. Even so Sparta already dominated, since this was the only Peloponnesian state with its own inscription. And in the years that followed, the other allies were rapidly elided from the collective memory. Thermopylae became Sparta's battle, and has remained Sparta's battle to the present. Sparta dominates Herodotus' narrative. And Sparta still dominates the modern site as it dominated the ancient site. The epigram for the Spartan dead mentioned by Herodotus read:

> Go tell the Spartans, passer-by,
> that here obedient to their words we lie.

He gives no author but later sources attributed it to the great lyric poet Simonides. The epigram has been much admired and has generated countless translations, beginning with the Roman Cicero, and has inspired imitations on modern war memorials across the world. The poem has all the austere terseness of the archaic and classical Greek epigram at is economical best, able to summon up a depth of experience in a few brisk words, with emotion at most suggested, never fulsomely expressed: here understated courage and unostentatious pride in having done their duty. The epigram still stands at the site, though the inscription is modern. It is written on a stone on top of the hill of the last stand.

The appropriation of Thermopylae for Sparta was driven in part by the dynamics of the war itself and in part by later developments. Athens and Sparta were the dominant powers in the war. The tensions between them, which went back into the sixth century, were exacerbated during the war against the invader by differences both of policy and of interest. After the war Athens took the lead in pursuing the anti-Persian cause and rapidly acquired a maritime empire. The result was a growing rift with Sparta which erupted half a century later in the Peloponnesian War. This was a war which, like the Cold War which dominated the second half of the twentieth century, divided the Greek world into two camps between Athens and Sparta. All of this sharpened the tendency to read the Persian Wars in terms of 'Athenian' and 'Spartan' achievements, and to blur and even erase the part played by all the other Greek states who resisted the invaders. Hence Salamis, a collaborative naval battle where Athens supplied the greatest number of ships and the winning strategy, was viewed even just a few years later as Athens' great achievement (Pindar, *Pythian* 1.75–6 in the 470s). In the same way, Thermopylae was Sparta's battle.

And it was very good for Sparta's image. Sparta was already a source of awe and puzzlement for the Greeks long before the invasion. Spartan culture was unique in Greece. It was part agrarian community, part boot camp. The Spartan elite were the top of a pyramid whose bottom was made up of the populations of Laconia and neighbouring Messenia, which Sparta had conquered. These populations, collectively termed 'helots', had been reduced to something between serfdom and slavery. The availability of a slave workforce to work the land allowed the Spartans to become a military caste. Freed from the daily demands of agriculture, they were able to train themselves to a level of fighting fitness unparalleled in a Greek world where most fighting was done by citizen militias. But the military ethos was not just free choice. The Spartans were sitting on a volcano of potential revolt, and the helots did rebel from time to time. The need to keep the helots down was reflected in some key Spartan customs. They annually declared war on the helots so that they could kill them with impunity. As part of this militaristic culture youths were raised and trained collectively by the state. Part of their training was in the *krypteia*, 'the secret/hidden service', a body which would move around at night, killing the most promising helots in order to prevent insurrection.

This military culture made Sparta the most powerful and feared land force in Greece long before the Persian invasion. The awe that Sparta inspired was enhanced by ingrained secrecy. It was Spartan practice intermittently to eject foreigners in a custom called *xenelasia* (literally 'driving out foreigners'), another unique practice—Greek states in general were happy to have non-natives permanently settled among them, even if they never gave them equal rights with their citizens. The expulsions made direct access to information about Sparta difficult. Spartans were also notoriously reluctant to give away information about military matters, even in the past, as the Athenian historian Thucydides found when he was researching his history of the Peloponnesian War. He could not get figures for the Spartan forces at the Battle of Mantinea in 418, 'because of the secrecy of the Spartan way of life' (Thuc. 5.68.2). For most Greeks Sparta was a little like Russia for Churchill, 'a riddle wrapped in a mystery inside an enigma'.

The aura of invincibility (together with the fact that as leader of the Peloponnesian League Sparta could bring a large number of allied troops into the field to supplement its own) made it inevitable that Sparta would be the leader of the Greek alliance in a world which had yet to experience Athenian naval power; Salamis was still to come. The Persians, at least the fighting men, shared the Greek nervousness about Sparta. Although Herodotus is probably right to represent the Persians as overconfident (they had a lot to be confident about), Hydarnes' troops knew enough about Sparta to be wary when they encountered an unidentified force 1,000 strong on Kallidromon as they marched around the Greek position in the Middle Gate at Thermopylae (Hdt. 7.218):

> When they saw men arming themselves, they were amazed; they were expecting no obstacles to appear and they had run into an army. At this point Hydarnes, frightened that the Phocians might be Spartans, asked Ephialtes where the force was from and on learning the facts he lined up the Persians for battle.

They had already received a bloody nose in the pass but the anxiety goes back further, since the Persians had long been aware of Sparta's fighting capacity. It was no accident that, when Aristagoras, the rebellious Persian vassal at Miletus, went in search of Greek allies to help foment revolt against Persia among the Greek cities in Ionia in the early 490s, his first call was at Sparta (Hdt. 5.49). Athens was a second thought.

Thermopylae added enormously to Sparta's already high reputation and helped to buff up what has been called the 'Spartan mirage', the legendary status of Sparta as a unique society and a uniquely effective fighting force. This was not just about status but had profound practical implications. As any boxer knows, if you can go into a fight with your opponent largely convinced that you are the better fighter, you have done half the job before you enter the ring. The impact of Thermopylae for Sparta's image can be seen in a variety of ways. It resonates throughout Herodotus' narrative of Thermopylae, where the focus remains primarily on Sparta, but especially in the conversation he puts into the mouth of Xerxes and the exiled Spartan king Damaratus (Hdt. 7.101–4) about two months before the battle, when the Persian army and fleet are gathered at Doriscus in Thrace to the far north. The cultural contrast between east and west which runs through the *History* reaches a climax in this book, especially in the antithesis between the Greek love of freedom and Persian despotism. But it is at its sharpest in this exchange. Xerxes asks if the Greeks will resist him, when they are so hopelessly outnumbered. He rejects outright the possibility that they will stand their ground, when there is no absolute royal power to compel them. The conversation is Herodotus' invention and is clearly modelled on an exchange in Aeschylus' *Persians*, in which the mother of Xerxes quizzes the chorus of Persian counsellors about distant Athens (*Persians* 230–44). She like Herodotus' Xerxes is puzzled that men can fight effectively without coercion from above. What matters, however, is not whether this exchange really took place but how Herodotus wants us to see the contrasting forces. We are poised here at the moment before Xerxes launches his army south. He is talking about the whole of Greece, which he is about to invade. But the position in the text invites us to see this as a preparation for the first encounter at Thermopylae, where his confident assumptions will be tested. So does Damaratus' famous response, which, though it embraces principles which most Greeks would recognize, focuses only on the Spartans:

> Though they are free, they are not wholly free: have a master, the law [*or* tradition—*the Greek is ambiguous*], whom they dread far more than your men dread you. They do whatever it bids. And its bidding is always the same, that they must never flee from battle before any mass of men, but must stay at their post and conquer or die.

This is one of the most inspiring moments of the History. And it has a strong element of truth: the Greeks were proud of their subservience only to the impersonal force of law, even if they did not always live up to their ideals. But sadly the Spartan tradition which Damaratus offers Xerxes is a fiction. The Spartans knew how to retreat both before and after Thermopylae; they had to or every Spartan defeat would be annihilation (and, good as they were, Spartan armies did experience defeats). They had withdrawn about a month or so before from the original defensive position at Tempe to the north, when it became clear that they could be outflanked by the Persians; and the Spartan commander at Plataea, Pausanias, was in the act of pulling back his troops when the Persians attacked (Hdt. 9.52–7). This is Herodotus (through Damaratus) reading backward from the legendary Thermopylae itself, not forward from the world before the battle. But the process again had begun before him. The epitaph for the Spartans quoted by Herodotus already makes the point, less dramatically and more tersely than Damaratus:

> Go tell the Spartans, passer-by,
> that here obedient to their words we lie.

The word I have translated as 'words', *rhemasi*, from the noun *rhema*, is profoundly ambiguous; that is one of the features which make this text so resonant. The basic meaning is 'something said'. But the related word *rhetra*, again essentially just 'something said', is the term used for the Spartan political and military system ('covenant', 'ordinance') ascribed to the semi- (perhaps wholly) mythical figure Lycurgus which governed so many aspects of Spartan life down to the classical period. So *rhemasi* here suggests 'laws', 'tradition'. But it could also suggest 'command':

> Go tell the Spartans, passer-by,
> that here by their commands we lie.

Whether law, tradition, or command, the epigram suggests that the word from Sparta is 'fight and die', which is what they did at Thermopylae. This epigram too must date to the 470s. So the myth was at work long before Herodotus gave Damaratus his rousing speech.

More eloquent even than Damaratus' claim is the account in Thucydides (Thuc. 4.30–40) of an incident in the Peloponnesian War. A small force of Spartan hoplites became trapped by a much larger Athenian force on the island of Sphacteria off the coast of Pylos in the Peloponnese in 425. They were hopelessly outnumbered by lightly armed troops better suited to the terrain, capable of rapid advance and retreat, and able to deploy slings and arrows. A chance fire had destroyed any cover and the Spartan hoplites were exposed to unremitting missile attack, without water under the relentless Greek sun. Finally they were outflanked by a force using a path of which they were unaware. Facing annihilation, they surrendered. Comparison with Thermopylae was inevitable and the analogy was noted by Thucydides. The surrender staggered the Greeks. Thucydides observes (Thuc. 4.40):

> This was the greatest shock to Greece of all that happened in the war; for they did not believe that the Spartans would ever give up their arms, either from hunger or in any other extremity, but would hold on to them and die fighting to the utmost.

The shock which reverberated round the Greek world after Sphacteria is a measure of how much the last stand at Thermopylae magnified the Greek image of Sparta. Spartans win or (less often) lose but do not surrender. The legend of ice cold courage under pressure was fed further by the anecdotal tradition. Most famous was the story of Dieneces cited by Herodotus (Hdt. 7.226). Warned by 'some man from Trachis' that the Persian archers were so numerous that when they loosed their bows, the arrows blotted out the sun, 'unperturbed' he answered that this was 'good news, . . . because the battle would be in the shade and not in the sunlight'. The anecdote improved with age. By the time it is recorded by Plutarch in the Roman period (*Sayings of the Spartans* 225B) and by John of Stobi (Stob. 3.7.45) in the early Byzantine period it has become simply: 'That's agreeable, because we'll be fighting in the shade.' This was the version known to Cicero, who translated it into Latin (*Tusculan Disputations* 1.101).

There were other stories. Herodotus tells of two men recuperating from eye infections who had the option of returning home (Hdt. 7.229–31). One, Eurytus, had himself led by his helot servant to the battle line; when they got to the fighting, the slave ran off but Eurytus joined the line and died with his comrades. His conduct was bad news for the other invalid, Aristodemus, who chose to go home, where he was subjected to a kind of social death:

> None of the Spartiates would light fire for him or talk to him and he was disgraced, given the name 'Aristodemus the runaway'.

He died the next year at Plataea, fighting as a berserker in a vain attempt to purge the taint of cowardice. Herodotus judged him the best fighter at Plataea (Hdt. 9.71) but the Spartans withheld any honour because he had willed his death, in contrast to others who had faced death bravely though they wanted to live. Herodotus was offended by the unfairness but the message reinforced the iron image of Sparta; this was a culture with no second chances. Finally there was the case of Pantites (Hdt. 7.232), who survived the battle because he was sent as a messenger to Thessaly. He too was shamed on his return to Sparta and hanged himself. His story mirrors that of Aristodemus, though more simply. It repeats the point that for a Spartan death is better than dishonour. Some of this is apocryphal. Certainly the Dieneces story looks suspect, largely because it provided the opportunity for a bon mot. The Spartans were famously men of action and not words, good at making a pithy point but not lovers of long speeches, and this exchange epitomized both taciturnity and courage under fire. The anonymity of his informant ('some man from Trachis') points this way. So perhaps does his name. It occurs nowhere else and could be an invention. It means 'unceasing', hence 'unbroken', 'enduring', 'unflinching'. One cannot be sure, since this is a culture where most names have a meaning; so etymologies can just be chance coincidence. But the name is suggestive. The same applies to Pantites, which means (ironically) 'fully honoured' or (without irony) 'fully requited/punished'.

True or not, these stories had gained currency outside Sparta by the second half of the century. They burnished the Spartan image of a culture whose citizens viewed death as the lesser evil. Such stories (and the dramatic reality of the last stand) fed into a trend later in the century for aristocratic members of other states to lionize Spartan society and to ape Spartan dress, appearance, and manners. As always, we are best informed about Athens, but the practice must have been widespread. So great was Sparta's stature that this admiration survived the surrender at Sphacteria undiminished. It even outlasted the Battle of Leuctra in 371 and its aftermath, when Thebes inflicted a decisive military defeat on Sparta and followed it up with a policy of liberating and strengthening Sparta's neighbours, surrounding Sparta with a ring of steel, which meant that it was never again the leading power in Greece. But the admiration persisted, and still does.

As much as Sparta's battle, this was—and remains—Leonidas' battle. Apart from his death and his marriage (to the formidable Gorgo, daughter of the notorious king Cleomenes) little is known about Leonidas. The seal was set on his reputation by Herodotus, though the work had again begun very soon after the battle. Herodotus notes that a stone lion stood on his tomb at Thermopylae near the hill of the last stand (Hdt. 7.225). The lion could have been used for the collective dead; but it was reserved for Leonidas. The image is rich in associations. Most obviously it puns on Leonidas' name, since the Greek for lion is *leon*. Pun, however, is too pale a term. The Greeks lived in a world where the hand of the divine is working unseen everywhere, and seemingly chance verbal gestures, naming someone, even a random utterance, can point fleetingly to a divine pattern usually invisible to human beings. From this perspective (and in retrospect) Leonidas was not accidentally named 'son of the lion'; that was his nature. More than this, the lion has a distinctive position in archaic Greek art and Greek epic as the noblest fighting beast. Epic heroes are often compared with lions at their moment of glory or death in battle. So one effect of the wordplay was to summon up the lion of the Homeric simile, the ideal symbol of the warrior at his most courageous and lethal. The same wordplay also lurks behind the oracle reported at Herodotus 7.220, foretelling the death of Leonidas as the price for success:

> For you, dwellers in spacious Sparta,
> either your great glorious city is by Persian men
> laid waste, or if not that, from Heracles' line

the bounds of Lacedaemon will mourn a dead king.
The might of bulls or lions will not check him
with matching strength; for he has the might of Zeus. And I say
he will not stop until he rends one of these utterly.

The tale of the victory which can only be won by the sacrifice of a member of the royal family is familiar from Greek mythology. The presence of an archetypal story pattern reinforces the natural suspicion that what we have here is an oracle composed after Leonidas' death. What matters, however, is not its authenticity but the way it again plays with Leonidas as the son of the lion. The lion at Thermopylae is long gone. But Leonidas still dominates the site. His is the statue on the monument commemorating the battle across the road from the final hill (Figure 21).

Figure 21. Statue of Leonidas at Thermopylae

The hagiography of Leonidas continued in song. The master lyric poet Simonides had celebrated Thermopylae in a choral song of which only a fragment survives (PMG 531 = F261P):

> For those who died at Thermopylae
> glorious is the fate, fine the destiny,
> the tomb is an altar, for lament remembrance, their commiseration
>   is praise.
> A shroud like this neither mildew
> nor all-conquering time will obscure.
> This precinct of brave men has won as attendant the good report
> of Greece. Witness is Leonidas,
> king of Sparta, who has left behind the great
> adornment of courage and ever-fresh fame.

Whether it was a song devoted specifically to the battle or Thermopylae was mentioned in the context of another celebration is unclear from the fragment. The great battles of the Persian Wars were made the basis of public celebrations with specially commissioned songs of praise. Thermopylae must have received its own song or songs of celebration, and for all we know this could be one. What matters here is that Leonidas is separated out from the rest of the dead. And he is already presented in terms which suggest the heroes of Homer. This is clearly visible in the last line, which echoes the ceaseless quest of the epic hero for *kleos aphthiton*, 'immortal renown'.

Herodotus could not ignore models like this which fitted so neatly into his view of the war and of his own project. As we saw in Chapter 2, Homer is a constant presence in Herodotus' text, always close to the surface even when he is not named, literary model and target of competition at one and the same time. This epic dimension is everywhere in Herodotus but it is most prominent in book 7, in the lead-up to the first major encounter between the invaders and the loyalist Greeks. Leonidas and Xerxes never meet but the struggle between them is presented as a duel. Each is given an illustrious genealogy stretching back over generations (Hdt. 7.11, 204). Each is presented as the finest physical specimen in the army he commands (Hdt. 7.187,

204). Each is motivated by an heroic desire for glory. This is brought out in Xerxes' case by the decision to go to war at the beginning of Herodotus' account of the invasion, where Mardonius dangles before him the prospect of fame (Hdt. 7.5), and it emerges again in his conversation with his uncle Artabanus as they pause before crossing the Hellespont, where he dismisses his uncle's anxieties on the ground that nothing great is ever achieved by dwelling on the risks (7.50):

> Gains generally come to people who are willing to act but to those who calculate everything and are timid they don't.

This is a world view which has its origin in the stark choice of death and glory faced by the Homeric hero, expressed memorably in the speach of the doomed Lycian king Sarpedon (*Iliad* 12.309–28):

> At once he spoke to Glaucus, son of Hippolochus:
> 'Glaucus, why then are you and I honoured above all
> with seat of honour, meats and filled cups
> in Lycia, and all look upon us as if we were gods,
> and we have a a great estate marked out by the banks of Xanthus,
> good land, vineyard and wheat bearing field?
> So now we must in the front ranks of the Lycians
> take our stand, and go to meet the fierce heat of battle,
> so that men among the heavy armoured Lycians may say of us:
> "In truth, not inglorious are the men who rule Lycia,
> our kings, and feed upon the fat sheep
> and drink the choice sweet wine, but their valour is
> noble, since they fight in the front ranks of the Lycians."
> My friend, if somehow you and I, escaping this war,
> might live on forever, ageless and immortal,
> I would not myself be fighting in the front ranks
> nor would I send you to battle which gives men glory.
> But now, since the fates of death stand close over us
> without number, which no mortal can flee or escape,
> let us go, and offer someone cause to boast or he to us.'

With Leonidas it is not the decision to fight but the decision to die that is ascribed to a desire for glory (Hdt. 7.220). Leonidas is not the only

Greek, or even the only Spartan, to choose to die. He debates with his troops. But the sense of the hero standing as an individual on the battlefield is increased by Herodotus' simultaneous claim that he knows the names of all the Spartan dead and yet refuses to reveal them. The effect is to concentrate the spotlight on a handful of warriors, in particular Leonidas. Among the other features which align the account of Thermopylae with epic is the fight for the dead warrior's body (Hdt. 7.225.1):

> There was a great struggle between the Persians and Spartans over Leonidas' body, until the Greek by their prowess rescued it and routed their enemies four times. The battle went on until the men with Ephialtes arrived.

This is one of only two passages in his work which narrate a struggle for a corpse. This is a regular motif in epic, where Greeks and Trojans fight either to retain possession of a dead foe or to rescue a dead comrade's body. Fighting over bodies was not just a literary device, of course. It happened in the real world. Battles ebb and flow, especially hard-fought battles like this one. The body of a commander has a value which justifies a fight to deny it to the enemy, just as its capture has enormous implications for morale for both sides. This was probably not invention. The point, however, is not what happened but what Herodotus wants us to know, and the effect here is to underscore yet again the sense that this battle, for all that it is fought in a very un-Homeric way with the hoplite line replacing the individual duels of the Homeric battlefield, is the direct descendant of the fighting in Greek epic.

The heroic contest between Xerxes and Leonidas has one last ironic twist. Xerxes and Leonidas alike lay claim to heroic status. Only one of them pays the hero's price. But for the real punchline we have to wait until the aftermath of Salamis in book 8. Leonidas stands and dies. After witnessing the defeat at Salamis, Xerxes (at least Herodotus' Xerxes) takes fright and speeds to the Hellespont to get back into

Asia before the Greeks can cut him off. Both are tested but only one of them passes the test for true heroism. This point is made by the traveller Pausanias (Paus. 3.4.7–8). Both Xerxes and Leonidas (he says) were towering figures; but Xerxes' greatness was confined to the march, Leonidas proved his in battle. In Pausanias' opinion Leonidas did not just surpass Xerxes. He was the greatest of all the Greeks who fought the eastern barbarian, greater even than Achilles. It is both rare and remarkable for a historical figure to be favourably compared with Achilles in this way. Indeed Pausanias insists that but for the betrayal by Ephialtes Leonidas would have stopped the Persians in their tracks and prevented all the destruction that followed.

This privileging of Leonidas was at its most marked in Sparta. Pausanias tells us (Paus. 3.14.1) that the Spartans brought his bones home forty years after his death at Thermopylae, and that athletic games were held in his honour and annual speeches of praise were delivered. Both honours were shared with the other great Spartan commander in the Persian Wars, the general Pausanias who master-minded the victory in the land battle at Plataea. The games were open only to Spartans. We are not told how far back they go. The same passage in Pausanias tells us that the names of all those who fought at Thermopylae were inscribed on a stone slab. But they did not share Leonidas' games. The privileging here goes deeper, however. Both the recovery of the bones and the regular celebration point to another aspect of Leonidas' heroic status. The Greek term 'hero' can refer to legendary figures like Achilles, belonging to what we would call Bronze Age Greece. But it also has another meaning, with reference to Greek cult. The hero in this sense is a figure somewhere between man and god who receives worship. Unlike the gods, who are immortal, heroes in this sense are mortals, but they are dead mortals. Dead mortals who still possess power. Figures whose lives or deaths had been marked by exceptional circumstances for good or ill could receive cult honours after death. Like the gods they had the power to help and harm. Unlike gods, who were worshipped all over Greece (though usually with specific local roles and titles) and who could impact on events across the world, heroes were local in two senses: their worship was usually confined to a single area and their power was closely associated (like that of modern saints) with the location of their remains. And while it was relatively rare for new gods to be introduced, new hero cults were being created throughout the historical period. Leonidas was evidently (unlike the rest of the dead from Thermopylae) a hero in this more solid, cultic sense, not just in his depiction by writers such as Herodotus as something like a Homeric warrior. We have a Spartan parallel in the search for the remains of Agamemnon's son Orestes (Hdt. 1.67–8) in the sixth century, at a time when Sparta needed supernatural aid against Tegea. Pausanias tells us that the Spartans were still honouring Leonidas and the general Pausanias in his day, more than half a millennium after Thermopylae. In a Sparta which had long since lost political independence to Rome and was no longer a serious fighting force, the nostalgic appeal of the commanders of the Persian Wars (both to locals and to tourists) must have been all the greater.

The myths began early and grew with time. The process is already at work in Herodotus. Before hostilities commence Xerxes, impatient that the enemy fail to flee as he expects, sends a scout to reconnoitre the Greek position. As he nears the Greek camp (Hdt 7.208), he is quietly ignored. He finds the Spartans outside their wall, calmly exercising or combing their hair as they await the Persian attack. Damaratus explains to Xerxes that Spartan warriors adorn their head when they are about to face the prospect of death. Whether this is true or not is impossible to say; but unlike other Greeks the Spartans always wore their hair long and there is something sublime in the way they calmly go about their coiffure and their daily exercise in casual indifference to the presence of a vast opposing army. For later writers in a more rhetorical age something more dramatic was needed. Diodorus of Sicily (Diod. Sic. 11.5.4–5) has an uplifting but rather grandiloquent exchange:

> When the Persians had set up camp by the river Spercheius, Xerxes sent messengers to Thermopylae, to see among other things their attitude to

the war with him. And he instructed them to announce that King Xerxes ordered them all to put down all their weapons and to withdraw to their homeland without danger and be allies of the Persians. And he undertook that if they did this he would give the Greeks territory far better than the one they currently inhabited. Leonidas and his men after listening to the messengers replied that as allies of the king they would be more useful with their weapons and that if they were compelled to wage war they would fight more nobly with them for their freedom. And as to the territory which he promised to give, that it was the Greek tradition to acquire land not through cowardice but through courage.

This loquacity is very un-Spartan. The ancients were fascinated by the dense expressiveness of Spartan ('Laconic') brevity and this was an event which invited it, as with Dieneces and the arrow cloud. Plutarch has a better version in a brief anecdote in his *Sayings of the Spartans* (225C), in which Xerxes sends a written message to Leonidas demanding that he hand over his weapons; Leonidas famously replies 'come and get them', *molōn labe*. As a terse gesture of defiance this has only one equal in Greek history, the (apocryphal) response of General Metaxas on 28 October 1940 to the Italian demand to enter Greek territory—*Ochi*, 'No'. The reply in Plutarch, like *ochi*, is too good to waste and the words *molōn labe* are engraved on the base of Leonidas' statues at Thermopylae and in Sparta. This is one of a cluster of sayings attributed to Leonidas in Plutarch, all attached to Thermopylae, his only (but large) footprint in the sands of time. The other star item is the famous order to his men to 'breakfast in the knowledge that they will dine in Hades' (*Sayings of the Spartans* 225D). The saying goes back at least a century and a half earlier, since it occurs already in Diodorus of Sicily (Diod. Sic. 11.9.4).

The same desire to expand the mythology around the battle can be seen in the claim in later sources, derived from Ephorus, that the Greeks at Thermopylae made a sortie into the Persian camp. This too had its elaborations. The *Minor Parallels*, which survives in the Plutarch corpus, has Leonidas not only break through to the Persian camp but actually take the crown off Xerxes (*Minor Parallels* 306D).

The story persists in modern times. It appears in George Croly's 'Death of Leonidas' of 1822 (nicely combined with an echo of the 'dine in hell' motif):

> And still the Greek rush'd on
> Beneath the fiery fold,
> Till, like a rising sun,
> Shone Xerxes' tent of gold.
> They found a royal feast,
> His midnight banquet, there!
> And the treasures of the East
> Lay beneath the Doric spear.
> Then sat to the repast
> The bravest of the brave!
> That feast must be their last,
> That spot must be their grave.

Croly liked the story, which appears again in his 'Leonidas'. It has a romantic glamour but we should probably take it as an extension of the process of heroicization of Leonidas which began in the fifth century. It is not enough now to die courageously by standing one's ground against overwhelming odds. A spectacular act of courage is needed. The effect is also to heighten the element of drama. Thermopylae becomes a nail-biting near-miss. The Greeks come within a whisker of ending the war there and then.

Though the Battle of Leuctra in 371 and the Theban invasions of the Peloponnese which followed put an end to Sparta's invincibility, they did not end Spartan ambitions. Sparta made intermittent attempts during the fourth century and after to regain something like its old power. But it was never again the dominant force in Greece. This did nothing, however, to suppress the Spartan mirage. In the period after Alexander there was a growing tendency for the Greeks to look back to the fifth century as a golden age. The defeat of Persia, one of the great surprises in European history, was part of this age of glory. Sparta itself looked back nostalgically to this better world, and within Spartan culture there were recurrent attempts to recreate the better past. Spartan choruses performed songs celebrating the glorious

Spartan past well into the era after Alexander (Athenaeus 15.678b–c). Presumably Thermopylae was part of that tradition.

But long before this Thermopylae had become collective Greek property. Sparta never developed a rhetorical tradition. But other city states did, especially Athens. Although our evidence is patchy, there is enough to show that Thermopylae was widely used in oratory of the classical period. It appears most often in the work of Isocrates, writing in the first half of the fourth century. His constant return to the topic allows us to glimpse its flexibility as a rhetorical motif.

Unsurprisingly the battle features as a recurrent example of courage against insuperable odds, most obviously in his *Archidamus* (§99). The dramatic date of the speech (really a pamphlet for reading) is in the 360s, after Spartan power had been drastically reduced. The 'speaker' is the Spartan crown prince Archidamus. This is the most perfunctory use of Thermopylae, which appears as one of a number of instances of Spartan success against overpowering odds. More often the battle is given a more overtly moralizing twist. This is the case in Isocrates' use of the battle in his last speech, the *Panathenaicus*, completed at the end of his life in 338. In a section designed to show that Athens' history is superior to that of Sparta, he attacks Sparta's misuse of its military power and introduces Thermopylae by way of contrast as a defeat whose moral worth outweighs the city's ruthless successes (*Panathenaicus* 187):

> But I might apply this argument to the disaster which befell the Spartans at Thermopylae. All who have heard of it praise and admire it more than the battles which were victorious but won over adversaries against whom they should never have been fought.

The iconic status of Thermopylae as a battle fought in the cause of Greek freedom made it a potent symbol in any discussion of Greek battles fought against outsiders. Here the Greeks set a precedent which has persisted to the present. This is the way Isocrates uses the battle in his *Panegyricus*, written about 380. Like the *Panathenaicus* this essay was written to be read, not declaimed; like *Panathenaicus* it belongs broadly to what the Greeks called *epideictic*, ceremonial/display oratory. The suggestion of display is unfortunate, since, though it was not written to achieve an immediate result (unlike speeches for the courts and for political debate), much of this kind of oratory was designed to inspire, especially in speeches delivered (as this one pretends to be) at Panhellenic festivals, where the themes tended to be about Greek unity. This speech argues the case for the abandonment of the relentless inter-Greek warfare, to be replaced by a Greek coalition against Persia. It idealizes the Persian Wars as a period when the two states competed to serve, and save, Greece. In this context the picture of the two rival states complementing each other at Thermopylae and Artemisium against the eastern foe offers a model for what should now be done. As Isocrates tells it (*Panegyricus* 90–2):

It was this king [that is, Xerxes] who had grown so proud and achieved such mighty tasks, and who had made himself master of so many, that our ancestors and the Spartans set out to meet, dividing the danger. The Spartans went to Thermopylae to oppose the land forces with a thousand picked soldiers of their own, taking along a few of their allies, intending to block the Persians in the narrow pass from advancing farther. Our ancestors sailed to Artemisium, manning sixty triremes against the whole of the enemy fleet. . . . But though they displayed equal courage, they did not meet the same fortunes. The Spartans were utterly destroyed. Although in spirit they won, in body they were worn down; it would be wrong to say that they were defeated, since not one of them chose to flee.

Isocrates returned to the case for a Greek campaign against Persia in 346 in his *Philip*, effectively an open letter to the king of Macedon. By now the political reality in Greece had changed. Sparta was a shadow of its former self and Athens had been losing territory to Macedon for over a decade. If anyone could realize Isocrates' dream, it was Philip. But Isocrates, though a little naïve, was no fool. Philip had to channel his relentless expansionism and his aggression away from Greek cities and turn it against the barbarian. By rekindling the collaborative spirit of the Persian Wars, he would become Greece's benefactor. In this context both Spartan and Athenian imperialism are dismissed in favour of their contribution to the freedom of the Greeks (*Philip* 147–8):

> No, all this [i.e. the record of the Athenian empire] has brought many complaints against Athens, while the Battle of Marathon, the naval battle at Salamis, and most of all the fact that they abandoned their own territory for the deliverance of Greece are praised by all mankind. They take the same view of the Spartans also. They admire the defeat at Thermopylae more than their many victories. They love and come to honour the trophy which was set up by the barbarians over the Spartans, while they view with distaste the trophies erected by the Spartans over their enemies. The former is regarded as a proof of courage, the latter of greed.

This Panhellenic dimension of Thermopylae is a constantly recurring theme in Athenian oratory of the fourth century BC. In a funeral speech for the Athenian war dead from the 390s the speechwriter Lysias (Lys. 2.30–1) writes:

> The Athenians, for their part, boarded their ships and went to defend Artemisium, while the Spartans and some of their allies went to meet the enemy at Thermopylae. They judged that the narrowness of the ground would allow them to keep the passage safe. The contest for both took place at the same time and the Athenians won the sea-fight, while the Spartans, though not falling short in spirit, but deceived as to the numbers both of those they expected to stand guard and of those whom they had to face, were destroyed, not defeated by their adversaries, but slain where they were stationed to fight.

The Athenian funeral orations for the war dead were ceremonial public speeches which honoured the newly slain by placing their achievement in the context of a long Athenian tradition of (as they saw it) just and selfless warfare. They used the mythic and historical background not just to honour the dead but more broadly to honour Athenian culture and inspire others to risk their lives in defence of the city. The Persian Wars were an important part of this background.

But appeals to the Persian Wars also had a place in the cut and thrust of real political debate. One (relatively) early example is Xenophon's account of the Athenian decision to help Sparta in 370 BC (*History of Greece* 6.5.43). After Thebes smashed the Spartan army at Leuctra in 371, the Thebans began a series of raids into the Peloponnese designed to break Sparta's hold there and strangle it in the longer term by empowering its enemies. Athens' decision was not easy, since the Athenians had begun the century as a Spartan vassal after their defeat in the Peloponnesian War and had then spent much of the last three decades at war with Sparta. However, the Athenians had more to fear from an unassailable Theban ascendancy, especially as Thebes was a close neighbour unlike the more distant Sparta, and in the end they sided with Sparta. History and even myth always played a part in political debate and an ambassador from Corinth to Athens, as well as rehearsing the pragmatic case for giving aid, also appealed to Sparta's record in defence of Greece:

> If ever again danger should come to Greece from barbarians, whom would you trust more than the Spartans? Who would you more gladly put at your side than these, whose men, posted at Thermopylae, chose all of them to fight and die rather than to live and admit the barbarian to Greece? So surely it is right for both you and us to show profound goodwill toward them, both because they proved brave men alongside you and because we can expect them to prove themselves again?

Athens knew where its interests lay. The ambassador had no need to play on fear of the barbarian. But the prospect of a Persian attack (however unlikely) remained a real possibility in the minds of the Greeks. Less than two decades earlier the Great King had intervened to broker a peace (the King's Peace, also known as the Peace of Antalcidas) between the Greek states to end the Corinthian War, a peace guaranteed by the threat of war from the king in the event of non-compliance.

The idea of Thermopylae as the archetypal fight against the threat from an expansionist outsider also made it useful in Athens' later struggle against Macedon. Toward the end of the first half of the fourth century, from the hurly-burly of Greek states competing for dominance, quite unexpectedly the northern backwater Macedon began to emerge as a major force under her wily, energetic, and ruthless king Philip. Macedon steadily and relentlessly expanded its control over northern Greece and sought opportunities to extend its influence further south. After the Battle of Chaeronea in 338 BC it finally became the controlling power in Greece. Macedon had its own anti-Persian rhetoric: both Philip and his son Alexander the Great harboured ambitions (spectacularly realized by Alexander) to invade the Persian empire. Ostensibly this was to avenge Persian aggression against Greece in the fifth century and the humiliation of the King's Peace in the fourth. But it also offered an opportunity to expand Macedonian power and wealth with the vast resources of the east. However, there was an additional factor. For some, perhaps many, in central and southern Greece, the Macedonians did not count as Greeks at all. The Macedonian royal house had been insisting since at least the early fifth century that they were as Greek as anyone to the south, and both Philip and his son actively sought ways to place themselves at the heart of Greek culture. War against Persia offered yet another opportunity to win acknowledgement and respect from the Greek powers but also at one and the same time to confirm the status of Macedon as the leading power in Greece and demonstrate its superiority to the older powers.

Athens for its part tended to regard the Macedonians as barbarous upstarts and Athenians hostile to Macedon found it useful to present Philip as an alien threat to Greece. So they harked back to the Persian Wars as a model for a unified Greek stand against the aggressor, and especially the non-Greek aggressor. The faction which pressed the case for vigorous action against Macedon lost the war with the Athenian defeat at Chaeronea in 338. But arguably they won the peace, not least because of the inspirational vision they presented of Athens as the hereditary champion of Greece which never shirked its duty. The vision was arguably all the more important in a defeated

Athens which had become a Macedonian vassal. One strand of the rhetoric they deployed in the constant struggles for influence within Athens, played out in both the Assembly and the law courts, was the argument that for Athens there was no honourable alternative to the heroic choice it made. It is in this context that the anti-Macedonian Hyperides brings in Thermopylae in a trial in 334, when he was attacked by a shadowy figure named Diondas for proposing public honours for his political ally Demosthenes, another implacable opponent of Macedon. The case survives in a fragmentary text only recently rescued (Diondas 176r):

> Best thing of all, I think, is to win, or, if it should happen, to fail fighting for the sort of cause for which we fought.... But consider that the Spartans fought at Corinth and won, but at Thermopylae all were destroyed. But nevertheless the victory is never mentioned but everyone praises the defeat.

The point is essentially the same as that pressed repeatedly by Isocrates, that a noble defeat is better than an ignoble victory, though this time the game is being played for real stakes. Like Sparta for Thermopylae, Athens will be remembered as the city which made the heroic choice and did what was right.

My last example from surviving Athenian oratory is the *Leocrates* of the Athenian politician Lycurgus (not to be confused with the legendary Spartan legislator). Leocrates left Athens after the defeat at Chaeronea. Lycurgus tried to make an example of him by prosecuting him for treason. The legal basis for the charge was poor and Lycurgus threw all of his immense moral authority into the prosecution, drawing heavily on poetry, myth, and stirring historical example. He also threw Thermoplyae into the mix. Like Isocrates (and probably under his influence) he paints a picture of glorious rivalry between Athens and Sparta in the service of Greece. After quoting at length lines from the Spartan martial poet Tyrtaeus on the nobility of patriotic death in battle he observes (Lycurg. *Leocrates* 108–9):

Fine and useful words indeed, gentlemen, for those prepared to listen. Such was the view of courage by the men who heard these verses that they competed for the leadership with our city. And quite right. For the deeds on both sides were glorious in the extreme. Our ancestors defeated the barbarians who first set foot on Attic soil and made absolutely clear that courage triumphs over wealth and and virtue over numbers. And the Spartans took their stand at Thermopylae and though their fortune was not the same, in courage they surpassed all mankind. And so at their tombs there are inscribed true testimonies to their virtue for all the Greeks to see. For them:

> 'Go tell the Spartans, passer-by,
> that here obedient to their laws we lie.'

And for your ancestors:

> 'Fighting for Greece Athens at Marathon
> laid low the might of the gilded Medes.'

These are fine lines to remember, men of Athens. They bring praise to the doers and for the city eternal renown. But not what Leocrates has done. Of his own accord he disgraced the renown the city has accumulated over all time. So if you kill him, you will convince all Greece that you too despise acts like this.

One point of detail here was to prove crucial for the reception of Thermopylae. We saw that the original epigram had *rhemasi*, 'command', 'tradition'. Lycurgus substitutes *nomimois* ('laws'/'traditions'). The effect is to put the emphasis more firmly on to law rather than military directive. Lycurgus could be passing on an already existing variant. But he needs to bolster his shaky legal case with parallels and examples; so this version may be his own. Ultimately it was this version, not Herodotus', which prevailed.

There is a recurring ambivalence in the Athenian treatment of Thermopylae. Thermopylae was a tale of remarkable courage and our sources never deny this. But there is an element of Athenian one-upmanship in the way Thermopylae is paired with Salamis or Marathon, especially in the cliché that the Spartans in the pass were 'not defeated in spirit' but overwhelmed by the numbers. This is not dismissive in itself: it is a commonplace which we also meet in the praise of Athenian war dead killed in a lost cause. But, when paired with a note that the Athenians won at Salamis, it gives Athens the edge. A noble defeat is fine but a noble victory is better.

Thermopylae also featured in the epideictic tradition which persisted long after the classical period into a Greek world where Rome was the dominant power and into a world where Christianity was the established religion. The classical period was for Greeks under Rome a golden age, and events and texts of the period remained invaluable as models. Much of the rhetoric continued strands we have already seen. The rhetorician Menander writing in the third century AD rather predictably selects Thermopylae in his *Divisions in Epideictic Rhetoric* as an example of courage for use in cases where the cause is noble but the outcome is failure, and for courage in a common cause. More imaginatively Maximus of Tyre, a writer of undemanding philosophical works in the second century AD, uses Thermopylae in passing in his Essay 24 (2e), *Whether Farmers or Fighters are More Useful to a City*, to press the case for the warrior: 'If the Spartans had been farmers, who would have taken his stand at Thermopylae with Leonidas?' This is, however, an Aunt Sally, since he then flips the argument in favour of the farmer.

Not all epideictic oratory was as serious as this. One of its major strands was praise and blame and already in the fifth century BC rhetoricians were demonstrating their skills with a variety of speeches on calculatedly unpromising, unexpected, or outlandish topics: praise of mice, praise of death, defence speeches for notorious mythic miscreants. At one level this is entirely trivial and playful. But since it also demonstrates the cleverness of the author, it could generate serious business in the form of paying pupils. This playful element continued in the later tradition. Thermopylae plays a passing role in an entertaining exchange within this tradition. The orator Dio Chrysostom, writing early in the second century AD, composed a *Praise of Hair* which included the celebrated incident at Thermopylae where the Persian scout sees the Spartans calmly dressing their hair in preparation for the fight; his conclusion, not unreasonably, was that even the austere Spartans took hair grooming seriously. The (balding) teacher of rhetoric Synesius, writing almost three centuries later, responded with a *Praise of Baldness*. Of Thermopylae he remarks (§15):

> It is worth while recalling how the Lacedaemonians dressed their hair before the Battle of Thermopylae. Dio calls this a great battle because the Spartans combed their hair before it, though not one survived in the wake of this evil omen.

Against this he sets the story from Plutarch (*Sayings of Kings and Commanders* 180B) which has Alexander order his general Parmenio to make the Macedonians shave their beards before the crushing defeat of the Persians at Gaugamela in 331 BC. Lack of hair has the practical advantage that the enemy has nothing to grip in close combat. The debating point is nicely made. This time the Greeks won.

Rather more serious is the other diachronic exchange, between Aristides and Libanius. Aelius Aristides was a rhetorician of the second century AD. One of his (now lost) speeches, *Against the Dancers*, was a critique of pantomime performers. Pantomime was a virtuoso balletic performance which was very popular but (as often with anything popular) frowned on by some moralists. Aristides had addressed his speech to the Spartans, probably both because of their earlier reputation for austerity and because they had by this time become enthusiastic enough about pantomime to include pantomime competitions in their festivals. The celebrated fourth-century orator Libanius, the friend of the emperor Julian, responded with a defence, *Reply to Aristides in Defence of the Dancers*. The famous hair incident is again given an outing (no doubt under Dio's influence); one of Aristides' complaints had been the way the artists tended their hair and Libanius retorts that the Spartans at Thermopylae did the same (§50).

Though most uses of Thermopylae were literal (if not always accurate), the battle could be used to support other kinds of courage than military and collective. Origen when defending Christianity in his *Reply to Celsus* uses the battle (2.17) to counter Celsus' claim that any sane man, unlike the Jesus of the scriptures, would avoid certain death: Leonidas too knew at Thermopylae that he would die but did not turn back.

Thermopylae also served as a gold standard of courage and sacrifice for the historians, as it does in modern times, sometimes with complex results. The sixth-century writer Agathias uses it in his account of an engagement during the defence of Constantinople against the Kutrigurs by the ageing Belisarius in 559. The comparison with the Persian Wars was unavoidable. The essential features are retained: overwhelming odds and an alien invader threatening freedom and civilization. The defending force is attacked by a cavalry division of 2,000 men. But Belisarius turns the tables on the enemy. With a force of 200 lightly armed troops and cavalry he sets an ambush in a valley for the enemy cavalry and puts them to flight, inflicting heavy losses. Like Belisarius himself, Agathias turns the example on its head (*Histories* 5.19.1–2):

> Such was the confidence and discipline, I believe, which filled them that (to compare very small with great) they could boast an achievement like the one they ascribe to Leonidas' Spartans at Thermopylae, when already under attack from Xerxes. But the Spartans were slaughtered to a man and their only glory was in dying without disgrace after killing many of the Persians. But Belisarius and his Romans, while showing Spartan courage, put all the enemy to flight by force and killed vast numbers of them without suffering anything untoward themselves worth mentioning.

Rather more mundane, not to say bathetic, is the use of the parallel by the verbose fourteenth-century historian Nicephorus Gregoras in his *Roman History*. The parallel crops up in his account of the civil wars in the Byzantine empire which marked the accession of John VI Kantakouzenos. The use is striking in that usually the example of Thermopylae is reserved for foreign wars. Nicephorus makes the three hundred a model for an undistinguished manoeuvre by a force opposed to Katakouzenos in 1342 (*Roman History* 2.627) to bar his passage through a valley in Thrace. Thermopylae returns later in the account of an event in the same year (*Roman History* 2.636–7), when Kantakouzenos finds himself drawn into battle with limited manpower. His forces camp all night expecting the worst. In a fine moment he inspires his men 'with that famous saying of Leonidas at Thermopylae in reverse: "Let us dine today so that we can breakfast in Hades." ' In the event breakfast in Hades has to wait; they extricate themselves.

It was almost inevitable that Thermopylae would also have an afterlife in Rome, which looked to Greece for cultural, architectural, and literary models. The Roman reception, especially by Cicero, was of crucial importance for the longer term future of the motif, since moderns from the Renaissance onward experienced Greece through Rome. The incident recurs often in Roman historical sources as a narrative detail. But as in Greece it also plays a role in rhetorical and philosophical works, serving as the absolute yardstick for courage and self-sacrifice. It was well enough established in the rhetorical tradition to form the subject of one of the recurrent *suasoriae*, exercises in persuasion. This type of exercise, which formed part of the underpinning of the training for the Roman public speaker, used historical and mythic examples as the context for arguing either or both sides of a dilemma. We are lucky to have a collection of such exercises (with the models offered by leading Roman, and less often Greek, orators) in the *Suasoriae* of the elder Seneca, a distinguished rhetorician (and father of the stoic philosopher), whose life straddled the first centuries BC/AD. The standard topics for the exercises included a debate set on day three of the battle (§2) in which the 300 Spartans deliberate whether they too should flee. The model responses show a stronger grasp of rhetoric than of history, but what matters for our purposes is the iconic status of the event as an extreme choice between life and honour. The dilemma allowed some of the best minds to display their originality in argument. It also prompted another play on the famous 'dine in hell' motif.

There is said to be a very clever remark of Dorion (not on this exercise, it's true, but on this topic); he made Leonidas say to the three hundred (which I think is also in Herodotus): 'Take breakfast knowing you will dine in Hades.' Asilius Sabinus, the wittiest joker among the rhetoricians . . . said: 'I would have accepted for breakfast, but declined for dinner.'

The Roman philosophical tradition like the Greek also picked up the example of Thermopylae. Cicero uses it in *De Finibus* (*On the Ends of Good and Ill*) 2.94, together with that of the Theban general Epaminondas, as the extreme example of the noble death when he discusses how the philosopher Epicurus treated death. The parallel is a conscious paradox, since, as he observes, philosophers usually die in their beds. Cicero uses Thermopylae more extensively in another philosophical work, *Tusculan Disputations* (1.101), in which he includes famous quotations from the anecdotal tradition. Thermopylae follows a clutch of examples from Roman history of soldiers who put the long-term survival of their country above their own lives. It serves along with the deaths of the Athenians Theramenes and Socrates as an example of high-minded contempt for death to support his argument that death is not something to be feared. One detail in Cicero's use of Thermopylae was to prove influential. He included a Latin translation of the Greek epitaph for the Spartan dead which was discussed earlier in this chapter. His version runs:

> Tell Sparta, stranger, that you saw us lying here,
> Because we obeyed our fatherland's sacred laws.

The abstraction of the country ('Sparta', 'fatherland', not the 'Spartans' of the original), the choice of the 'laws' version of the Greek, and the sacralization of the laws explicitly raise patriotism to an absolute ideal which demands the ultimate sacrifice. The appeal to sight ('you saw us', not 'we lie') creates a personal relationship between the dead and the imaginary viewer. Cicero's version was to have a profound impact in the modern era.

The incident recurs again in (the younger) Seneca's *On Benefits* (6.31) and *Moral Letters* (82.19–21). The use in *Moral Letters* is the more straightforward. The Spartans at Thermopylae appear in an argument against fear of death. The passage in *On Benefits* is more interesting. There Seneca draws heavily on Herodotus' conversation between Xerxes and Damaratus. His Damaratus goes further in showing an uncanny ability to predict the engagement at Thermopylae in detail. The incident is used to demonstrate the importance for men of power and influence to have friends and advisers who speak with candour. Seneca's version ends rather more positively than Herodotus' in line with his overall argument. In Herodotus (Hdt. 7.105) Damaratus' reward for his candour is a dismissive guffaw from the king. In Seneca he is offered anything he chooses and selects an honour which Persian kings reserve for themselves, to ride in a chariot into Sardis wearing a crown, in effect a Roman triumph.

One recurrent feature in all of this is the commingling of Greek and Roman examples. Seneca in the *Moral Letters* links Thermopylae with the Fabii, a Roman clan who according to legend took upon themselves the task of defending Rome against the Veii. Over 300 of them were trapped and killed at the Battle of Cremera in northern Italy. The story clearly owes a lot to Thermopylae. It even takes place at almost the same time, 477 BC. Though Roman writers were happy to use Greek examples, they did not rely solely on the Greeks. The mingling simultaneously both elevates the status of the home-grown examples by associating them with famous Greek examples and asserts Rome's own claim to equal and better the Greeks. Rome's admiration for Greece often came with a degree of discomfort, motivated in part by an awareness of the scale of cultural borrowing and resultant sense of inferiority, and partly by Roman disdain for the decline which made Greece just another Roman province.

The most explicit instance is the use by the historian and politician Cato, the most Roman of all Romans, writing in the first half of the second century BC. In a fragment of his history preserved three centuries later by Aulus Gellius in his compilation work *Attic Nights*, Cato tells of an engagement in 258 BC in Sicily during the first of Rome's wars against Carthage (3.7). The Romans find themselves cornered by the enemy, who (unlike Xerxes in 480) have got there first and taken the superior position.

A tribune (one of the middle-ranking officers in the Roman army) volunteered to lead a suicide squad of 400 men in a diversionary move to draw the enemy into an attack while the main corps extricated itself. The ruse succeeded and the army escaped, though the Roman diversionary force was wiped out, except for the tribune who was found seriously wounded. He recovered to serve his country bravely on many future occasions. Cato feels compelled to observe:

> [B]y leading aside that force he saved the rest of the army. But it makes a huge difference where you place that service! Leonidas the Spartan performed a similar exploit at Thermopylae. For his valour all Greece honoured him with glory and enormous gratitude in memorials of the highest distinction; they showed their gratitude for that deed of his with pictures, statues, praises, histories, and in other ways; but the tribune of the soldiers, who had done the same thing and saved the day, gained small glory for his deeds.

Thermopylae remains for Cato the exemplar but its use is ambiguous. The Roman by implication surpasses the Greek, in that he rescues the whole army, and he does it without glory or the need for it. The tribune is variously named in our sources but not by Cato (as far as we can see). This may be part of his point. For the Roman the deed itself is enough. But Cato suppresses another detail, that the tribune was awarded a military honour (Pliny, *Natural History* 22.11). He also seems unaware of the irony (Cato was not noted for his sense of humour) that Leonidas gave his life for Greece, while his Roman counterpart survived; he gave his men. We should perhaps also bear in mind that, quite apart from his deep-seated hostility to the influence of Greek culture in Rome, Cato had a personal stake in Thermopylae. He had served with distinction in the battle fought at Thermopylae against Antiochus III in 191 BC and he personally believed that his intervention saved the day for Rome (Plutarch, *Cato the Elder* 14). Cato was no more afflicted by modesty than he was by a sense of humour, and it may have irked him that Thermopylae always belonged to Leonidas. He had missed the party by three centuries.

9

The Myth in the Modern Era

The reception of the battle in the modern era demands a book in itself. As the definitive heroic act and the last word in patriotism, its roots have spread across civic rhetoric and monuments, over poetry and art, over the novel and the cinema. All I can do here is sketch some of the more striking appropriations. Already in Renaissance texts it is the archetypal noble defeat. It features briefly in Montaigne's essay *Des cannibales* (§16) in the sixteenth century, where Leonidas' defeat outranks the great victories of antiquity. Disconcertingly for the European, he projects Leonidas and the Spartans on to the Amerindians in his praise of their fortitude. But it was in the eighteenth century and afterward that Thermopylae really came into its own. The battle adopts different guises, often superimposed: the iconic battle for freedom; the struggle against the threatening alien outsider, the model for the noble defeat in a great cause. The appeal to Thermopylae is often, at least to the outside viewer, loaded with irony.

In the age of revolution, at the end of the eighteenth century, Thermopylae exercised a powerful appeal as the model for patriotic commitment to the cause of liberty. Nowhere was the appeal more natural than in the Greek struggle for independence. The classical world was the basis for civilized education, and nostalgia for classical Greece and revolutionary ideas coalesced in the foreign support for the cause of Greek freedom. The struggle against Persia in this context was what it was for Herodotus, a national struggle for liberty against an alien aggressor. And it was both natural and easy to replace the Persians with the current oppressor from the East, the Turks. Inevitably Thermopylae and the other sites of the Persian Wars helped to define both Greece and current hopes for Greek freedom. The desire to restore the Greek past was fed by the Grand Tour, which brought the sites of Greek history off the page and into the physical world for the north European elite and so introduced them to the gulf between the glories of antiquity and the abject present. The battle becomes the basis for ringing cries for the liberation of Greece in a spate of *Thermopylae* poems, from the German Philhellene Wilhelm Müller to the Anglo-Indian Derozio and others, and again in George Croly's 1822 poem 'Leonidas':

> But there are none to hear;
> Greece is a hopeless slave.
> Leonidas! no hand is near
> to lift thy fiery falchion now:
> no warrior makes the warrior's vow
> upon thy sea-wash'd grave.
> The voice that should be raised by men,
> must now be given by wave and glen.
>
> And it is given! the surge—
> the tree—the rock—the sand—
> on freedom's kneeling spirit urge,
> in sounds that speak but to the free,
> the memory of thine and thee!
> The vision of thy band
> still gleams within the glorious dell,
> where their gore hallow'd, as it fell!
>
> And is thy grandeur done?
> Mother of men like these!
> Has not thy outcry gone
> where justice has an ear to hear?
> Be holy! God shall guide thy spear;
> till in thy crimson'd seas
> are plunged the chain and scimitar,
> Greece shall be a new-born star!

Thermopylae is firmly embedded in Byron's aspirations for Greece in his colossally successful *Childe Harold's Pilgrimage*, based on his travels in southern Europe at the end of the first decade of the nine-teenth century:

> Fair Greece! sad relic of departed worth!
> Immortal, though no more; though fallen, great!
> Who now shall lead thy scatter'd children forth,
> And long accustom'd bondage uncreate?
> Not such thy sons who whilome did await,
> The hopeless warriors of a willing doom,
> In bleak Thermopylae's sepulchral strait—
> Oh! who that gallant spirit shall resume,
> Leap from Eurotas' banks, and call thee from the tomb?
>
> (Canto II. 693–701)

So too for Byron's associate William Haygarth, for whom Britain was to assume the role of Leonidas in the face of a complacent world, in his poem *Greece* published in 1814:

> And O my country! let thy voice be heard.
> Amid the din of battle, like the cry
> Of the wild eagle in the tempest's roar;
> When Hellas rises to assert her rights,
> Be not far from her: let thy chieftains sage
> Direct the onset, and thy hardy sons
> Be foremost in the fight which Britons love,
> The fight for liberty.
>
> .   .   .   .
>
> Thou stand'st alone
> With thy few warriors in the narrow pass,
> The world's Thermopylae
>
> (662–9, 687–9)

With the liberation of Greece seen as the restoration of an idealized past it was inevitable that Greece's supporters and admirers would map events in the War of Independence on to moments in classical history. The Turkish siege and capture of Missolonghi on the north coast of the Corinthian Gulf becomes Thermopylae, with the dashing Souliot leader Markos Botzaris who lost his life in the fighting there as the new Leonidas. Thermopylae features in Pushkin's 'Arise o Greece' as one of the places shaken by battle, probably with reference to the Battle of Alamana fought just outside the pass in 1821. Much of this mapping was projected on to Greece from Romantic lovers of a lost past. But Greece was not passive in this process. The continuity between Greece past and Greece present was a vision readily embraced by Greek politicians and intellectuals, many of whom had been educated in northern Europe and exposed to the radical ideas of the Enlightenment, including the notion that Sparta was itself a model of liberty. Thermopylae and Leonidas feature in Byron's 1811 'Translation of the Famous Greek War Song':

> Sparta, Sparta, why in slumbers
> Lethargic dost thou lie?
> Awake, and join thy numbers
> With Athens, old ally!
> Leonidas recalling,
> That chief of ancient song,
> Who saved ye once from falling,
> The terrible! the strong!
> Who made that bold diversion
> In old Thermopylæ,
> And warring with the Persian
> To keep his country free;
> With his three hundred waging
> The battle, long he stood,
> And like a lion raging,
> Expired in seas of blood.

So too in Elizabeth Barrett Browning's 'Riga's Last Song' of 1826, visibly influenced by Byron, with its assimilation of recent Souliot resistance against the Turks to Marathon and Thermopylae:

> I looked on the mountains of proud Souli,
> And the mountains they seemed to look on me;
> I spoke my thought on Marathon's plain,
> And Marathon seemed to speak again!
> And as I journeyed on my way,

> I saw an infant group at play;
> One shouted aloud in his childish glee,
> And showed me the heights of Thermopylæ!

But the link with Thermopylae was not imposed by Byron or anyone else. It was there in the Greek original of Byron's 'War Song', the so-called 'Greek Marseillaise' attributed (almost certainly falsely) to Rigas Velestinlis, the first 'martyr' to the cause of independence, which was in circulation by the last years of the eighteenth century:

> Sparta, Sparta, why do you sleep
> your deep lethargic sleep.
> Awake, call to Athens
> your unfailing ally.
> Remember Leonidas
> the renowned hero,
> the man of praise,
> fearsome and dread.
>
> .   .   .   .   .
>
> When in Thermopylae
> he masters the war
> and annihilates the Persians.
> With three hundred men
> he advances to the centre
> and like a lion enraged
> he wades in their blood.

When Alexandros Ypsilantis, leader of the abortive uprising against the Turks in the Danubian provinces in 1821, was in prison in Hungary after the defeat at Drăgăşani, the German philhellene poet Wilhelm Müller saw him as Leonidas. But Ypsilantis himself had included Leonidas and Thermopylae among the dense list of Greek heroes of old invoked in the call to arms in his leaflet *Fight for Faith and Motherland*. Again, Odysseas Androutsos was welcomed in Athens in 1822 with a song:

> Like a new Leonidas
> he appears at Thermopylae
> Odysseus the valiant.

He fires like lightning
the guns of the Greeks
at the heart of tyrants.

The comparison was inevitable in the case of Androutsos, who commanded a band of 120 men who held out against a force of 6,000 Turkish troops at Gravia Inn in 1821, a month after the defeat at Alamana. The small band had inflicted heavy casualties on the Turks and deterred them from proceeding further south to attack the insurgents in the Peloponnese.

The same radical new thinking which recruited Leonidas to the cause of freedom in the case of Greece also enlisted him in the service of Revolutionary France; that plus the association of Leonidas with the ultimate in patriotism. The appropriation of Thermopylae for the Revolutionary cause emerges in the 1790s with the three-act historical play of Loaisel-Tréogate, *Le Combat des Thermopyles; ou L'École des guerriers* ('The Battle of Thermopylae or The School for Warriors'), staged in Paris in 1795, and Pixérecourt's one-act 'patriotic tableau' of 1799, *Léonidas, ou Le Départ des Spartiates* ('Leonidas or the Departure of the Spartans').

More ambiguous is the response of David in his painting *Leonidas at Thermopylae* (Figure 22). Napoleon was nonplussed by the choice of theme: 'How wrong you are to put your energy into painting those defeated.' His reaction is understandable. David had chosen not only a defeat but a moment of calm before the battle, a moment of inaction and reflection rather than action. In the foreground, at the centre of the canvas, the Spartan king sits, nude, looking toward but not directly at the viewer. Instead of an intense expression of resolve his gaze reflects a contemplative calm. For anyone wanting a full-blooded battle scene, in the context of continuing hostilities between France and most of Europe, the image is not just a puzzle but a disappointment. According to David's pamphlet devoted to the painting, Leonidas 'meditates with a type of tenderness at the imminent and inevitable death of his friends'. However, the choice makes sense against the

Figure 22. *Leonidas at Thermopylae* by David

backdrop of the artist's own experience of the turbulent years of the French Revolution. He had seen a great cause destroy its adherents, and he had come to doubt, at least temporarily, the wisdom of his own choice of the active rather than the artistic life. David had committed wholeheartedly to the revolutionary cause and had even served (and spoken) in the National Convention He had been closely associated with Maximilien Robespierre and found himself in prison after Robespierre's fall and death. The work was started in 1798–9. Artist and subject probably shared their reflections on the inevitability of death. The painting was not finally completed and exhibited until 1814, by which time the world had changed again. In the intervening years David had been taken up by Napoleon and had seen France rise to become the dominant power in Europe. But in the year the painting was exhibited Napoleon's seemingly irresistible progress had come to an end and the emperor had abdicated. The great Enlightenment project which had begun with the Revolution had petered out.

David never said so but it is difficult not to see Napoleon himself in the doomed and pensive Leonidas. The similarities must have grown for David in the year or so after the glorious return of Napoleon from his first exile. The final defeat of Napoleon at Waterloo was followed by the emperor's exile to St Helena and that of David to Belgium when he was proscribed on the restoration of the Bourbons. The relevance of the work to David himself was noted by contemporaries.

David's *Leonidas* experienced a new application in the 1820s, when a number of his paintings including the *Leonidas* featured in the exhibition in support of the Greek cause organized by philhellenes in Paris during the siege of Missolonghi in 1825–6. Now it was recruited for the cause of Greek independence. It was in the same context that Michel Pichat's *Leonidas*, previously banned because it was tainted with republicanism, was staged to great acclaim. After this, Thermopylae largely disappeared as a source of collective inspiration in France, displaced by other models of heroism.

Waterloo itself provides the setting for one of the other celebrated re-enactments of Thermopylae in Napoleonic France. The anecdote is located during the retreat of the Imperial Guard after its courageous but unsuccessful advance at Waterloo. Called upon to surrender by a British officer, Pierre Cambronne replied: 'La garde meurt et ne se rend pas' ('The Guard dies and does not surrender'). The alternative version has him say simply 'Merde!' ('Shit!'), which gave rise to a famous euphemism, 'le mot Cambronne' ('the Cambronne word') and even to 'Cambronne' as equivalent to 'shit'. The story is probably apocryphal in both versions, though it arose only days after the battle. The more ornate response was recorded first in the *Journal général de France* on 24 June, six days after the French defeat, in an account by the journalist and dramatist Rougemont, who may have invented it. The story had a profound appeal in a France which had seen its hopes of revival dashed and which now lay at the mercy of its enemies. At this point it was believed that Cambronne had died. In fact it transpired that he had been captured by the British. The British officer who captured him, Colonel Sir Hugh Halkett, denied that either reply had been made by Cambronne, and according to some accounts he had been wounded in the head and so was in no condition to orate. Cambronne himself survived for another twenty-seven years but never gave his own version. But you can't keep a good story down and the legend once set in motion persisted. It owes a lot of its stamina (and the link to Thermopylae) to Victor Hugo's account in *Les Misérables* (which popularized the *merde* version):

> The victor of the Battle of Waterloo was not Napoleon, defeated. It was not Wellington, giving way at four, despairing at five. It was not Blücher, who never fought at all. The victor of the Battle of Waterloo was Cambronne. To blast with such a word the thunder which is killing you, that is victory.
>
> . . . To make the last of words the first by blending it with the glory of France, to close Waterloo insolently with carnival, to finish Léonidas with Rabelais, to sum up this victory in a supreme word impossible to utter, to lose the field and safeguard history, to have the laughter on your side after this carnage, this is immense.

Cambronne's claim to the mantle of Leonidas may be no better than that of thousands who fought at Waterloo. But the awkward fact of capture and survival did him no harm. He has a square and a Métro station in Paris named after him. His refusal to accept the proud words ascribed to him did not prevent his home town of Nantes from honouring him with a statue inscribed: 'La garde meurt et ne se rend pas' (Figure 23).

The power of Thermopylae to extract victory from defeat is played out again in two American debacles. As Waterloo shows, Thermopylae fits neatly into narratives of patriotism and commitment to a national destiny. This heady mixture gave the story a powerful appeal when the expanding New World of America met setbacks at the Alamo and Little Bighorn. The last stand at the Alamo entered American folklore within days of the fighting. The basic facts are easily told. A garrison of roughly 200 Texian insurgents (including a few Tejanos among the Anglos) was besieged at the Alamo mission near San Antonio from 23 February to 5 March 1836 by a vastly

Figure 23. Statue of Cambronne at Nantes

superior force of perhaps 1,800 Mexicans under General Antonio López de Santa Anna. Early on 6 March the Mexicans attacked and overran the mission after fierce fighting and annihilated the garrison (Figure 24). The broad narrative is straightforward, though the details are confused and contested.

Although the Texan rebellion provided the springboard for territorial acquisition, the aims of the rebels were both mixed and confused. Some were certainly secessionists, who favoured annexation by the United States of America. But for many it began as an issue of state rights against the increasing centralization of the newly installed dictator Santa Anna. Initially the colonists had sought to achieve their goals by peaceful means. But the heavy-handedness of the Mexican response pushed its opponents toward secession, and Texan independence was formally declared on 2 March 1836, when the siege was already under way and only four days before the massacre. Like Thermopylae, the

Figure 24. Remains of the Alamo mission

defeat at the Alamo was followed by a dramatic reversal, when Texan forces decisively defeated the Mexican army at San Jacinto just a few weeks later on 21 April and captured Santa Anna himself.

Unlike Thermopylae, however, the enemy here was no invader; this was Mexican soil and the rebels were settlers initially encouraged by the Mexican government. The defence was not part of a shared national cause of liberation or even expansion; the call for help issued by the garrison commander, William B. Travis, was largely ignored in the USA. But the USA had been interested in acquiring Texas in the 1820s, and President Andrew Jackson had offered to buy it in 1829. After the secession of Texas in 1836 the prospect of annexation remained a live issue in US politics, though contentious because of the Texan practice of slavery, long a source of fierce division in the USA, and Mexico's refusal to recognize Texas' independence. Texas was formally annexed in 1845 and the subsequent Mexican–American War of 1846–8 ended with Mexico ceding to the US all its territory north of the Rio Grande. These included Alta California, which meant that the USA now finally stretched to the Pacific. Against this background it is not surprising that the battle was retrospectively recruited to the cause of manifest destiny. This idea, which fuelled American expansionism in the nineteenth century, held that the American people were not only justified but obliged to expand across the whole continent. The defence at the Alamo became a myth almost immediately. The battle inevitably invited comparison with Thermopylae: a spirited defence against dramatically superior odds, a last stand culminating in massacre, and fought against an enemy both racially and religiously (as Catholic) alien. The link was being made within days. The first printed account in the *Telegraph and Texas Register* of 24 March 1836 already refers to the battle as 'the Thermopylae of Texas' and the theme was picked up in subsequent reports.

As often, Thermopylae is not just the archetype but the model which has been superseded. The first Alamo monument (erected in Austin Texas in 1841) bore a quotation: 'Thermopylae had her messenger of defeat but the Alamo had none.' The authorship is disputed, but the claim that the last stand at the Alamo outdid the original (nobody survived the Alamo) is unmistakeable, if contentious. The defenders clearly stood their ground and died virtually, if not literally, to a man, either in the fighting or in the subsequent summary executions of the small number who surrendered. In the loss of life for the defenders and in the dramatic disparity between the contestants it resembled Thermopylae. Like Thermopylae the defenders inflicted heavy casualties on their attackers (though like everything else about the battle that too is contentious). Finally, the defenders at the Alamo, like the Spartans, were champions of a very specific freedom, freedom from external control. The Spartans fought for Greek autonomy while practising one of the most restrictive of Greek political systems. Texas practised slavery; Mexico did not.

There is a final nice detail which links the two battles. The 'Come and get them' challenge found in Plutarch has a parallel not directly at the Alamo but in the events at Gonzales which helped spark the conflict. The story goes that, when the Mexican army came to seize a (not particularly useful) cannon, the defenders had a flag with the words 'Come and take it'. The town of Gonzales still celebrates an annual 'Come and take it' festival in October.

Thermopylae resurfaces once more after the defeat at the Little Bighorn, known to the Indians as the Battle of the Greasy Grass. In

1876, amid continuing friction between white settlers and the Indians of the plains, exacerbated by the discovery of gold in the Dakota Black Hills, the US army undertook to pacify the tribes who were resisting the government policy of taking away their land and pushing them into reservations. This was the context for the attack by the 7th Cavalry under George Armstrong Custer on a large camp on 25 June. The details are mired in obscurity and controversy. But it seems that Custer thought he would be attacking a nearly defenceless village. Instead he found himself hopelessly outnumbered by combined forces from several tribes, mainly Lakota and Cheyenne. In the fierce fighting that followed Custer was killed and his command was wiped out (see Figure 25). The defeat has all the necessary ingredients for 'Thermopylization': a doomed command which fights to the last against overwhelming odds, a battle against a threatening and alien force, which in 1876 is what the Native American was even when

Figure 25. Last stand hill Little Bighorn

defending his own land. Again like Thermopylae (and the Alamo), it was the prelude to a dramatic reversal of fortune for the victors, who were broken within a few years of the battle. Unlike the Alamo, however, Little Bighorn was complicated from the start. It did not matter so much that Custer's action was colonialist aggression in support of legalized plunder rather than a courageous defence of national liberty. The real problem was that the massacre could be seen as an unnecessary waste of life. This view figured prominently in the early discussion, and got in the way of a narrative of heroic self-sacrifice in the cause of manifest destiny. The army high command was keen to distance itself from the failure and Custer's death deprived him of any right of reply. Early newspaper reports put the disaster down to his rashness. The subsequent absorption of the Indians into a US which was now a single state from sea to sea meant that they were no longer unambiguous outsiders; this sets Little Bighorn apart from other iconic last stands. Already, before the Sioux Wars of the 1870s, there were influential voices which opposed the brutal treatment of the Indians. But there was from the start an opposing position and the heroization of Custer gained ground in the days and months imme-diately after his death, in both poetry and art. The comparison with Thermopylae too began early, with Edgar Fawcett making the con-nection just two months after the battle:

> So from thy sorrowing country shalt thou win
> rank beside all her loyalest and her best
> thou new Leonidas with thy noble kin
> slain in that wild Thermopylae of the west.

The heroization was taken up by the twentieth-century cinema in *They Died with Their Boots On,* starring Errol Flynn as a dashing and honourable Custer. It was released in November 1941 only weeks before the Japanese attack on Pearl Harbor, a coincidence which did no harm to the box-office takings. The battle had already featured in the 1926 movie *General Custer at the Little Big Horn,* again with a positive portrayal of Custer, and in the more thoughtful *The Scarlet West* in 1925, whose hero is a Native American caught between cultures and loyalties. The anti-heroic tradition too was taken up by the cinema, in *Little Big Man*, released 1970 in an era disillusioned by war in Vietnam. But long before this the battle had been turned into popular entertainment by Buffalo Bill Cody in his re-enactments of the battle in his Wild West Show from as early as 1886.

The appropriation of Thermopylae for modern war found its way into public monuments. The nineteenth century saw the rise of the cult of the dead in many parts of the Western world, both public and private, in cemeteries, in art, in poetry, and in prose. This was also the great age of the nation state with its centralizing claim on the absolute loyalty of its citizens. The two trends coalesced in the proliferation of public monuments for the war dead which begins around the middle of the century. The tendency to memorialize the ordinary casualties of war was given added impetus in the early twentieth century by the First World War. The unimaginable scale of the carnage demanded national expressions of both grief and gratitude, and (when so many voices publicly criticized the justification for conflict on this scale and the way in which the war had been conducted) a memorial to the cause for which they fought and died. Memorials to the war dead proliferate both on the battlefields and in towns and cities of the combatant nations.

Unlike its enemies, however, Germany had to come to terms not only with loss of life on an industrial scale but also with defeat and humiliation, which gave added urgency to the need to justify the national cause for which so many died. Thermopylae as a model for commitment to country and to duty at any cost had been prominent in nineteenth-century German education. Both the battle and Sparta more generally had enormous appeal for the cause of German nationalism and the end of the nineteenth and the beginning of the twentieth centuries saw a significant rise in German admiration for Sparta. This included features often ignored by Sparta's more squeamish modern admirers—its ruthless exploitation of the helots and its equally ruthless eugenics, reflected in the practice of exposing weak infants to natural selection by the elements in order to maintain the purity of the breeding/fighting stock. Sparta's allure increased in the wake of defeat in the Great War, not only for the military and the politicians but also for academics. Many in public life and higher education were hostile to democracy, and this hostility enhanced the admiration for authoritarian Sparta, an admiration which was given further stimulus by the rise of National Socialism and Hitler's own fascination with Sparta. This admiration was seized on and magnified by Nazi ideologues, which gave them a classical antecedent for their notions on race. Sparta could be held up as the first society devoted to the unflinching pursuit of an ideal of racial purity.

The impact of Thermopylae on the memorialization of the war dead is visible only in the constant presence of the famous epigram to the Spartan dead:

> Wanderer kommst Du nach Deutschland, verkundige dorten Du habest
> Uns hier liegen gesehen, wie das Gesetz es befahl.
>
> (Traveller, go tell them there in Germany that you have
> Seen us lying here as the law commanded.)

Variations on this inscription appear in a number of German memorials to the losses in the war. But this version, the inscription on the memorial to the dead at the Langemarck cemetery, is the most famous, and the closest to the original (German) lines, which are Schiller's translation of Cicero's version of the Thermopylae epigram, with 'Germany' substituted for Schiller's 'Sparta'. Langemarck was close to the site of a disastrous German offensive during the First Battle of Ypres in 1914, in which inexperienced volunteer troops found themselves facing British veterans. Like Thermopylae Langemarck passed rapidly from history to myth. The presence of students (in reality a minority) among the casualties, and the report from the German high command on 11 November 1914 immediately after the engagement that the troops advanced singing 'Deutschland über alles' added both to the pathos of the loss and the sense of heroic self-sacrifice; they also made the battle a valuable recruit to propaganda for the war. The value of Langemarck as the archetype for sacrifice in a patriotic cause grew after the German defeat and the battle played an important role in Nazi propaganda; Hitler himself (who had served near the scene of the engagement) visited the cemetery in 1940. Though the German source for the inscription was Schiller, Schiller never intended the lines as a freestanding epigram. They appear in his meditative poem 'Der Spaziergang' ('The Walk'), of 1795. The appeal to Schiller is rich in irony. Schiller's poem reflects on the relationship between man and nature, and in a world convulsed by the French Revolution untrammelled human nature was a frightening force; nature needed to be harnessed to ordered civilization, productivity, and progress. It is profoundly ironic that his lines were subsequently used to commemorate carnage in the first truly industrialized war.

The Greek battle, again often read through the famous epigram for the Spartans attributed to Simonides, takes on a more ambiguous colour in anglophone responses to the First World War, mainly because it tends to appear in poetry rather than state monuments. This relocation allows for recognition of horror and waste as well as courage and sacrifice. Certainly transparent readings of the war as a refighting of the Greek battle for freedom occur. W. Macneile Dixon's 'To Fellow Travellers in Greece' of 1914 presents the war in Europe (in a rather eclectic mixture) as a renewed battle for the democratic values of Athens fought by the British troops as new Spartans, with the Germans as the Persian invader. The war itself is seen as a divinely instigated test to avert complacency. Possibly the finest poetic use of Thermopylae in this vein is Laurence Binyon's 'For the Fallen', also written in 1914, which draws (unusually) on Simonides' choral tribute to the fallen in the fourth and seventh stanzas:

> They shall grow not old, as we that are left grow old:
> Age shall not weary them, nor the years condemn.
> At the going down of the sun and in the morning
> We will remember them.
>
> .   .   .   .

> As the stars that shall be bright when we are dust,
> Moving in marches upon the heavenly plain,
> As the stars that are starry in the time of our darkness,
> To the end, to the end, they remain.

His soldiers are granted immortality through death, in the spirit of Greek heroism. Spared decay, they are frozen perpetually in the beauty of youth like a modern Achilles. But both Thermopylae and its memorialist can also be recruited, like contemporary poetry on the war in general, to confront the uncomfortable realities of conflict or its causes. The most famous is H. W. Garrod's terse 'Neuve Chapelle', published in 1919:

> Tell them at home there's nothing here to hide.
> We took our orders, asked no questions, died.

The epitaph is 'laconic' in its austere brevity. The lines celebrate unflinching courage without glamorizing or heroizing their death. But the celebration is complicated by the ambiguous first line. They have no shame to hide; but the line implies that others may, whether those who sent them, or those who commanded, or those who stayed at home and dodged the war. And the second line can be read to suggest that there were questions to be asked. The disillusion is more barbed still in Godfrey Elton's 1925 version of 'Simonides'/Cicero:

> Tell the professors, you that pass us by
> They taught political economy
> And here obedient to its law we lie.

These Spartans have died not for a great cause but for an impersonal and inexorable political-economic law—that idea that competition for resources and power between modern industrial states makes war inevitable. There is no 'fatherland', no higher ideal to make sense of their fate, not even a government or military hierarchy, only the professors of politics and economics who expound the abstract principles which squander lives remotely. Equally bleak is A. E. Housman's 'The Oracles'. Professor of Latin at University College London from

1892 to 1911, Housman was steeped in the classical tradition even more than Elton. In 'The Oracles' he goes back beyond the battle itself to the story in Herodotus (Hdt. 7.220) that the oracle of Apollo at Delphi had predicted that the price for the rescue of Greece was the death of a Spartan king (the italics are Housman's):

'Tis mute, the word they went to hear on high Dodona mountain
    When winds were in the oakenshaws and all the cauldrons tolled,
And mute's the midland navel-stone beside the singing fountain,
    And echoes list to silence now where gods told lies of old.

I took my question to the shrine that has not ceased from speaking,
    The heart within, that tells the truth and tells it twice as plain;
And from the cave of oracles I hear the priestess shrieking
    That she and I should surely die and never live again.

Oh priestess, what you cry is clear, and sound good sense I think it;
    But let the screaming echoes rest, and froth your mouth no more.
'Tis true there's better boose than brine, but he that drowns must drink it;
    And oh, my lass, the news is news that men have heard before.

The King with half the East at heel is marched from lands of morning;
    Their fighters drink the rivers up, their shafts benight the air.
And he that stands must die for nought, and home there's no returning.
    The Spartans on the sea-wet rock sat down and combed their hair.

Herodotus spoke only of Delphi but Housman adds the oracle of Zeus at Dodona in north-west Greece in order to magnify the ineffectual role of the oracles and to create a bleak sense of the inadequacy of religion and the failure of belief—the only reliable guide is the human heart. Unusually among modern responses to Thermopylae Housman picks up the story of the Spartan grooming to end with a richly homoerotic image of masculine beauty. But where Herodotus used the anecdote to stress Spartan courage, Housman uses it to underscore the waste of war: '*he that stands must die for nought*'. As Gideon Nisbet has pointed out, this poem was not in fact composed for or during the war; it had first appeared in 1903. But after 1914 it could not but be read against the background of the enormous loss of life in the war.

The war with its waste and cost became a recurrent theme for Housman. The same bleak vision is found in his 'Epitaph on an Army of Mercenaries' of 1917.

> These, in the day when heaven was falling,
>   The hour when earth's foundations fled,
> Followed their mercenary calling
>   And took their wages and are dead.
> Their shoulders held the sky suspended;
>   They stood, and earth's foundations stay;
> What God abandoned, these defended,
>   And saved the sum of things for pay.

The poem was dedicated to the Old Contemptibles, the professional soldiers of the original British Expeditionary Force sent to fight on the western front, most of whom were dead by the time he wrote. The classical image is different and mythology replaces historical precedent—here they are like Atlas, holding up the sky. But as in 'The Oracles', human beings fight and die in an indifferent world abandoned by divinity. The common soldiers save what God could not. Heroism exists. It is noble and beautiful but it has no meaning. This reading finds an echo many decades later in Margaret Atwood's evocation of Thermopylae to express the gap between the undeniable beauty of the ideals of courage and self-sacrifice and the ugliness of war in her 1995 poem 'The Loneliness of the Military Historian':

> True, valour sometimes counts for something,
> as at Thermopylae. Sometimes being right—
> though ultimate virtue, by agreed tradition,
> is decided by the winner.
> Sometimes men throw themselves on grenades
> and burst like paper bags of guts
> to save their comrades.
> I can admire that.
> But rats and cholera have won many wars.
> Those, and potatoes,
> or the absence of them.
> It's no use pinning all those medals

across the chests of the dead.
Impressive, but I know too much.
Grand exploits merely depress me.

Of all the modern political appeals to the model of Thermopylae the most notorious is Goering's radio broadcast during the battle for Stalingrad. The fight for Stalingrad was the high-water mark of German expansion. Operation Barbarossa had seen the German army sweep almost effortlessly across the steppes of Russia in a repeat of the disastrous decision of Napoleon to invade a country with vast strategic depth; that is, the space to be traversed in order to deliver a knockout blow. The invasion was hampered by inadequate planning and poor logistics. Hitler's disdain for his generals and insistence on taking the major decisions led to confused strategy. When the army failed to take Moscow in December 1941, Hitler turned his attention to Stalingrad. After a seemingly irresistible advance which almost took the city, the German army met with fierce resistance in a battle which turned into one of the most brutal sieges in modern warfare, fought among the ruins of the city (Figure 26). It lasted over five months, from 23 August 1942 to 2 February 1943. A determined and well-planned Russian counter-attack eventually isolated the German salient at Stalingrad in an area which came to be known as *Der Kessel*, 'the cauldron'. It proved impossible to supply the encircled forces by air despite determined efforts by the Luftwaffe. An attempt by Panzer divisions to break through to the German Sixth Army in Stalingrad failed. The latter found itself under siege with fuel, ammunition, and supplies steadily dwindling, and subject to the most appalling starvation and cold. Shielded from (and deaf to) the truth, Hitler refused to contemplate surrender. The army at Stalingrad was left to its fate and the German people were kept in ignorance of the real state of affairs by a very effective propaganda machine. Useful as a means of tying down Soviet forces, the Sixth Army was still more important for Hitler as a mythic example of tenacity and courage for the German people, increasingly so as the tide of war turned against them. Unfortunately for him the forces at Stalingrad were not working from the same

Figure 26. Ruins of Stalingrad

script. The mythic value was brought out clearly in the speech by Hermann Goering on Saturday 30 January 1943, who had the job of indicating the full scale of the defeat which threatened in the east. Goering alluded to a number of annihilating defeats, historical and mythic, including Thermopylae, and went on:

> One day it will be said thus: when you come to Germany, tell them you have seen us lying at Stalingrad, as the law has commanded, the law of the security of our people. And this law each of you carries in your breast, the law to die for Germany, for the life of Germany is the hope of every law. And not just you, the young soldiers on your heroic mission, your sacrifice is obligatory for the whole German folk, not that it moans or argues about whether this or that is necessary, whether the warriors at Stalingrad must stand their ground or not—they have to stand their ground, the law so commanded it, the law of honour, but also beyond all things the law of warfare, and this law of warfare matters for no other goal than the rescue of our people.

In its way the speech was brilliant. It presented annihilating defeat as a prelude to victory. With its use of the famous epigram for the Spartans it appealed not just to the story of Thermopylae and the immortality bestowed by the epigram, and beyond that to the lionization of Sparta in Nazi ideology, but also to the physical memorials of the First World War. It played (explicitly) to the racism always close to the surface in appropriations of Thermopylae by claiming that the survival of the race depended on heroic sacrifice and it cast the catastrophic failure of the expansionist dream as a defensive act, more than that, a defence of Europe and not just Germany. The description of the young soldiers in pursuit of the classical heroic ideal masked for the people at home the horrors of life in the Cauldron. For at least some units not engaged at Stalingrad it may have helped to reinforce the readiness to fight to the last man. At Stalingrad, however, the broadcast was heard with a mixture of outrage (at the thought of the fat Reichsmarschall in the comfort of Berlin preaching to the starving troops in the freezing Russian cold), cynicism, and gallows humour. They rightly recognized it as their funeral speech. The invitation either to commit suicide or to die in an act of final heroism was bolstered by a clutch of awards to the senior officers, including General (now Field Marshal) Friedrich von Paulus, the commander of the Sixth Army, who recognized the promotion for what it was. But few took up the invitation to make a glorious end. The army surrendered just days later. The greatest irony of this, the most blatant distortion of the Battle of Thermopylae in history, is that these Spartans refused to die. There was no 'come and take them' as in Leonidas' legendary response to the Persian invitation to surrender; they laid down their weapons, though in the event countless thousands were to die anyway from exposure, mistreatment, and Russian reprisals. Joseph Goebbels struggled vainly in his broadcast on the day after the surrender to present the fate of the Sixth Army as annihilation in the patriotic cause. By this time, however, in a development which presaged the growing difficulties of information control in the age of mass media, the Russians had arranged a media blitz which meant that the truth was out, even in Germany. The epigram, however, still retained its appeal and was useful for the mythologization of the Wehrmacht as a 'clean' military machine untainted by the ideology of National Socialism (manifestly untrue of the Russian front and questionable at best elsewhere). It was used in 1955 by Erich von Manstein, the superior officer who left Paulus to his fate, in his self-serving but successful memoir, *Verlorene Siege* ('Lost Victories'), which heroized the fighters of Stalingrad, though von Manstein never showed any personal inclination to take on the role of Leonidas.

But even in the war years after Stalingrad the mythology retained its hold over the diehard imagination in Germany. Thermopylae was the inspiration for the Luftwaffe Leonidas-Staffel (Leonidas Squadron), created as the Reich collapsed to slow down the Russian advance with suicide missions. And Hitler himself to the end invoked Leonidas' last stand as the ultimate validation of self-destructive resistance in preference to survival and subjugation.

Goering's use of Thermopylae to mythologize the doomed Stalingrad salient finds an echo in another disastrous offensive a decade later in what proved to be the last days of French colonial rule in Indo-China. An abortive French attempt to deliver a knockout blow against the Vietminh insurgents in northern Vietnam left the French forces surrounded, undersupplied and outgunned and facing a numerically superior and determined enemy. The Battle of Dien Bien Phu lasted from 13 March to 7 May 1954. On 19 April, as the French position was becoming desperate, the US Undersecretary of State, General Walter Bedell Smith stated: 'insofar as the free world is concerned, the French Union forces at Dien Bien Phu are fighting a modern Thermopylae'; that is, as bulwark against the advance of communism in east Asia. He failed to persuade the European nations to intervene to support the French. After fierce fighting the French forces were overrun and had to surrender. At the Geneva peace conference which followed, France recognized Vietnamese independence. A temporary partition of Vietnam (which in the event lasted until several years after American withdrawal in 1973 after an equally disastrous war) was agreed and by the end of the year the French had withdrawn from the north. They lingered on to support the south but finally quit the country in 1956.

However, the twentieth century did not invent the appeal to the great defensive last stand to commemorate losses in expansionist or imperialist wars. Long before this, Thermopylae had appeared in the memorial to the dead (more specifically to the Natal Carbineers, who fought on the British side) at Isandlwana in KwaZulu-Natal:

> Not theirs to save the day
> but where they stood,
> falling to dye the earth
> with brave men's blood
> for England's sake and duty.
> Be their name sacred
> among us. Neither
> praise nor blame
> add to their epitaph.
> But let it be simple as that which
> marked Thermopylae.
> Tell it in England those
> that pass us by,
> here, faithful to their charge,
> her soldiers lie.

In 1879 a British army entered Zulu territory to enforce an edict from the British High Commissioner for Southern Africa, Sir Henry Bartle Frere, but essentially to break the power of the Zulus as an independent nation. One of its columns was wiped out at Isandlwana. In an age when Africa was being carved up by imperial powers which saw themselves as bringing the light of Christianity and civilization to backward heathens, the appropriation of Thermopylae made a kind of sense, although the Zulus might have seen things differently. The echo of the epigram to the Spartans at the end of the inscription is unmissable. The epigram is also used (without mention of Thermopylae) in the inscription in the cemetery at Waggon Hill to the British soldiers and officers who died in the Boer War:

> Tell England, you that pass this monument.
> We died for her and rest here quite content.[1]

The ease with which Thermopylae could be deployed as a bulwark for the imperial project can also be seen in the literature of the period, as in Doyle's 'Private of the Buffs':

Let dusky Indians whine and kneel;
  An English lad must die.
And thus, with eyes that would not shrink,
  With knee to man unbent,
Unfaltering on its dreadful brink,
  To his red grave he went.

Vain, mightiest fleets, of iron fram'd;
  Vain, those all-shattering guns;
Unless proud England keep, untam'd,
  The strong heart of her sons.
So, let his name through Europe ring—
  A man of mean estate,
Who died, as firm as Sparta's king
  Because his soul was great.

The subject, Private John Moyse, was reportedly executed for his refusal to kowtow to his Chinese captors. Sadly the whole incident is probably fiction. But as with the Zulu Wars the Greek last-ditch resistance to the foreign invader is applied not to a glorious death in defence of freedom but to the British imperialist project, and in this case to one of its most discreditable policies. The context was the Second Opium War of 1856–60, fought to force China to open its doors to British trade. One important goal was to crush resistance from the Chinese authorities to sales of the opium produced by the British in India. The trade was lucrative for the East India Company (and helped to balance the cost of imports of tea from China). But the handsome profits came at enormous cost for the millions of addicts among the Chinese and the inevitable collateral damage on families and the social fabric.

For all the cynicism or jingoism in the appropriation of Thermopylae the battle retained its currency as the gold standard for heroic self-sacrifice. Or more precisely not so much the battle as its reverberation in the epigram attributed to Simonides. It can be heard behind the famous inscription to the Allied dead at the Battle of Kohima in India in the Second World War:

> When you go home
> Tell them of us and say
> For their tomorrow
> We gave our today.

The ridge at Kohima on the India–Burma border was the site of fierce fighting between Japanese and combined British and Indian forces from early April to late June 1944, when Japanese forces invaded India from the east through Burma in Operation U-Go. It's not hard to see why the Thermopylae parallel suggested itself. In both battles the invaders looked like an unstoppable force. In a rapid offensive the Japanese armies had overrun South East Asia and the British forces had been forced unceremoniously out of Burma, falling back on Imphal in the Naga Hills in north-east India. Japanese success at Imphal and Kohima would cut British lines of communication, block the Americans from sending supplies to China, and bottle the British up in India, even conceivably precipitate the collapse of the Raj. The hill station at Kohima is on the only road from Imphal to the supply depot at Dimapur and the only major route linking India and Burma. It was vital for any counter-offensive, making it—like Thermopylae—both a strategic prize and a pinch point. And although the two armies rapidly reached a rough equilibrium, initially at Kohima as at Thermopylae the invaders were met by a numerically inferior defending force (1,500 against about 13,000), leading to a viciously fought hand-to-hand siege which lasted for thirteen days before support could be sent. Unlike Thermopylae the defenders at Kohima held out but the battle was close-fought. Since this was one of the last Japanese offensives of the war, Kohima was also one of the battles which tipped the balance against Japan. Although Kohima (in comparison with many other battles in this conflict) is relatively little known, it was voted one of Britain's greatest battles in 2013 in a poll conducted by the National Army Museum, only just behind Rorke's Drift. It was not just a British battle, however, since Indian regiments fought alongside British. But it was 'the last great stand of empire' (the subtitle of Fergal Keane's book on the battle). It both stopped Japan's expansion in its tracks and marked the last days of the British Raj, which the Japanese commander Renya Mataguchi had hoped to topple. India received its independence only three years after the battle and the rest of the empire was dismantled in the next two decades.

Although universally recognized as the Kohima memorial, the poem predates the inscription. It was published in 1919 and was one of a number of war epitaphs composed by the classicist J. M. Edmonds. The presence of 'Simonides' is unmistakable in the combination 'go home, tell them'. But Edmonds's free version distances itself both from the Greek original and from the institutionalized Ciceronian insertions. For Cicero's 'fatherland', 'laws', and 'obedience' he substitutes the notion of sacrifice as a gift freely bestowed by the dead on those at home. He retains the sense of trade or balance in the Greek original (life or obedience) but substitutes a different accounting, neatly underlined by the time-motif (tomorrow for the many at home bought by death today for the few on the battlefield). This injects a more pronounced emotional effect than the model, while retaining the deceptive simplicity of the Greek and avoiding excessive sentiment. 'Go home' like 'we lie' notes that these warriors will never return home, but it makes its point economically and with restraint. Edmonds's text actually read 'for your tomorrows *these gave their* today', placing the anonymous passer-by between the dead fighters and the audience at home. Whether he misremembered Edmonds or remembered his Herodotus, the author of the Kohima text, Major John Etry-Leal (himself a classicist), substituted the first person and brought the epitaph closer to the Greek original (Figure 27). In the process he enhanced the emotional force of the inscription by givng the dead a voice and so creating a direct contact between them and their beneficiaries.

The epigram also lurks behind the Polish memorial at Monte Cassino, the most ferocious battle in the Allied advance through

Figure 27. Kohima Memorial

Italy in 1943–4 and one of the fiercest in the whole of the war in the west. The fighting centred on the great medieval abbey atop a steep hill. Convinced that the Germans were using or would use the abbey either for surveillance or defence, the Allied forces reduced it to rubble (Figure 28) but in the process provided an ideal defensive position for the Germans, who now occupied the site. Monte Cassino has more in common with Stalingrad than Thermopylae. Both battles were fought amid ruins and in dug-in positions in conditions comparable with those of the First World War. Here as at Stalingrad Hitler ordered his forces to defend their position to the last as a means of halting what he presented as a war of annihilation against Germany. The attacking forces lost 55,000 men before soldiers from II Polish Corps finally took the hill and raised the Polish flag (initially a pennant of the 12th Podolski Lancers). The Poles had been involved in some of the toughest fighting and this, together with their iconic role (comparable to the

Figure 28. Ruins of Monte Cassino

raising of the US flag on Iwo Jima), is reflected in the inscription in the Polish cemetery at the site:

> Przechodniu powiedz Polsce
> żeśmy polegli
> wierni w jej służbie
>
> Passer-by, tell Poland
> that we died
> faithful to its service

Despite its presence at Stalingrad, Kohima, and Monte Cassino, Thermopylae plays a smaller role in the Second World War than in the First. Poetry makes less use of it, though the Second World War has a less distinctive voice in poetry in general. The déjà vu of yet another global war picking up the unfinished business of the previous one meant that there was less room both for the innocent idealism and for the disillusion of the earlier conflict. And unlike the First World War the fight against fascism both had and still has a reputation for being a 'good' war. One of the relatively few responses is J. E. Brookes's 'Thermopylae 1941', written in the grim prisoner-of-war camp at Salonika after his capture by the Germans in Crete, about the (abandoned) position at Thermopylae. Brookes and another member of the Australian and New Zealand Army Corps, Blue, are dug in at Thermopylae until they get the order to retreat. Brookes with his classical knowledge is aware of the burden of history. Blue is dismissive:

> The soul of Sparta stirred, could but the brave
> Leonidas renew his mortal span
> instead of merely turning in his grave,
> and all his hoplites, perished to a man,
> but resurrect themselves. . . . I said 'They wore
> long hair, the Spartans, a visible proof
> that they were free, not helots, and before
> the battle they would gravely sit aloof
> and garland it with flowers.' Bluey spat.

Brookes's knowledge of Herodotus is used to point up the gap between legend and the mundane boredom of real war, and there is equal irony in the gap between his classical learning and his complete ignorance as a frontline soldier of what is actually going on. But there is none of the bitterness of the non-establishment responses to the earlier war; the poem leaves the cause for which they fight intact at the end:

> But as we drove away I must confess
> it felt like a desertion. Those few men
> with flowers in their hair were heroes! Yes!

Allusions to Thermopylae in civic monuments fade after the Second World War. The battle does, however, make a striking appearance in former President Bill Clinton's speech at the dedication in September 2011 of the memorial to the dead of United Flight 93, though not on the memorial itself. The passengers of Flight 93 foiled the terrorist hijack of the plane (part of the 9/11 attack on the USA in 2001) by storming the cockpit to prevent it being crashed into the centre of Washington DC, at the cost of their lives. Thermopylae figures in his brief speech, together with the Alamo, complete with the famous Dieneces anecdote ('And the enemy said: "We are going to fill the air with so many arrows that it will be dark." And the Spartans said: "Fine, we will fight in the shade." '). As so often the aim is to underscore the differences as much as the similarities between the ancient exemplar and its modern equivalent. This is not conventional warfare but a civilian response to terrorism, and there is no trace here of the notion, which recurs in the epigram in its different guises, of doing one's duty:

> This is something different. For at the Alamo and Thermopylae they were soldiers. They knew what they had to do. Your loved ones just happened to be on a plane . . . They saved the capital from attack, they saved God knows how many lives. They saved the terrorists from claiming the symbolic victory of smashing the center of American government. And they did it as citizens.[2]

The reason Clinton could use Thermopylae in this way on a major public occasion is that despite its absence from the monuments the battle retains a firm place in popular culture in video and board games, novels, and most importantly cinema. Of the novels the best known is Steven Pressfield's *Gates of Fire*. The date, 1998, inevitably invites the reader to think in terms of the First Gulf War against Saddam Hussain, though in fact it is difficult to find any allusion, even indirect, to contemporary politics. If recent events make an impact it is largely in the gritty depiction of military life, which owes much to cinematic presentations of the US military.

The area of popular culture where the battle does maintain its political voice is cinema. The story has been told twice in mainstream Hollywood movies. Its first cinema outing was in *The 300 Spartans* in 1962. This was the golden age of the sword and sandal epic on screen and Thermopylae offered a great opportunity for heroics. Politically the Cold War was at its height and with it the Manichaean sense that the world was divided into good and bad. Though the film was released before the events, this was the year of the Cuban crisis in which Kennedy and Khrushchev faced off over the Russian decision to base missiles in Cuba. Only three years earlier Fidel Castro had overthrown the pro-American Batista and put in place a Communist regime which looked toward, and depended on, Soviet Russia. A century and a half earlier James Monroe had enunciated the principle that the Americas were the backyard of the USA and no foreign power could be allowed to gain a toehold there. Subsequent administrations had upheld the principle as an article of faith. The film was also released just a year after the Bay of Pigs fiasco, in which the CIA had orchestrated an unsuccessful attempt by Cuban exiles to invade the island to over-throw the Castro regime. For its narrative to work Thermopylae requires little or no acquaintance with the classical world. The story is easily told: aggressors who threaten civilization as we know it and defenders who fight for freedom. It is not only with the lens of retrospect that the political aspects of the film advertise themselves to the viewer. But it is only the historical context that gives this film a wider resonance. Nothing in the costumes or the incidents points unambiguously to any contemporary relevance. Even Xerxes' ambi-tion to conquer the whole of the West ('It was my father's dream: one world, one master') has its origin in Herodotus. Only the voice-over at the close reaches explicitly beyond historical epic:

> But it was more than a victory for Greece. It was a stirring example to free people throughout the world of what a few brave men can accomplish once they refuse to submit to tyranny.

Contemporary commentators also saw an allusion to the Cold War.

Where contemporary politics may have lurked behind the 1962 film, it is stamped in Day-Glo colours on Zack Snyder's 2007 movie *300*. Its origin in a graphic novel allows *300* to create both more exaggerated battle scenes and an enemy which is pure caricature. The Xerxes in this film, seen only briefly, is part bejewelled effeminate, part sci-fi monster, crudely but graphically catching both the sense of menace and the degeneracy traditionally associated with the East.

Hostile critics see the film as based on a crude East–West contrast but the reality is more precise. Xerxes' Persian army becomes unambiguously modern with a form of battledress inspired by the Arabs of films such as *Lawrence of Arabia*. This is West versus Middle East. The identity of the foe inevitably suggests Iran, a long-standing US bugbear since the overthrow of the Shah and the seizure of US diplomats and embassy workers in Tehran in 1979, and a continuing source of anxiety for the West because of its nuclear programme. But the timing suggests that Iran is not the only current enemy behind Xerxes' army. The graphic novel of 1998 which inspired the film was written in the wake of the Gulf War fought in response to Sadam Hussain's invasion of Kuwait in 1990. Although Iraq was forced to withdraw from Kuwait, that war had left unfinished business, since Sadam remained in power. The US and its allies returned to the fray in 2003 with a full-scale invasion of Iraq, this time in the so-called 'war on terror' triggered by the destruction of the Twin Towers of the World Trade Center in September 2001. The film was released two months after the 'surge' of military action in Iraq announced by George.W. Bush in January 2007 and was in production during the breakdown of public order and the interfaith fighting which followed the successful overthrow of the Sadam regime. Ultimately the enemy is a vague Middle Eastern amalgam, Iran–Iraq with a subtext of Islam. In its use of Thermopylae to play out contemporary conflicts between the forces of civilization and its enemies, the cinema reverts to a practice established by the French theatre of the late eighteenth and early nineteenth centuries. The comic-book visual style may explain why we find a cluster of video games at this point which make use of Thermopylae.

Where *The 300 Spartans* and *300* read contemporary politics into ancient history, *Go Tell the Spartans* sets Vietnam against an implied backdrop of Thermopylae. The film was released in 1978 but its dramatic date is 1964, when US troops were technically 'advisers'. Not long afterwards they were to be sucked into a disastrous war which still scars the collective American psyche. The plot centres on a unit of troops embroiled in a war in which the enemy is elusive, the loyalties of the civilian population are unclear, and the local authorities they are aiding are incorrigibly corrupt. It ends with the destruction of the Vietnamese rearguard and all but one of the Americans who stay with them. The explicit appeal to Thermopylae comes in a scene which gives the film its title, itself derived from the memorial verses to the Spartan dead. The film picks up on the location and role of the epigram by featuring an inscription on the entrance to a cemetery of French soldiers found by the American troops. Since the film starts with a screentext which briefly notes the failure of the French to hold their colonies in Indo-China, the cemetery anticipates the eventual failure of American intervention in Vietnam. The commanding officer explicitly contrasts the war in Vietnam with the war of liberation in Europe against Nazi Germany. Here Thermopylae is the archetype of the doomed enterprise, both the immediate mission of these troops and the US presence in Vietnam as a whole. Thermopylae is also the archetypal patriotic battle, and the irony here is that, as the characters repeatedly point out, this is not America's affair—'it's their war'. They are the interlopers. At the close the lone American survivor, spared by a wounded Viet Cong soldier who has him in his sights, turns to him and says: 'I'm going home, Charlie ... if they'll let me'.

The Last Samurai, released in 2003, is less tied to contemporary events than the other films we have looked at. The film injects an American officer into the 1877 Satsuma revolt of the Samurai against the modernizing Meiji government. Firmly on the side of the Samurai, it presents a romantic view of the conflict, with the warrior caste as the resistance, seeking to preserve a traditional way of life threatened with extinction by a regime corrupted by its desire to embrace the west, here represented principally by the presence of US military advisers. Thermopylae puts in a brief appearance near the end. The American, Algren, mentions it to his Samurai friend Katsumoto, just before the Samurai with traditional armour and weaponry engage with government forces equipped with modern artillery and rifles. Initially the government troops are teased into exposing themselves to attack and severely mauled. But they are rapidly reinforced and the Samurai are slaughtered by machine-gun fire when they launch a suicidal cavalry charge. Just before this final charge Thermopylae puts in a second appearance, when the American finishes his account of Thermopylae by revealing that the Spartans were wiped out to a man. Katsumoto's response is to smile. Though the enemy, in the form of the US as the representative of Westernization, is like Herodotus' Persians an outsider, the existential threat is cultural. Thermopylae is used to ennoble a final stand for a disappearing world against its destruction by modernity with its machines and its subservience to money.

Although the collective (and literal) political symbolism of Thermopylae predominated in the nineteenth and twentieth centuries, the battle is occasionally made to carry a different message. The most famous example is the moving 'Thermopylae' ($\Theta\epsilon\rho\mu\sigma\pi\dot{\nu}\lambda\epsilon\varsigma$) of Constantine Cavafy published in 1903, one of the finest evocations of the last stand of the Greeks in any language:

> Honour to those who in their life
> define and guard Thermopylae.
> Never abandoning their duty,
> just and straight in all their acts
> but with pity also and compassion;
> generous when they are rich, and when
> poor, again generous in small ways,
> still helping as much as they can;
> always speaking the truth,
> yet without hate for those who lie.
> And even more honour is their due
> when they foresee (and many do foresee)
> that Ephialtes will appear in the end
> that the Medes at the end will come through.]

Here the past is brought into the present in a very different way from those we have seen so far. The last stand at the pass is not relived in a single military engagement but is endlessly re-enacted in daily life. Gone are the Spartans and their military ethos. There is no hint of war at all except in the opening and closing metaphors of the guard at the pass and the ultimate defeat by the Persians. Instead the last stand becomes a way of living one's life ('in their life', 'in all their acts'—'στην ζωή των', 'σ' όλες των τες πράξεις') with integrity, while retaining both generosity and compassion for those who fall short. This is not war but struggle. It is as applicable to private life as to public, and it celebrates a more mundane but no less admirable kind of heroism than the uses of the battle to honour or celebrate those who serve a national or ideological cause. Fittingly Leonidas never puts in an appearance; this is not about great men. But like Leonidas their heroism too ultimately rests in persisting in a doomed cause. Failure and betrayal are inseparable from life.

We are equally far from the military sphere in Emily Dickinson's staccato '"Go tell it"—What a Message':

> 'Go tell it'—What a Message—
> To whom—is specified—
> Not murmur—not endearment—
> But simply—we—obeyed—
> Obeyed—a Lure—a Longing?
> Oh Nature—none of this—
> To Law—said sweet   Thermopylae
> I give my dying Kiss—

Dickinson does not only allude to the famous couplet, she answers it back with a question. It has been suggested, plausibly, that the inspiration is the relationship of Dickinson (herself from a family of lawyers) with the judge Otis Lewis Lord. Sweet Thermopylae is not a place but a person and the 'law' which he obeys is not the higher calling of patriotism in Cicero's translation of 'Simonides' but his legal duties which keep them apart and to which (in this poem) he has sacrificed his health. Commitment here is individual, not collective. And the price is paid not just by the person who commits but by those left behind. Sylvia Plath too in a more sombre tone draws the battle into her private world in 'Letter in November', published in 1965 two years after her death:

> O love, O celibate.
> Nobody but me

Walks the waist high wet.
The irreplaceable
Golds bleed and deepen, the mouths of Thermopylae.

This complex poem, located at the point where the year turns toward winter, swings between celebration of nature and despair. The sensuous colours embodied in the gold of the apples and the leaves give way (as the yellow of the leaves turns to red) to the contemplation of death in the image of Thermopylae. But this is private death, a multiplicity of individual Thermopylae, not a grand collective stand.

This expanded view of the battle also inspires Dimitri Hadzi's abstract sculpture *Thermopylae* of 1966 (Figure 29). Though Hadzi chose a theme which reflected his Greek extraction, the inspiration was in part American, John F. Kennedy's book *Profiles in Courage*. The work presents a powerful image of physical struggle between massive

Figure 29. Dimitri Hadzi: *Thermopylae*

figures. But Kennedy's book is about moral rather than physical courage. The battle here is neither literal nor necessarily collective.

As we saw above, one striking feature of the period since the Second World War is the silence of the monuments. The losses in modern wars continue to receive commemoration in large monumental public works. But Thermopylae no longer figures in physical memorials to the war dead. We are far from the age of revolution or the birth of the nation state, when the classical past was implicated in every area of education and public life. But Thermopylae has retained its place in political rhetoric, and its enduring hold on the collective imagination is reflected in its continued presence in the world of culture and entertainment.

We have come a long way from the pass in central Greece in a hot August in 480 BC. And we are not at the end of the story. That is for others to tell.

10

And Finally…

So was Thermopylae a great battle?

If by 'great' we mean 'big', either in duration or in scale, the answer is mixed. Though short in comparison to many nineteenth- and twentieth-century battles, by the standards of hoplite warfare this was a relatively long engagement. Just how long the average hoplite battle (if there ever was such a thing) lasted has been a matter of dispute. Ancient sources rarely give us a precise indication. With sources from the classical period and earlier the problem is still greater, because the hour had yet to be invented. The term *hora* meant 'season' or 'period'. The idea of dividing the day and night into equal shorter periods does not emerge until the fourth century BC and the term *hora* as 'hour' only gained wide currency in the era after Alexander. Time tended to be measured either by the length of one's shadow or by activity patterns. Thus, for instance, Xerxes ordered his final attack at Thermopylae 'at the time when the marketplace (*agora*) is at its fullest' (Hdt. 7.223), that is mid- to late morning. You can't really set your watch by this. But we can get some sense of what counted as a long engagement from those occasions when ancient writers under- score the duration of a battle by fixing beginning and end. Herodotus, for instance, (Hdt. 7.167) tells us that the Battle of Himera in Sicily between the Greeks and Phoenicians lasted 'from dawn to late even- ing', perhaps fourteen hours. This and similar indicators suggest that a full day was a very long time for a battle. So probably when two armies met in the Graeco-Roman world, the result was decided in a few hours. At three days, even with intervals, Thermopylae was a long encounter by ancient standards. The fighting was prolonged and arduous during those three days and the final phase on Kolonos hill must have dragged on before the Persian commanders tired of the delay and the casualties, and ordered the archers to finish off the defenders. Its duration was made possible only by the nature of the terrain and the fortification work carried out by the Spartans, making it closer to a siege than a conventional infantry clash. Taken alone, that duration might not amount to much. But it was made more striking by the enormous imbalance between the armies.

In size, whether we measure numbers engaged or losses relative or absolute, Thermopylae was small by comparison with the industrial scale which warfare has assumed in the modern world. This comparison would of course rule out any battle before the modern era. But even in ancient terms, although the Persian army was almost certainly the largest ever seen in Greece in its day, the total number engaged was dwarfed by subsequent battles in Greece. The Spartan losses were probably excruciatingly painful for Sparta itself, especially for the relatively small population of full Spartiates, but for Greece as a whole this was no more than a skirmish. And even Sparta was able both to turn out in force and to take the lead in the climactic engagement at Plataea in the following year. The Persian losses were greater but not significant given the size of the army, as far as we can gauge this.

But there is no rule of thumb which links size to significance in war or in anything else. So how significant was Thermopylae? If by significant we mean decisive, the answer is a firm negative. The battle had no direct impact on the facts on the ground. It did not destroy the military capability of either side, and so effectively end the conflict. Nor did it tilt the balance between victory and defeat. The Greeks lost, and lost unambiguously. The bulk of the survivors retreated in haste, the rearguard was annihilated, and the Persians were left in control of the field and the Greek dead. But this was no knockout blow. Greek resistance wavered, but it continued not just in the immediate aftermath of the battle, to give victory in the naval battle at Salamis, but into the following year, when the Greeks delivered a decisive blow at

Plataea in 479. On the other hand, though the Greeks put up a spirited resistance, they did not stop the invaders. The Persian advance was slowed but only briefly; they were able to overrun the whole of Greece as far as the Isthmus of Corinth. They even burned Athens. Even the eventual defeat did no real harm to Persia, if one sets aside, as the Persian king could, the immense losses in the land and sea engagements overall, the vast suffering of a retreating army, and the consequent devastation for the families back home. Herodotus depicts the war as an unmitigated disaster for Persia and Aeschylus presents the defeat as shaking the authority of the monarchy and the traditions of Persia (*Persians* 584–90). But this is the Greek view of Persian history. Xerxes could reasonably claim success for his expedition. He had physically destroyed Athens before he left Greece immediately after the Battle of Salamis. This was important, since part of his mission was to punish Athens for the defeat of his father's expedition at Marathon in 490. Immediately after capturing and sacking Athens he sent a glowing report of his achievement back home to Persia (Hdt. 8.54). His departure after Salamis meant that he had no direct connection with the subsequent defeat at Plataea, which he could blame on his general Mardonius. And Mardonius (like Custer after the Little Big Horn) was conveniently dead. Persian royal propaganda was highly effective and, unlike Greece, there was no official space or opportunity for competing narratives. So his account would be the only one available. And his authority was not seriously challenged on his return. He continued to rule until he was assassinated in 466, fourteen years after he crossed into Greece. Paul Davis in his book on the hundred most decisive battles in ancient and modern history rightly excludes it, while including both Marathon in 490 and Salamis a month or so after Thermopylae.

The battle was not entirely without immediate practical results. It cost Xerxes time. He held back for four days before ordering the first attack (Hdt. 7.210). The fighting then cost him another three days. Herodotus claims (Hdt. 8.25) that Xerxes for the whole of the following day displayed the dead to his troops before moving out on the day after. So he spent eight days altogether at the pass. This delay was on top of an already slow descent through Greece. He had taken from April or thereabouts to late August to get from Abydos in the Dardanelles to Thermopylae. Herodotus gives us the impression that he was not in a hurry. Although this may be his own inference, it accords with the facts, since this is a long time to advance without resistance, receiving the surrender of city after city. It has been suggested that he deliberately slowed his advance to coincide with the Carnea and the Olympic Games in order to exploit the Spartan reluctance to fight at that period and the distraction to the Greeks generally caused by the Olympic festival. The idea is appealing. But the Persians did not need to worry about Greek numbers; and the benefit of any reduction in opposition forces would come at great potential cost in terms of Persian supplies, morale, discipline, and possibly desertions as the army dawdled. Xerxes may have misjudged his enemy and assumed that most of Greece would capitulate without a fight rather than risk obliteration. But his delay was to prove costly. Unless he could deal a knockout blow to the Greeks, his army was virtually forced to over-winter before waiting for the next campaigning season. This in turn had implications for the army's supplies, which were certainly a problem in the next year (Hdt. 9.45.2). And the defeat at Salamis meant that the army could not be provisioned from the sea and was forced to rely on Greek allies such as Thebes and plunder from captured territory. By the end of the winter the Persian commissariat, for all its efficiency, must have been seriously stretched. Thermopylae helped sow the seeds of ultimate defeat by adding to the Persian delay. But only to a limited extent; the roots of the delay were elsewhere.

However, it would be a mistake to dismiss Thermopylae out of hand. For several months the Greeks had watched as the Persian military machine slowly but inexorably descended into Greece. In the process Xerxes had accepted the surrender of Greek and non-Greek peoples on the peninsula. Called upon to give earth and water, the traditional Persian diplomatic protocol for accepting Persian authority, either as vassal or as ally, all had complied rather than risk being crushed.

Other Greek states not in the immediate path of the invasion had also complied. Some of the cities and peoples whom Xerxes recruited en route had provided levies, swelling his already large forces. The result in Herodotus' narrative is a slowly moving but unstoppable progress, which resembles a snowball gathering seemingly limitless momentum. All this stopped at Thermopylae. Though they had ample time to retreat before the enemy engaged, the defenders held their ground. And for a period they consistently outfought a far larger force. They proved that the Persians were not invincible and undermined the psychological advantage they had enjoyed up until then.

Herodotus draws our attention to this psychological dimension. Apart from any desire to stop the Persians, the Spartans were at Thermopylae to stiffen Greek resolve (Hdt. 7.206), and though the point is made with reference to the Greeks immediately in Xerxes' path, it applies to all Greek waverers. This was to be an example. His Leonidas, on arriving at Thermopylae, in his appeal to the Greeks in the vicinity for aid insists that the Persians can be resisted successfully (Hdt. 7.203):

> It was not a god invading Greece but a mortal. And there was and would never be a mortal whose fate did not include misfortune, and the greatest misfortune to the greatest of them. It was to be expected that the invader, as a mortal, might fail in his intent.

Herodotus makes this an implied answer to the awed statement which he puts into the mouth of 'a man from the Hellespont' in 7.56, when Xerxes at the height of his achievement crosses the Dardanelles on the magnificent bridge which his engineers have built on his orders:

> O Zeus, why have you taken mortal form and called yourself Xerxes instead of Zeus and propose to demolish Greece by leading the whole world against it? You could have done this without all these.

Herodotus had no access to formal records of any speeches, public or private, and even his living eyewitness informants must have struggled to remember anything said in the distant past. His speeches are at best conjectural reconstructions and probably mostly invention. The 'man from the Hellespont' looks like a transparent mask for Herodotus' attempt to recreate the impact of Xerxes' achievement, and the uncanny unconscious dialogue between this invented character and Leonidas suggests that both are the work of Herodotus. But what matters is less the archival status of the speeches than their contribution. Their job is to draw out the views of participants as Herodotus saw them, not to reproduce data from records. And the psychology is real. Herodotus and his audience lived in a world in which the gods were believed to intervene in human life at all levels and in which events were explained in theological as well as empirical terms. All this is familiar from Greek tragedy; but it is not a literary fiction; it is life as the Greeks saw it. Herodotus and his speakers do effectively express Xerxes' own pride in his achievement and his confidence in his prospects, the seemingly superhuman power he wields, and the consequent illusion of invincibility and the impact on observers near and far. He also stresses (Hdt. 7.184) that Xerxes' army was 'unscathed' until Thermopylae, which was the very first setback for the Persians.

Thermopylae worked no miracles. It was recognized immediately as a serious military setback for the Greek cause and it caused alarm. The Persians now had unimpeded access to central Greece and there was no immediate prospect of assembling an army which could defeat them on land, especially out in the open, unlike the following year at Plataea. The Greek strategy had always been defensive and its main goal had been to stop the Persians as far north as was possible. This had amounted to finding a geophysical feature which could act as a safety barrier—first the mountain ranges of Olympus and Ossa which divided Macedonia from Thessaly, then the mass of Kallidromon and Oeta at the southern end of the Thessalian plain. In the Peloponnese the response to the news of the battle was to start fortifying the Isthmus of Corinth (Hdt. 8.70–3) on the same principle, as the only serious remaining geophysical obstacle. At the same time at Salamis the forces from the southern half of Greece still wanted, or at least some did, to fall back beyond the Isthmus and leave the northern half to its fate (Hdt. 8.74). The Greeks remained as divided as they had been throughout. The Athenian general, the wily Themistocles, famously had to force the issue. When he was losing the argument with the proponents of retreat, he sent a false message to the Persians telling Xerxes that the Greeks intended to flee (Hdt. 8.75). This was almost the truth; they just had not quite made up their minds. We should not let any romantic attachment to the glory that was Greece blind us to the alarm and division which persisted in the Greek camp.

This division persisted even after Salamis, when despite the destruction of the Persian fleet the Greeks still confronted an enormous foreign army in the heart of Greece. But there was no automatic flight. Which in turn means that all the ambiguities of Thermopylae were as visible to the Greeks at close quarters as they are to us two and a half millennia away. It was a defeat for the Greeks but it was also a hard-won victory for the Persians. And the opposition could have been sustained longer with a larger Greek force in the pass and on the mountain path. The stand at Thermopylae offered some support to those who took the view that Persian victory was not a foregone conclusion. This was less important for Athens than for other states. One of the Persian goals was to punish Athens for the defeat of the earlier expedition at Marathon and for its aid to the Ionian revolt before that. So at this stage Athens had nothing to gain from capitulating; the choice was either fight or flee. But there were other states north of the Peloponnese which were less exposed, those of northwest Greece, Megara, Euboea and Aegina, to which we can add the islands of the central Aegean. Though capitulation would not guarantee safety, the Persians had dealt leniently with Greek states which went over to their side. So the others had far less reason to fight to the last than Athens. The adherence of many of these to the Greek cause was to some extent of only symbolic and psychological significance. But that should not be underrated. And collectively they were important at Salamis, since the states outside the Peloponnese (excepting Athens, which provided almost half the fleet) provided 25 per cent of the Greek fighting ships. The island state of Aegina in the Saronic Gulf was especially important, since most Greeks thought that they were the best fighters at Salamis (Hdt. 8.93). In the run-up to that battle all these needed to feel that they stood a chance.

More important than any support for a more optimistic view of Greek prospects, Thermopylae also tested and confirmed the viability of the preferred Greek strategy, though this was a happy side-effect rather than a strategic aim. The Greeks from the start realized that they needed terrain which would neutralize the numerical advantage enjoyed by the Persians. They can never have had good figures for the enemy, even though they did send out spies. But their spies will have confirmed the vast scale of the expedition. And although our sources do not mention it, the Persian advance must have pushed before it large crowds of displaced people in flight and bringing accounts of the vast army moving steadily through Greece. The Greeks knew that any battle site needed to be chosen with a view to turning those enormous numbers into a weakness, or at least to balancing the odds. The strategy was initiated first in Tempe, where the Greeks would have faced the Persians in a narrow ravine. It was never put to the test, since the Greek commanders were advised that the Persians could easily outflank their position. Thermopylae was chosen on a similar principle, with the added advantage that it allowed the Greeks to deal with the threat presented by the Persian fleet. The battle confirmed the wisdom of the Greek strategy. For three successive days Xerxes threw his forces at the Greeks and the only reason they were overrun on the third was because of the flanking manoeuvre. Certainly the Persians concluded that the Greeks had chosen their position well. Herodotus tells us (Hdt. 9.13.3) that the lesson of Thermopylae was instrumental in Mardonius' choice of position at Plataea next year:

> The reason Mardonius marched away was that Attica was not a land fit for cavalry, and if he were defeated in a battle, there was no line of retreat except by a route [i.e. through Mount Cithaeron] so narrow that a few men could check him. He therefore planned to withdraw to Thebes and give battle there near a friendly city at his back and on ground suitable for cavalry.

The choice of Salamis allowed the Greeks to repeat the strategy of Tempe and Thermopylae, this time at sea, by drawing the Persians into the narrow channel between Salamis and the coast of Attica, where the smaller Greek fleet could manoeuvre, and the Persians would not only be unable to use their superior naval skills but would struggle to avoid colliding with each other. Even in space more favourable to the Greeks Themistocles was taking an enormous risk, since a Greek defeat at Salamis, unlike the defeat at Thermopylae, would have broken, possibly destroyed, the Greek fleet. The Persians would then have been able to mop up all of Greece north of the Isthmus of Corinth and to land troops in the Peloponnese in locations of their choosing, if the southern states decided to hold out and fortify the isthmus. But it was a risk that paid off.

But Themistocles was not the only one taking a risk. Xerxes too was taking a chance in engaging the Greek fleet. Xerxes thought he had the Greeks cooped up in the bay of Salamis. He had already found that if he could bottle up his enemy in a narrow space from the front and rear, he could dislodge or destroy them. The Persians were keen to bring the Greeks to battle (Hdt. 8.66–9) and were evidently ready to believe that the Greeks would flee, as indeed many of them wanted. Xerxes needed to break the Greek resistance soon, if he was to avoid another campaign season in Greece. So he blocked the strait between the island of Salamis and the mainland from the east to prevent a Greek escape in that direction, while sending the bulk of the fleet into the strait in an arc designed to overlap the Greek line and prevent them from slipping away to the west (Hdt. 8.76). He clearly thought he was dealing with a demoralized and divided enemy, who would be reluctant to fight, and either be readily defeated in battle or inclined to surrender. The move was not foolish, but Xerxes did not need to engage the Greek fleet. He could have blockaded it with part of his fleet and moved on by land and sea. And there is all the difference in the world between catching a small land force in a pincer movement, using numbers to bludgeon them, and manoeuvring a large fleet in a confined space which leaves only limited room for movement.

In Diodorus (Diod. Sic. 11.17.2; cf. Plutarch *Themistocles* 12) Xerxes sends part of his force round Salamis to enter the strait from the west and box in the Greeks from both directions. This was what he had originally attempted at Artemisium, when he sent part of his fleet eastward around Euboea; the encirclement failed only because the fleet was hit by a storm. But there is no reason to believe that Diodorus had access to an independent source for his account and we should accept Herodotus' version. Aeschylus' account in *Persians* 366–8 seems to agree with Herodotus; and Aeschylus lived through the events and even fought at Marathon. If instead of advancing his fleet in a line from the east he had used precisely the same encirclement manoeuvre and advanced simultaneously on both fronts, Xerxes might have repeated his success at Thermopylae. He could have squeezed the Greeks into a tighter space where they would have impeded each other. It would probably not have needed skilful tactics, just weight of numbers. He did not.

There is another way of assessing the value of Thermopylae. What if the Greeks had won? There was no prospect of reversing the Persian gains with the resources at their disposal. The most they could have achieved was to halt Xerxes' advance. Persian Greece would have

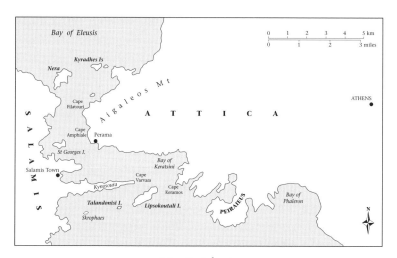

Map 6. Salamis

stopped at Malis. Though a Greek victory would have caused temporary relief and even jubilation, it would ultimately have been catastrophic for the Greek cause. There is no reason to imagine that the Persian threat would have gone away. The greater part of the invading army would probably have withdrawn, since it was too large to be supplied in the longer term in Greece. Northern Greece would either have been garrisoned by a residual Persian presence or held by Greek vassals of Persia. Either way the southern Greeks would have faced Persian-dominated territories with the pass and (for now) Phocis as the uneasy boundary between free and occupied Greece. Forced to settle with northern Greece for the time being, the Persians would have been able to wait until the endless Greek bickering offered an opportunity to intervene and push south. And they could be confident that it would. Persia had been expanding its empire for half a century or more, and ultimately it would want to tidy up the map of Greece. But it would now be working from a firmer and nearer base. A Greek victory at Thermopylae would only have postponed the absorption of Greece into the Persian empire. So the best outcome for the battle may be the one we have. Success drew Xerxes on to risk his forces disastrously at Salamis. With more time to consolidate the position in Greece and consider his options, Xerxes, and with him Persia, might have behaved differently, and the result too might have been different. So would the history of Europe. From this perspective the Greek losses were a price worth paying.

To claim more than this for Thermopylae would be to exaggerate, and even this may be too much for many. In the end what earns Thermopylae its place among the great battles is its hold on the imagination rather than any measurable impact on events. The vast inequality between the forces makes it an unambiguous model of courage under pressure. The decision at the end to stay and die enhances this sense of abnormal courage and dedication to a cause. This remains the case even in an age which recognizes the stultifying limitations of Spartan society and the irony that the heroes of Greek freedom were the most oppressive of all the Greek states in terms of

internal liberty. And this sense of abnormal courage is already embedded in our earliest narrative of the events in Herodotus, which
emphatically presents the Greek resistance at Thermopylae in heroic
terms. The issues at stake add to its iconic status. This was a battle to
defend native soil against an outsider, and it is easier to glorify a
defensive battle than one in pursuit of wealth, land, and empire,
even if the battle has since been used to glorify just such actions.

Here we come to one of the main reasons that Thermopylae has
held its place as *the* last stand for freedom against insuperable
odds, even though greater disparities have occurred since. This was
the first encounter between invader and defender in the greater of the
two Persian expeditions. And this first encounter is presented by
Herodotus as a clash between cultures. It forms part of a narrative of
a perennial clash between East and West which goes back beyond
the records (Hdt. 7.20). How can free men who are not ruled by a
master or driven by the lash be expected to stand their ground,
asks Herodotus' Xerxes (Hdt. 7.103), prompting from Herodotus'
Damaratus one of the most inspiring definitions of freedom ever
spoken. For Herodotus this is not really about race. The factors
which lead Persia to defeat are common to humanity (psychological,
social, political, theological), not exclusive to any one race. And they
are not innate, but acquired or cultivated. His Greeks are capable of
all the brutality and error of his barbarians and his barbarians are
capable of courage, wisdom, judgement, and restraint; Plutarch famously called him *philobarbaros*, 'barbarophile' (*On the Malice of Herodotus*
857A). In his insistence that error and crime are common to humanity
he resembles his great predecessor, the tragedian Aeschylus. But the
clash of cultures has frequently metamorphosed in the reception of
Thermopylae into a clash between races: and the issue of the defence
of civilization against the alien other turns up with alarming regularity.

All these factors give the battle an appeal far beyond its significance
in the world of events. But the final factor to note is Herodotus. He did
not invent his way of reading the battle or the war, and many of the
features just outlined recur in ancient sources which seem to be

making little, if any, use of Herodotus. This is most visible in the Greek orators. Though they may have read Herodotus, they are addressing audiences of hundreds or thousands of Athenian citizens who for the most part will not have acquired their understanding of the Persian Wars or any other era of Greek history from texts but from oral tradition. The picture changes when we get to Rome, where our speakers and writers are addressing a relatively (sometimes extremely) privileged group who can be expected to know their Greek texts, including Herodotus. This shift is greater still when we reach the Renaissance, when knowledge of the ancient world was acquired from and communicated through Greek and Roman texts which the accidents of survival had reduced dramatically. The few surviving sources which deal in any detail with events in the wars became critical for the perception of the war and the battle. This means Herodotus, Diodorus, the essayist Plutarch and Justin's precis of Pompeius Trogus; but most of all Herodotus. Not only is his account dramatic, gripping, inspiring, and profoundly moving. It is also the first. So the most significant reason for the place of Thermopylae in a series devoted to great battles is probably Herodotus.

NOTES

Chapter 2

1. An Achaemenid cylinder seal in the Metropolitan Museum of Art, NYC, which shows a king armed with bow and spear slaying a Greek hoplite, gives a sense of how the campaign might have been presented as a success story (see Figure 30). It has been suggested that the occasion is Thermopylae and the hoplite Leonidas but the seal could relate to the Ionian Revolt, Marathon, or the campaigns of 480/479 BC. Since the king did not fight in person in any of these, we are not looking at a literal reality whichever we choose.
2. The term 'Yaunâ' derives from 'Ionian', one of the three main dialectal (and for the Greeks tribal) divisions of the ethnic Greeks. This also served as a generic term for the Greeks of the eastern seaboard of the Aegean (though not all the Greeks there were Ionian) for the neighbouring peoples who

Figure 30. Achaemenid cylinder seal

215

encountered the eastern Greeks. This term was then extended to the Greeks of the Greek peninsula. It persists as the term for Greece in the Middle East, as for instance the Turkish 'Yunanistan'.

Chapter 9

1. Thermopylae is also invoked in an anonymous poem printed in the *Cape Times* on 20 February 1879 in praise of the successful defence of Rorke's Drift on the same day:

> For in that little fortress
> Five score at most held out,
> While twice two thousand Zulus
> Raised high their battle shout.
> 'Twas but a hundred heroes—
> Leonidas had three—
> Yet have they made of that stockade
> A new Thermopylae!

The comparison here is more apt (despite some shaky arithmetic), since the British force held out against odds of 20 to 1, though almost all the fighters at Rorke's Drift survived.

2. In recent years Thermopylae has featured more in challenges to state authority than in civic rhetoric. The 'come and get them' (*molōn labe*) of Plutarch's Leonidas has been adopted by the US gun lobby, often in the original alphabet (ΜΟΛΩΝ ΛΑΒΕ), in its resistance to legislation affecting the right to buy and own arms. The phrase appears on websites, T-shirts, mugs and bumper stickers. Leonidas' challenge (which resembles a slogan already popular in the 1970s, 'They'll get my gun when they can pry it from my cold dead fingers/cold dead hands') casts the gun lobby as the defenders of freedom against an overbearing attack on that freedom and aptly captures the perception by the US libertarian right of the state as a threatening and invasive presence.

   Battle and battlefield were also claimed by the rightwing Greek *Golden Dawn* (*Chrysi Avgi*), which rose in prominence during the global financial crisis early in the new millenium and the refugee crisis, when Greece became the main entry point for migrants entering Europe from the east. From 2012 until its collapse *Chrysi Avgi* used Thermopylae and especially Leonidas' statue as a location for militaristic rallies. The choice of model presents them as outnumbered but determined defenders of freedom and lays exclusive claim to Greek patriotism. It emphasizes their ultranationalist political agenda and especially their violent anti-immigration position, presenting them as the sole bastion preventing Greece from being overrun by a tide of non-Christian foreigners.

FURTHER READING

A book like this stands unashamedly on the shoulders of generations of serious researchers across a number of fields. It has not been possible to acknowledge specific influences in the text, though individual authors will immediately recognize their work. What follows is not a full bibliography of the battle, its evaluation and its reception. The theme is far too vast for that. It simply lists a number of works which the reader may find useful in following up and testing the narratives and arguments in this book. The list is broken down by category but inevitably the boundaries between the categories are fluid and some works could be cited many times. Some works are edited collections; in most such cases I have simply listed the collection rather than the chapters I've drawn on and left the reader to browse. For the reader's benefit I flag with an asterisk a number of works which offer a ready access to some central issues. The choice is (inevitably) subjective. If the reader wants a quick update on the issues, the obvious first port of call would be Matthew and Trundle (eds.), *Beyond the Gates of Fire*, cited below, which treats briefly a number of the issues addressed in this book and is recent enough to incorporate most of the modern discussion.

The Persian Wars

Burn, A. R., *Persia and the Greeks* (London, 1962).

*Cawkwell, G., *The Greek Wars: The Failure of Persia* (Oxford, 2006).

Flower, M. A., 'Appendix R: The Size of Xerxes' Expeditionary Force', in Robert B. Strassler (ed.) and A. L. Purvis (trans.), *The Landmark Herodotus, The Histories* (New York, 2007), 819–23.

Flower, M. A., and Marincola, J., *Herodotus, Histories Book IX* (Cambridge, 2002).

*Green, P., *The Greco-Persian Wars* (Berkeley and Los Angeles, 1996)

Grundy, G. B., *The Great Persian War and Its Preliminaries: A Study of the Evidence, Literary and Topographical* (Oxford, 1901).

Hammond, N. G. L., 'The Expedition of Xerxes', in J. Boardman, N. G. L. Hammond, D. M. Lewis, and M. Ostwald (eds.), *The Cambridge Ancient History*, iv (Cambridge, 1988), 518–91.

Hignett, C., *Xerxes' Invasion of Greece* (Oxford, 1963),

*Holland, Tom, *Persian Fire: The First World Empire and the Battle for the West* (London, 2005).

Kelly, T., 'Persian Propaganda—A Neglected Factor in Xerxes' Invasion of Greece and Herodotus', *Irania Antiqua* 38 (2003), 174–219.

Lazenby, J. F., *The Spartan Army* (Warminster, 1985).

*Lazenby, J. F., *The Defence of Greece, 490–479 B.C.* (Warminster, 1993).

Maurice, F., 'The Size of the Army of Xerxes in the Invasion of Greece 480 B.C.', *Journal of Hellenic Studies* 50 (1930), 210–35.

Munro, J. A. R., 'Observations on the Persian Wars 2: The Campaign of Xerxes', *Journal of Hellenic Studies* 22 (1902), 294–332.

Munro, J. A. R., 'Xerxes' Invasion of Greece', in J. B. Bury, S. A. Cook, and F. E. Adcock (eds.), (Cambridge, 1926), *The Cambridge Ancient History* iv. *The Persian Empire and the West*, 268–316.

Rahe, P. A., *The Grand Strategy of Classical Sparta: The Persian Challenge* (New Haven, 2015).

The Battle at Thermopylae

Bradford, E., *The Battle for the West: Thermopylae* (New York, 1980).

*Cartledge, P., *Thermopylae: The Battle that Changed the World* (London, 2005).

Dascalakis, A., *Problèmes historiques autour de la bataille des Thermopyles* (Paris, 1962).

Evans, J. A. S., 'The "Final Problem" at Thermopylae', *Greek, Roman and Byzantine Studies* 5 (1964), 231–7.

Hammond, N. G. L., 'Sparta at Thermopylae', *Historia* 45 (1996), 1–20.

*Matthew, C. A., and Trundle, M. (eds.), *Beyond the Gates of Fire: New Perspectives on the Battle of Thermopylae* (Barnsley, 2013).

Roisman, J., *The Classical Art of Command: Eight Greek Generals Who Shaped the History of Warfare* (Oxford, 2017).

Topography

Domínguez-Mondarero, A. J., 'The Archaic Period', in J. Pascual and M. F. Papakonstantinou (eds.), *Topography and History of Ancient Epicnemidian Locris* (Leiden, 2013), 445–70.

McInerney J., *The Folds of Parnassos: Land and Ethnicity in Ancient Phokis* (Austin, 1999).

Marinatos, S., 'Forschungen in Thermopylai', in M. Wegner (ed.), *Bericht über den VI internationalen Kongress für Archäologie, Berlin 21–26 August 1939* (Berlin, 1940), 333–9.

Müller, D., *Topographischer Bildkommentar zu den Historien Herodots: Griechenland* (Tübingen, 1987).

Pritchett, W. K., 'New Light on Thermopylai', *American Journal of Archaeology* 62 (1958), 203–13.

Pritchett, W. K., *Studies in Ancient Greek Topography, Part V* (Berkeley and Los Angeles, 1985).

*Rapp, G., 'The Topography of the Pass at Thermopylae circa 480 BC', in C. A. Matthew and M. Trundle (eds.), *Beyond the Gates of Fire: New Perspectives on the Battle of Thermopylae* (Barnsley, 2013), 39–59.

Sanchez-Moreno, F., 'Mountain Passes in Epicnemidian Locris', in J. Pascual and M. F. Papakonstantinou, *Topography and History of Ancient Epicnemidian Locris* (Leiden, 2013), 337–60.

Stählin, F., 'Thermopylen', article in *Paulys Real-Encyclopädie der classischen Altertumswissenschaft* (2nd edn.), by G. Wissowa et al., vol. VA (1934), 2.

Szemler, G. J, Cherf, W. J., and Kraft, J. C., *Thermopylai: Myth and Reality in 480 B.C.*, (Chicago, 1996).

Herodotus

Baragwanath, E., *Motivation and Narrative in Herodotus* (Oxford, 2008).

Fehling, D., *Herodotus and His 'Sources'*, trans. J. G. Howie (Leeds, 1989).

*Gould, J., *Herodotus* (London, 1989).

*Harrison, T., *Divinity and History: The Religion of Herodotus* (Oxford, 2000).

How, W. W., and Wells, J., *A Commentary on Herodotus in Two Volumes*, ii. *(Books V–IX)* (Oxford, 1912).

Lateiner, D., *The Historical Method of Herodotus* (Toronto, 1989).

Macan, R. W., *Herodotus, the Seventh Eighth and Ninth Books, with Introduction, Text, Apparatus, Commentary, Appendices, Indices, Maps* (London, 1908).

Munson, R. V., *Telling Wonders: Ethnographic and Political Discourse in the Work of Herodotus* (Ann Arbor, 2001).

Redfield, J., 'Herodotus the Tourist', *Classical Philology* 80 (1985), 97–118; repr. in T. Harrison (ed.), *Greeks and Barbarians* (New York, 2002), 24–49.

Other Ancient Sources

Bowen, A., *Plutarch: The Malice of Herodotus (de malignitate Herodoti). Translated with an Introduction and Commentary* (Warminster, 1992).

*Brosius, M., *The Persian Empire from Cyrus II to Xerxes, Translated and Edited with Notes* (London, 2000).

Flower, M. A., 'Simonides, Ephorus and Herodotus on the Battle of Thermopylae', *Classical Quarterly* 48 (1998), 365–79.

Kuhrt, A., *The Persian Empire: A Corpus of Sources from the Achaemenid Period* (London, 2007).

*Llewellyn-Jones, L., and Robson, J., *Ctesias' History of Persia: Tales of the Orient* (London, 2010).

Pretzler, M., *Pausanias: Travel Writing in Ancient Greece* (London, 2007; repr. Bristol, 2011).

Stronk, J. P., *Ctesias' Persian History: Part I, Introduction, Text and Translation* (Düsseldorf, 2010).

Sparta

*Cartledge, P., *Sparta and Lakonia: A Regional History 1300–362 B.C.* (London, 1979).

Cartledge, P., *Spartan Reflections* (London, 2001).

Hooker, J. T., 'Spartan Propaganda', in A. Powell (ed.), *Classical Sparta: Techniques Behind Her Success* (London, 1989), 122–41.

Powell, A. (ed.), *A Companion to Sparta*, 2 vols. (Chichester 2017).

The Persian Empire

Briant, P., *From Cyrus to Alexander*, trans P. T. Daniels (Einona Lake, IN, 2002).

Bridges, E., *Imagining Xerxes: Perspectives on a Persian King* (London, 2014).

*Brosius, M., *The Persians: An Introduction* (London, 2006).

Dandamaev, M. A., and Lukonin, V. G., *The Culture and Social Institutions of Ancient Iran*, trans. P. L. Kohl with D. J. Dadson (Cambridge, 1989).

Gershevitch, I., *The Cambridge History of Iran*, ii. *The Median and Achaemenian Periods* (Cambridge, 1985).

Kuhrt, A., *The Persian Empire: a Corpus of Sources from the Achaemenid Period* (London and New York 2007).

*Waters, M., *Ancient Persia: A Concise History of the Achaemenid Empire* (Cambridge, 2014).

Greek and Persian Weaponry and Warfare

Armayor, O. K., 'Herodotus' Catalogues of the Persian Empire in the Light of the Monuments and the Greek Literary Tradition', *Transactions of the American Philological Association* 108 (1978), 1–9.

Bardunias, P. M., and Ray, F. E., *Hoplites at War: A Comprehensive Analysis of Heavy Infantry Combat in the Greek World, 750–751 BCE* (Jefferson, NC, 2016).

Carey, B. T., Alfree, J., and Cairns, J. (2005), *Warfare in the Ancient World* (Barnsley, 2005).

Fink, D. L., *The Battle of Marathon in Scholarship: Research, Theories and Controversies since 1850* (Jefferson, NC, 2014).

Hanson, V. D., *The Western Way of War: Infantry Battle in Classical Greece* (Berkeley and Los Angeles, 2009).

Head, D., *The Achaemenid Persian Army* (Stockport, 1982).

Khorasani, M. M., *Arms and Armor from Iran: The Bronze Age to the End of the Qajar Period* (Tübingen, 2008).

Konijnendijk, R., '"Neither less valorous nor weaker": Persian Military Might and the Battle of Plataia', *Historia* 61 (2012), 1–17.

*Konijnendijk, R., *Classical GreekTtactics: A Cultural History* (Leiden, 2017).

Krentz, P., 'Hoplite Hell: How Hoplites Fought', in D. Kagan and G. F. Viggiano (eds.), *Men of Bronze* (Princeton, 2013), 134–56.

Matthew, C. A., *A Storm of Spears: Understanding the Greek Hoplite at War* (Barnsley, 2012).

Raaflaub, K. A., 'War and Society in Archaic and Classical Greece', in K. A. Raaflaub and N. S. Rosenstein (eds.), *War and Society in the Ancient and Medieval Worlds: Asia, the Mediterranean, Europe, and Mesoamerica* (Boston, 1999), 129–61.

Ray, F. E., *Land Battles in 5th Century BC Greece: A History and Analysis of 173 Engagements* (Jefferson, NC, 2009).

Schwartz, A., 'Large Weapons, Small Greeks: The Practical Limitations of Hoplite Weapons and Equipment', in D. Kagan and G. F. Viggiano (eds.), *Men of Bronze* (Princeton, 2013), 157–75.

Snodgrass, A. M., *Arms and Armour of the Greeks* (London, 1967).

Tuplin, C., 'All the King's Horse: In Search of Achaemenid Persian Cavalry', in G. Fagan and M. Trundle (eds.), *New Perspectives in Ancient Warfare* (Boston, 2010), 101–82.

Tuplin, C., 'Marathon: In Search of a Persian Perspective', in K. Buraselis and K. Meidani (eds.), *Marathon: The Battle and the Ancient Deme* (Athens, 2010), 251–71.

*Van Wees, H., *Greek Warfare: Myths and Realities* (London, 2004).

Thermopylae Refought

Brown, A. R., 'Banditry or Catastrophe? History, Archaeology, and Barbarian Raids on Roman Greece', in R. W. Mathison and D. Shanzer (eds.) *Romans, Barbarians, and the Transformation of the Roman World: Cultural Interaction and the Creation of Identity in Late Antiquity* (Farnham, 2011), 79–96.

Burns, T. S., *Barbarians within the Gates of Rome: A Study of Roman Military Policy and the Barbarians, ca 375–425 AD* (Indiana, 1994).

Cherf, W. S., 'Procopius *De aedificiis* 4.2.1–22 on the Thermopylae Frontier', *Byzantinische Zeitschrift* 104 (2011), 71–113.

*Cunliffe, B., *The Celts: A Very Short Introduction* (Oxford, 2003).

*Gregory, T., *A History of Byzantium* (2nd edn., Chichester, 2010).

Lock, P., *The Franks in the Aegean: 1204–1500* (New York, 1995).

Long, G., *Greece, Crete, and Syria* (Australia in the War of 1939–1945, series I, vol. ii, 1953).

McClymont, W. G., *The Official History of New Zealand in the Second World War 1939–1945: To Greece* (Wellington, 1959).

Mallan, C., and Davenport, C., 'Dexippus and the Gothic Invasions: Interpreting the New Vienna Fragment (*Codex Vindobonensis Hist. Gr.* 73, ff. 192v–193r)', *Journal of Roman Studies* 105 (2015), 202–26.

Martin, G., *Dexipp von Athen: Edition, Übersetzung und begleitende Studien* (Tübingen, 2016).

Martin, G., and Grusková, J., '"Dexippus Vindobonensis"? Ein neues Handschriftenfragment zum sog. Herulereinfall der Jahre 267/8', *Wiener Studien* 127 (2014), 101–20.

Millar, F. G. B., 'P. Herennius Dexippus: The Greek World and the Third-Century Invasions', *Journal of Roman Studies* 59 (1969), 12–29; repr. in Millar, *Rome, the Greek World and the East*, ii (Chapel Hill, NC, 2004), 265–97.

*Rankin, D., *Celts and the Classical World* (London, 1987).

Renfrew, C., *Archaeology and Language: The Puzzle of Indo-European Origins* (Cambridge, 1987).

Runciman, S., *Mistra: Byzantine Capital of the Peloponnese* (London, 1980).

*Stocking, C., and Hancock, E., *Swastika over the Acropolis: Re-interpreting the Nazi Invasion of Greece in WWII* (Leiden, 2013)

Tyquin, M., *Greece: February to April 1941* (Sydney, 2014).

*Waterfield, R., *Taken at the Flood: The Roman Conquest of Greece* (Oxford, 2014).

Reception of Sparta and Thermopylae Ancient and Modern

Albertz, A., *Exemplarisches Heldentum: Die Rezeptionsgeschichte der Schlacht an den Thermopylen von der Antike bis zur Gegenwart* (Munich, 2006).

Baumbach, M., 'Wanderer, kommst Du nack Sparta: zur Rezeption eines Simonides—Epigramms', *Poetica*, 32 (2000), 1–22.

Clough, E., 'Loyalty and Liberty: Thermopylae in Western Imagination' in T. Figueira ed. *Spartan Society* (Swansea, 2004) 363–84.

Davis, P. K., *100 Decisive Battles: From Ancient Times to th Present* (Oxford, 1999).

Dillery, J., 'The Roman Historians and the Greeks', in A. Feldherr (ed.), *The Cambridge Companion to the Roman Historians* (Cambridge, 2009), 77–107.

Gotter, U., 'Cato's *Origines*: The Historian and His Enemies', in A. Feldherr (ed.), *The Cambridge Companion to the Roman Historians* (Cambridge, 2009), 108–22.

Hodkinson, S., and Morris, I. M. (eds.), 'Sparta and the French Enlightenment', in *Sparta in Modern Thought: Politics, History and Culture* (Swansea, 2012).

Krebs, C., 'Leonidas Laco quidem simile apud Thermopylas fecit: Cato and Herodotus', *Bulletin of the Institute of Classical Studies* 49 (2006), 93–101.

Morris, I. M., '"To Make a New Thermopylae": Hellenism, Greek Liberation, and the Battle of Thermopylae', *Greece and Rome* 47 (2000), 211–30.

Morris, I. M., 'The Paradigm of Democracy: Sparta in the Enlightenment', in T. Figueira (ed.), *Spartan Society* (Swansea, 2004), 339–62.

Morris, I. M., 'Shrines of the Mighty: Rediscovering the Battlefields of the Persian Wars', in E. Bridges, E. Hall, and P. J. Rhodes (eds.) *Cultural Responses to the Persian Wars: Antiquity to the Third Millennium* (Oxford, 2007), 231–64.

Petrovic, A., *Kommentar zu den simonideischen Versinschriften* (Leiden, 2007).

*Rawson, E., *The Spartan Tradition in European Thought* (Oxford, 1969).

Rood, T., 'From Marathon to Waterloo: Byron, Battle Monuments, and the Persian Wars', in E. Bridges, E. Hall, and P. J. Rhodes (eds.) *Cultural Responses to the Persian Wars: Antiquity to the Third Millennium* (Oxford 2007), 267–97.

Van Steen G., *Liberating Hellenism from the Ottoman Empire: Comte de Marcellus and the Last of the Classics* (New York, 2010).

Ziogas I., 'Sparse Spartan Verse: Filling Gaps in the Thermopylae Epigram', *Ramus* 43 (2014), 1–19.

And specifically

…in modern poets

Davies, P., and Lander, H., 'Binyon's Simonides: The Relationship between Simonides' Encomium to the Dead at Thermopylae and Binyon's *For the Fallen*', paper delivered at the Poetics of War conference, UCL 17–18 June 2015, https://www.youtube.com/watch?v=A77Dtll6FBA&feature=youtu.be.

Dimaras, K., *A History of Modern Greek Literature*, trans. M. P. Gianos (Albany NY, 1972).

Güthenke, C., 'Nature in Arms: Greek Locality, Freedom and German Philhellenism', in C. Emden and D. Midgeley (eds.), *German Literature, History and the Nation: Papers from the Conference 'The Fragile Tradition', Cambridge 2002* (Oxford, 2004), ii. 93–118.

*Güthenke, C., *Placing Modern Greece: The Dynamics of Romantic Hellenism, 1770–1840* (Oxford, 2008).

Loeffelholz, M., *The Value of Emily Dickinson* (New York, 2016).

Ricks, D., *The Shade of Homer* (Cambridge, 1989).

*Roessel, D., *In Byron's Shadow: Modern Greece in the English and American Imagination* (Oxford, 2001).

*Vandiver, E., *Stand in the Trench, Achilles: Classical Receptions in British Poetry of the Great War* (Oxford, 2010).

…in Eighteenth-Century and Revolutionary France

Christesen, P., 'Spartan Land Tenure and French Socialism from Mably to Fustel de Coulanges', in S. Hodkinson and I. MacGregor Morris (eds.), *Sparta in Modern Thought: Politics, History and Culture* (Swansea, 2012), 165–230.

Glover, G., *Waterloo: Myth and Reality* (Barnsley, 2014).

*Johnson, D., *Jacques-Louis David: New Perspectives* (Newark, DE, 2006).

Winston, M., 'Spartans and Savages: Mirage and Myth in Eighteenth-Century France', in S. Hodkinson and I. MacGregor Morris (eds.), *Sparta in Modern Thought: Politics, History and Culture* (Swansea, 2012), 105–63.

…in the Third Reich

*Chapoutot, J., *Greeks, Romans, Germans: How the Nazis Usurped Europe's Classical Past*, trans. R. R. Nybakken (Oakland, CA, 2016).

Losemann, V., *Nationalsozialismus und Antike: Studien zur Entwicklung des Faches Alte Geschichte 1933–1945* (Hamburg, 1977).

Rebenich, S., 'From Thermopylae to Stalingrad: The Myth of Leonidas in German Historiography', in A. Powell and S.Hodkinson (eds.), *Sparta: Beyond the Mirage* (London, 2002), 323–49.

...in the movies

Combe, K., and Boyle, B., *Masculinity and Monstrosity in Contemporary Hollywood Films* (New York, 2013).

Fotheringham, L. S., 'The Positive Portrayal of Sparta in Late-Twentieth-Century Fiction', in S. Hodkinson and I. M. Morris (eds.), *Sparta in Modern Thought: Politics, History and Culture* (Swansea, 2012), 393–428.

Levene, D., 'Xerxes Goes to Hollywood', in E. Bridges, E. Hall, and P. J. Rhodes (eds.), *Cultural Responses to the Persian Wars: Antiquity to the Third Millennium* (Oxford, 2007), 383–403.

Nisbet, G., '"This is Cake-Town!": *300* (2006) and the Death of Allegory', in S. Hodkinson and I. M. Morris (eds.), *Sparta in Modern Thought: Politics, History and Culture* (Swansea, 2012), 429–58.

*Richards, J., *Hollywood's Ancient Worlds* (London, 2008).

*Wetta, F. J., and Novelli, M. A., *Last Stands from the Alamo to Benghazi: How Hollywood Turns Military Defeats into Moral Victories* (London, 2017).

The Greek War of Independence

*Athanassoglou-Kallmyer, N., *French Images from the Greek War of Independence, 1821–1830: Art and Politics under the Restoration* (New Haven, 1989).

Brewer, D., *The Greek War of Independence* (London, 2001).

Curta, F., *Edinburgh History of the Greeks, c. 500 to 1050: The Early Middle Ages* (Edinburgh, 2011).

Dascalakis, A., 'The Greek Marseillaise of Rhigas Velestinlis', *Balkan Studies* 7 (1966), 273–96,

Trencsenyi, B., and Kopecek, M. (eds.), *Discourses of Collective Identity in Central and Southeast Europe (1770–1945), Texts and Commentaries*, ii. *National Romanticism: The Formation of National Movements* (Budapest, 2007).

Alamo and Little Bighorn

*Buccholz, D., *The Battle of the Greasy Grass / Little Bighorn: Custer's Last Stand in Memory, History and Popular Culture* (London, 2012).

Dippie, B. W., '"What valor is": Artists and the Mythical Moment', in C. E. Rankin (ed.), *Legacy: New Perspectives on the Battle of the Little Bighorn* (Helena, MT, 1994), 209–30.

Hansen, T., *The Alamo Reader: A Study in History* (Mechanicsburg, PA, 2003).

Jenkins, J., 'The Thermopylae Quotation', *Southwestern Historical Quarterly* 94 (1990), 298–304.

*Lookingbill, B. D. (ed.), *A Companion to Custer and the Little Bighorn Campaign* (Chichester, 2015).

Pinheiro, J. C., *Missionaries of Republicanism: A Religious History of the Mexican–American War* (Oxford, 2014).

*Rankin, C. E. (ed.), *Legacy: New Perspectives on the Battle of the Little Bighorn* (Helena, MT, 1994).

Rosenberg, B. A., *Custer and the Epic of Defeat* (University Park, PA, 1974).

*Thompson, F. S., *The Alamo: A Cultural History* (Dallas, 2001).

*Tucker, P. T., *Exodus from the Alamo: The Anatomy of the Last Stand Myth* (Philadelphia, 2010).

*Winders, R. B., *Crisis in the Southwest: The United States, Mexico, and the Struggle over Texas* (Lanham, MD, 2002).

The Opium and Zulu Wars

Beckett, I. F. W., *Rorke's Drift and Isandlwana* (Oxford, 2019).

Greaves, A., and Mhkize, X., *The Tribe that Washed Its Spears: The Zulus at War* (Barnsley, 2013).

Knight, I., *The Zulu War 1879* (Oxford, 2014).

Laband, J., *Historical Dictionary of the Zulu Wars* (Lanham, MD, 2009).

*Laband, J., *Zulu Warriors: The Battle for the South African Frontier* (New Haven, 2014).

Murray, J., 'An African Thermopylae? The Battles of the Anglo-Zulu War', *Akroterion*, 54 (2009), 51–68.

*Ringmar, E., *Liberal Barbarism: The European Destruction of the Palace of the Emperor of China* (New York, 2013).

Stalingrad, Monte Cassino, and Kohima

*Beevor, A., *Stalingrad* (London, 1998).

Craig, W., *Enemy at the Gates: The Battle for Stalingrad* (New York, 1973).

Hellbeck, J., *Stalingrad: The City that Defeated the Third Reich*, trans. C. Tauchen and D. Bonfligio (New York, 2012).

*Keane, F., *Road of Bones: The Siege of Kohima 1944: The Epic Story of the Last Great Stand of Empire* (London, 2010).

Lyall Grant, I., *Burma: The Turning Point* (Chichester, 1993).

Parker, M., *Monte Cassino: The Story of the Hardest Fought Battle of World War Two* (London, 2003).

Roberts, G., *Victory at Stalingrad: The Battle that Changed History* (London, 2002).

Rutherford, J., *Combat and Genocide on the Eastern Front: The German Infantry's War, 1941–1944* Cambridge, 2014).

Sadler, J., *El Alamein: The Story of the Battle in the Words of the Soldiers* (Stroud, 2010).

Shirer, W. L., *The Rise and Fall of the Third Reich: A History of Nazi Germany* (New York. 1989).
*Wijers, J., *Winter Storm: The Battle for Stalingrad and the Operation to Rescue 6th Army* (Mechanicsburg, PA, 2014).
Ziemke, E., *Stalingrad to Berlin* (Washington DC, 1968).

Dien Bien Phu

Bradley, M. P., *Vietnam at War* (Oxford, 2009).
Davidson, P. B., *Vietnam at War: The History, 1946–1975* (Oxford, 1988).
Fall, B., *Hell in a Very Small Place: The Siege of Dien Bien Phu* (London, 1967).
Lawrence, M. A., and Logevall, F., *The First Vietnam War: Colonial Conflict and Cold War Crisis* (Cambridge, MA, 2007).
Schrader, C. P., *A War of Logistics: Parachutes and Porters in Indochina, 1945–1954* (Lexington, KY, 2015).

9/11

Langerwerf, L., '"And they did it as citizens": President Clinton on Thermopylae and United Airlines Flight 93', in Annemarie Ambühl (ed.), *Krieg der Sinne— Die Sinne im Krieg: Kriegsdarstellungen im Spannungsfeld zwischen antiker und moderner Kultur / War of the Senses—The Senses in War: Interactions and tensions between representations of war in classical and modern culture*, thersites, Journal for Transcultural Presences and Diachronic Identities from Antiquity to Date 4 (2016), 243–73.

Burial and Monuments

Arnold, C., *Necropolis: London and Its Dead* (London, 2009).
Laqueur, T. W., *The Work of the Dead: A Cultural History of Mortal Remains* (Princeton, 2015).
Mosse, G. M., *Fallen Soldiers: Reshaping the Memory of the World Wars* (Oxford, 1991).
Varley, K., *Under the Shadow of Defeat: The War of 1870–1871 in French Memory* (London, 2008).
Wheeler, M., *Heaven, Hell, and the Victorians* (Cambridge, 1994).

INDEX